FROMMER'S

COMPREHENSIVE TRAVEL GUIDE

LAS VEGAS '91-'92

by Mary Rakauskas

PRENTICE
HALL
PRESS

NEW YORK • LONDON • TORONTO • SYDNEY • TOKYO • SINGAPORE

FROMMER BOOKS

Published by Prentice Hall Press
A division of Simon & Schuster Inc.
15 Columbus Circle
New York, NY 10023

ISBN 0-13-333113-X
ISSN 0899-3262

Manufactured in the United States of America

CONTENTS

MAPS

To my gambling cronies—
Shirley and Marie

Inflation Alert

I don't have to tell you that costs will rise regardless of the level of inflation. For that reason it is quite possible that prices may be slightly higher at a given establishment when you read this book than they were at the time this information was collected. Be that as it may, I feel sure that these selections will still represent the best travel bargains in Las Vegas and its environs.

A Disclaimer

Although every effort was made to ensure the accuracy of the prices and travel information appearing in this book, it should be kept in mind that prices do fluctuate in the course of time and that information does change under the impact of the varied and volatile factors that affect the travel industry.

INTRODUCING LAS VEGAS

Las Vegas is a winning resort city. This top American vacation destination is a desert playland.

Las Vegas is in a construction frenzy of "the biggest," "the most," "the finest," and "the only"—with superlatives and hyperbole exploding daily. Owners of hotel/casino/resorts are rushing to catch up by refurbishing rooms, expanding casinos, and adding towers. As in any business, a few of those in status quo are slipping downward into auction or Chapter XI. The town is not just in its perpetual boom phase; its aim is to become the place to take the kids and the town to which to retire in luxury (well, almost) at a significantly lower cost (for the moment).

Bugsy Siegel would never recognize today's Las Vegas. At the end of 1989, The Mirage opened in all its volcano-erupting and waterfalling splendor. Even the most jaded would have to agree that Steve Wynn created a uniquely spectacular gaming, theatrical, dining, and relaxing environment. Seven months later in June 1990, Excalibur opened its 4,032-room when-knighthood-was-in-flower resort at the southern edge of the Strip. It's another of the total-entertainment Circus Circus Enterprises. And with the advent of Excalibur, MGM Grand's Kirk Kerkorian gobbled up 115 acres across the street for what is reported to become a movieland theme park and a 5,000-room hotel. The hotels seem to get bigger by the minute.

Las Vegas is on a roll. Growth and expansion have upped the projected hotel capacity to 85,000 rooms by the end of 1991. As of the moment, there's not an unemployed architect around. The city has graduated from a brief-stay attraction to one of the fastest-growing metropolitan areas in the country. It's become a town for families because of the success of the gaming industry, the appeal of the weather, the low cost of living, the wealth of jobs, and the great tax environment. (There's no state income tax—gaming revenues account for 40% of the state budget—and no corporate tax—companies are relocating to Las Vegas at the rate of two per month.) Right now Las Vegas has a population of about 700,000, but this number is expected to double by 1994.

Las Vegas has busted Hollywood's hand as the world's entertainment capital. You can see more name stars glowing onstage every night than MGM had on its movie lot during its entire history.

Some say that Las Vegas is an architectural disaster, housing a world of perpetual motion. Others say that Las Vegas personifies the American spirit—loud, brash, and aggressive—and is a place where hope springs eternal to overcome the odds and beat the system (how else to explain Las Vegas's $2-billion-a-year gross income?). Las Vegas is gambling. Stakes start at a paltry nickel in downtown slots and can go up to $10,000 or more on a single bet at gaming tables. One anonymous roller, known only as "Crawford," flew off in his own private plane after raking in $800,000 in winnings during one eight-hour spree. Some say that he breezed in from the Oklahoma oil fields. He tipped the cocktail waitresses with $500 chips, tossed down Bloody Marys throughout his red-hot streak, and had the whole town talking before he left.

In Las Vegas, craps and poker have been elevated from smoky back rooms to chandeliered and paneled casinos. Free drinks and cigarettes are courtesies extended to all rollers, but dedicated gamblers with weighty bankrolls are usually invited to posh private layouts. At those inner sanctums, full meals are among the wall-to-wall freebies.

When Bingo was rediscovered as a crowd pleaser, several hotels began to install 1,000-seat parlors. Now players lay down $1 or $2 per card to compete for cash prizes as large as $25,000 in some cases. Bingo is big business. So are blackjack and baccarat and roulette and keno.

Although these are reasons why more than 12 million visitors invade Las Vegas every year, the city has other magnetic appeals.

Where else but in Las Vegas can you play tennis on indoor courts at 4 or 5am? Las Vegas has more tennis courts open to public play than any city in the world, and it has well-known tennis pros giving instruction.

Golfers get their strokes in Vegas, too. No fewer than ten championship courses are open to play. PGA, Senior PGA, and LPGA tournaments are held there.

Where else but in Las Vegas can you order hefty ranchhand breakfasts at 7, 11, or 18 hours after the usual breakfast time? Clocks don't clock such things in Las Vegas, where time can be ignored by vacationers—and it usually is. "When you're having a ball," the Vegas philosophy goes, "who cares what time it is?" And you certainly can't tell the time of day inside a casino.

Where else but in Las Vegas can you dine while watching trapeze artists perform daredevil stunts or bicycling acrobats throw balloons to the kids? Carnival goings-on and breathtaking circus acts for both adults and children are staged at the peppermint-striped Big Top and hotel known as Circus Circus.

Las Vegas is built entirely for fun. It takes the ordinary and makes it extraordinary. It takes the extraordinary, adds imagination and dash, and turns it into a happening to beguile and amuse. Nothing is small, unless it's *the world's smallest.* Big is bigger. A hamburger is a "prime two-pound beefer." A hot dog is "a yard long." A disco is "where the stars all go to unwind." And an insignificant hole-in-the-wall dress shop will purport to have "the world's greatest collection of original designs."

If you stand on the Strip and watch traffic move bumper-to-bumper through the city, you'll see license plates from everywhere. Local taxis with names arranged in dice designs, sleek Porsches and Maseratis, recreation vehicles, pickup trucks, Hertz and Brooks rental cars, sand buggies, and motorcycles and scooters—a wheeling world flashes by in a constant flood. Budget-conscious tourists, Arabian sheiks, students on a fling, families detouring from the nearby great national parks, showbiz and rancher tycoons, Japanese businessmen, politicians, retired pensioners, urbane globetrotters, first-time travelers, and dedicated gamblers—they all find their way to Las Vegas. Some stay to live in the vivid city, thrilled with the always-something-to-do pace.

There's a lot to appeal to everyone in the Las Vegas desert playground. This guide hopefully will lead you to the things you enjoy most. Las Vegas is a cow town grown up, a boom town still booming, with an easy-to-take Out West welcome. You'll discover more bargains in beautiful hotel rooms, more fine places to wine and dine, and more entertainment in Las Vegas than in any other resort.

Because there are so many outstanding places at which to stay and things to see and do, I've covered them *selectively*—to keep this book from reaching encyclopedic length. I've personally checked each recommendation, and only places I consider worthy are included.

Although I've also stated rates and prices, please bear in mind that they're subject to change at any time. Usually they'll be fairly close to ranges quoted, if past experience holds true.

But change is inevitable in Las Vegas. And that's what makes it one helluva town. There's absolutely no other place like Las Vegas, Nevada!

---

1. History

NEVADA THEN

Las Vegas always has been a place to make a lot of money. But the Native Americans, who were there first, and the Mormons, who arrived 30 strong in 1855 to try their hand at farming, didn't fare as well as others. Those Mormons were shortly driven out by bands of Piute, who were in turn driven out; today the Piute are but a mini–minority group in Nevada's overall population.

When prospectors on their way to or from the California gold rush in the 1880s stopped off in Nevada, many hit pay dirt in gold and silver. Actually the first Nevada ore strike was in Pioche in 1870. (The town is 175 miles northeast of Las Vegas.) Diggings soon spread to other areas, and the search for the precious metals lasted through the early 1900s.

Rich ore veins eventually petered out, leaving sorry ghost towns scattered throughout the high and low desert wilderness that makes up much of Nevada. The landscape near these towns is pock-marked with abandoned mine shafts. Former mining centers at Searchlight, Goodsprings, Eldorado Canyon, Virginia City, and Rhyolite are among the many ghost towns you may visit. (Goodsprings is the closest to Las Vegas—35 miles, about an hour's drive—but it isn't much to rave about, unless you stop for a drink or two at the metal-lined-and-sheathed Pioneer Saloon. I'll deal with ghost towns in Chapter X.)

In 1905 the Union Pacific Railroad built a division point depot here, and that's when a parched and dusty tent town became the city of Las Vegas. Land speculation began then and climaxed in a two-day auction when 1,200 residential sites were sold for $265,000. The boom has been going on ever since. The future of Nevada's towns and cities in the early 1900s was entirely dependent on the iron horse. If the railroads came, the towns would survive; without the railroads, most were doomed to fade and fail.

Although gold and silver were dug until ore became so low-grade that it no longer attracted commercial mining operators, Nevada is still called the Silver State. It continues to hold its mining lure as one of the world's prime sources for semiprecious gems. Turquoise and fire opal are the two best-known gem rocks in the area, and there are many others.

NEVADA NOW

Nevada grew faster in the 1970s than any other state in the Union. More than 58% of the state's population (over 600,000) lives in Clark County, where Las Vegas is located, and the assessed valuation of property in the county passed the $6-billion mark during 1984. The population rise continues. Clark County is among the top five fastest-growing areas in the United States.

Nevada ranks second only to Alaska in land owned by the federal government. Some 47 million acres of the state are administered by the Bureau of Land Management. That's roughly two-thirds of Nevada. Much of this acreage is devoted to park and recreation areas, and Lake Mead alone has a shoreline of 550 miles and covers 163,000 acres. Distances out there, where the land is big and sparsely populated, are measured more in hours driven than in miles.

On lands that are privately owned, livestock production is the major preoccupation. Bing Crosby used to have a Nevada ranch, and Wayne Newton still does. Howard Hughes tried ranching at first, near Blue Diamond, northeast of Las Vegas, but problems associated with heavy poaching reportedly cost him $166,000 a year before he sold out.

After the slowdown in gold and silver mining, the next desert boom came with the construction of Hoover Dam in the 1930s. The dam was a shot in the arm for Las Vegas during the Depression, while the rest of the country was salving its poorness with such tunes as "Pennies from Heaven" and "I Found a Million Dollar Baby in the Five and Ten Cent Store." More than pennies were being made—and spent—in prospering Las Vegas.

Gambling, of course, always was popular among the freewheelers in this laissez-faire western state. But it went through many vicissitudes before it finally was legalized in 1931.

Some say that Clark Gable's first wife, Rhea, helped put Las Vegas on the map of national consciousness when she set up housekeeping there to get her divorce and lost as much as $12,000 in one sitting at the roulette tables. Gossip columnists sharpened their pencils and did their best. The publicity was hairy but effective.

Still others say that the real Vegas boom started with cross-countrying GIs and their spouses and camp followers, who referred to the town as "Lost Wages," during World War II. Nick the Greek, the legendary gambler, also attracted a great deal of attention to the Nevada oasis. Certainly personnel from the Nevada Test Site, from the Nuclear Rocket Development Station, and from several military bases (including huge Nellis Air Force Base, eight miles northeast of Las Vegas) contribute to the current economy as well as to the vast and scary blots of Yucca Flat, Jackson Flat, and Frenchman Flat, designated on the map as *Danger Zones* (where nuclear bombs have been tested).

Without a doubt, each of these elements has helped to make Las Vegas the boom town that it continues to be.

OFF-OFF-BROADWAY, NEVADA

According to *Nevada* magazine, blockbuster entertainment first made a stand in Nevada, not in Las Vegas but in the tiny town of Elko (pop. 3,800). There, Newt Crumley's Commercial Hotel paid jazzman Ted Lewis a whopping $12,000—that was way back in 1941—to serenade the cowboys and passing tourists. Business picked up so fast that other then-contemporary stars, such as Chico Marx, Paul Whiteman, and Ray Noble's orchestra, were successively booked.

The experiment made a big impression on neighboring hotels, but wartime travel restrictions and gasoline shortages brought it to an end, and it was 1945 before anything comparable to it was attempted. Then Bugsy Siegel opened the "Fabulous Flamingo" with a $25,000 booking of Xavier Cugat plus Abbott and Costello.

Competition turned into something fierce . . . and financial. Entertainers who were drawing "only" $20,000 either were on the skids or had agents who were dolts. Betty Hutton reportedly drew $100,000 for a brief stint at the Desert Inn. Million-dollar contracts have been reported since, and nobody knows exactly how much star luminaries toted home the last time they were out. But some years ago, Neil Diamond earned $650,000 (now a low-scale amount) for a four-night inaugural stint as headliner at the Aladdin's Theatre for the Performing Arts.

For the Stardust, over 25 years ago veteran booking agent Frank Sennes imported Paris's lavish Lido extravaganza. This, too, started a trend. Thematically many extravaganzas mirror each other, but they also try to outdo each other with technical wizardry, and the results are nothing short of amazing. With the rising cost of superstar entertainment, more and more hotels are adopting the less-expensive "spectacular" format.

At this writing, it's back to the big-star attractions and TV performers—Cher at The Mirage; Bill Cosby, Sarah Vaughan, and Julio Iglesias at Caesars Palace; Eddie Murphy at the Las Vegas Hilton; Englebert Humperdinck and the perennial Wayne Newton at Bally's–Las Vegas; and Dolly Parton and Kenny Rogers at the Golden Nugget.

Vegans call Las Vegas the Entertainment Capital of the World. Judged by the talent on hand on any one day and by salaries paid—a year's entertainment bill on the Strip has topped $200 million—there's justification for the claim. But there are always worriers. Some say that there may not always be enough top-caliber talent to go around.

If sell-out performances by Wayne Newton, Liza Minnelli, Frank Sinatra, Robert Goulet, and Paul Anka are any indication, the worriers are wasting their time. The Nashville Sound has brought a whole new breed of entertainer to Las Vegas. Such artists as Dolly Parton and the Gatlin Brothers continue to pack audiences in.

For a brief and flashy while a couple of years back, Las Vegas attempted to outdo *The Dirtiest Show in Town*. Sex was touted and sometimes spoofed tastefully, but more often it was strictly prurient. Local critics bellowed "Vulgar!" The producers of hard-core dirt had miscalculated their audiences. Too many people found the whole naked scene too boring—or, more to the point, too unentertaining—and they shunned the more blatant shows. Whereupon the trend switched back for the most part, although there are still big-name shows "for mature audiences."

SEVEN COME ELEVEN

The name of the game in Las Vegas is gambling. You can't ignore it, and it's almost impossible to avoid constant confrontation with the chance to take a chance—and another and another.

One-armed bandits crowd your route through the airport terminal and through supermarkets and drugstores; the little white ball whirls around countless roulette wheels in casinos everywhere, and stakes from 50¢ (although few) to over $10,000 are laid on the line at the craps tables.

Millions of dollars allegedly were skimmed out of casinos by some tout-trained early operators, but that was before the Nevada Gaming Control Board gained such strong authority over their operating procedures. Everybody agrees that today the operations

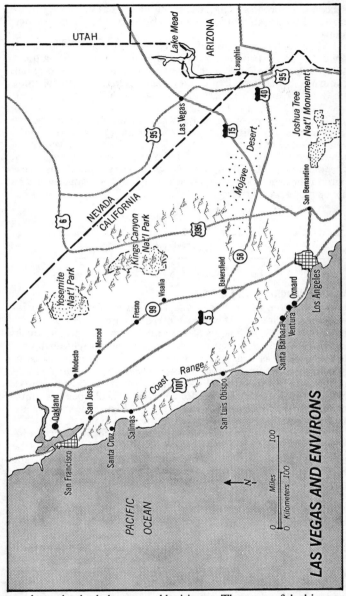

LAS VEGAS AND ENVIRONS

are almost boringly honest and legitimate. The entry of the big corporations (individual investors could no longer come up with the financing) into hotel and casino management has made a big difference, with the death or retirement of some of the old-time operators speeding the process along. A large number of Las Vegas casinos are operated by corporations rather than by individuals or by partnerships.

The Las Vegas boom looks as if it will never end. Major hotels are constantly expanding, and new ones are always popping up. A subsidiary "Strip," although never as successful as the original, came into being along Convention Center Drive with the opening of Kirk Kerkorian's International Hotel (now the Las Vegas Hilton) and Howard Hughes's Landmark.

Gaming Control Board regulations used to prohibit people with outside gambling interests from owning casinos in Nevada. But several years ago, the regulations were relaxed, and ever since a new influx of investment money has been pouring into the state in corporate helpings. It's impossible to stay very long in Las Vegas without hearing about this—and about how the hometown ways are being displaced by big business.

---

2. The People

WHO OWNS LAS VEGAS?

Ownership in Las Vegas is so intermeshed with corporate investment that it's almost impossible to determine exactly where the power lies. Big stockholders often control corporate decision making because of their immense investments, which are seldom known to the public. Las Vegas fits into the American free-enterprise complex in other strangely involved ways. The little old woman sitting next to you in a keno parlor, for instance, might conceivably own a hefty corner of Las Vegas because she has a block of stock or a chunk of money in a Minneapolis bank. The paradox is that she may not know that her investment money is being used in Las Vegas.

In spite of the convolutions of corporate finance, certain individuals (or their estates) stand out. Howard Hughes can't be ignored. Neither can Del Webb, Kirk Kerkorian, Bill Harrah, the Binion family (Benny died in 1989), and Jackie Gaughan. The monumental holdings of some of these people are staggering.

Howard Hughes

Howard Hughes, as one of the world's richest men, held center stage as a dashing figure all his life. As a pioneer pilot on world flights, he was an adventurer. As an escort to leading ladies in Hollywood, he was "an admirable and eligible contender" for the affections of some of the most famous stars. As a movie mogul, he made Jane Russell and her bust measurements famous. And, besides, he was a millionaire when millionaires were uncommon, a handsome guy with personality and charm who had everything going for him. Before he beat his retreat, he was a giant, a hero. He was

Hughes Aircraft. He was also the financing force behind one of the most abysmal failures in the aircraft industry—the Spruce Goose. Even years after his death, he is still one of the world's most talked-about or speculated-about men.

His Las Vegas holdings have included the Sands, Frontier, Desert Inn, and Landmark hotels. Add to the lineup Harold's Club (in Reno); considerable acreage adjoining McCarran Airport; options on about 500 old silver- and gold-mining claims in Nevada; and the immense Krupp ranch, where it is believed that Hughes lived part of the time.

Perhaps we'll never know the real Howard Hughes story. Clifford Irving's publishing hoax almost succeeded, partly because people were so curious about this mysterious millionaire. But when Irving and his wife went to jail, the public still knew nothing of Howard Hughes.

One of the most interesting portraits of Hughes to emerge since his death is James Phelan's *The Hidden Years*. Phelan, a journalist, had been keeping tabs on Hughes for about 20 years. When Hughes died, Phelan began to gather information from employees who had worked for Hughes as well as from other sources. His compelling portrait describes one of the world's richest men who died in a pitifully wretched condition—almost deaf and starving, with one of his legs atrophied and his body covered with bedsores. But even Phelan can only speculate why Hughes cut himself off from the world and allowed himself to degenerate to such a lowly state.

Kirk Kerkorian

Another name to reckon with in Las Vegas is Kirk Kerkorian, the publicity-shy entrepreneur. Kerkorian made a big splash in Las Vegas when he bought the Flamingo, but he was already well on his way with wheelings and dealings that included the purchase and eventual sale of the land on which Caesars Palace was built. Later he built the 1,500-room International Hotel (now the Las Vegas Hilton), Nevada's largest resort hotel.

For a while it appeared that Kerkorian might be tiring of Las Vegas involvements. He sold the Flamingo and the International to Hilton Hotels. At first it was reported that he would keep his gambling concessions in the hotels, but, no, Hilton bought those, too.

It's clear now that Kerkorian never did drop out of the Vegas scene. He did sell his personal interest in the Bonanza Casino, but he sold it to MGM, and MGM built the MGM (now Bally's) Grand Hotel. Among his recent interests have been the Sands Hotel and the Desert Inn. Small wonder that watching the moves of Vegas high financiers is like watching a billiard game: One shot, and the balls veer off in every direction.

Kerkorian is difficult to see, the bane of every reporter and gossip columnist in Las Vegas. One fortunate journalist, Susan Gould, after weeks of negotiation, was granted an interview with Kerkorian for a magazine. Some interview! Most of Susan's time with Kerkorian was spent on the tennis court, she revealed, where Kerkorian liked to work out with his attorney. Whenever Susan asked a question, Kerkorian, virtually wordless, nodded to his attorney to answer.

Still, Kerkorian is said to be a likable man, and he's a Vegas name to remember.

Born in Fresno, California, the son of an immigrant turkey farmer, Kerkorian made his money from a charter air service. He moved into Las Vegas with the purchase of the Flamingo for $12.5 million, a nice little deal, and made a pile (500% profit) on the sale of his land for Caesars Palace.

Del Webb

Also among the major hotel impresarios in Las Vegas was Del Webb, who died at 74 in July 1974. If there was ever to be a "Mr. Las Vegas," Webb was it, *nolo contendere*.

The son of a Fresno contractor, he began his working life as a carpenter in Phoenix, Arizona, his first job being to finish building a friend's grocery store. From this unpromising beginning, Webb built up a nationally known construction firm that, during World War II, was awarded numerous government contracts—airfields, hospitals, training bases, and prisoner-of-war camps. Inevitably his firm became associated with Hughes Aircraft—two giants together —and completed such projects as a radar system manufacturing plant and nuclear research laboratories.

By the end of the war, Webb began to look into Las Vegas and contracted to build the first of the new-style hotels—the Flamingo, formerly owned by Kerkorian. About the same time, Webb (who always prefaced the name of his properties with "Del Webb's . . .") became a co-owner of the New York Yankees, along with Dan Topping, retaining his interest until 1965, when he sold out to CBS. Some of his other interests were oil exploration and partnership in a movie company with Bing Crosby.

Webb's company specialized in constructing retirement communities, shopping centers, and resort hotels. He sold his Silverbird Hotel to Caesars World in July 1972. Impressively tall, Webb always wore a hat. With his death, the old order diminished. But his name lives on.

Bill Harrah

Big-time operators in Nevada can't be mentioned without including Reno's late Bill Harrah. His personal income was supposed to have passed the $40-million-a-year mark, and an authority at the Gaming Control Board once said that "he's the second man on the totem pole in Nevada, close to Howard Hughes in total value of holdings."

BIG-TIME GAMBLERS

Las Vegas has had its share of colorful characters, and most of them have been gamblers. The most colorful of the gamblers was certainly Nick the Greek.

Nick the Greek

The King of Gamblers from 1928 to 1949—and the man who may have done the most to put Las Vegas and its casino games on the map—was the legendary Nick the Greek (his real name was Nicholas Dandolos). In his time the famous gambler-philosopher won and lost more than $50 million, and he died poor. But at one time the Las Vegas Chamber of Commerce had more inquiries about the Greek than they had about another phenomenon, Boulder Dam.

Nick the Greek refused ownership of Las Vegas land in payment for gambling debts owed to him. He also spurned offers of other ventures, including hotel partnerships, that would have made him financially independent. (His name attracted business.) Nick preferred to gamble for his fortunes, claiming that he'd rather pay and lose. Raking in house percentages, he said, would have robbed him of the thrill of betting, even though he knew that he eventually would be among the victims of the house percentages, a loser.

Ed Sullivan and other celebrities attended Nick's funeral on December 30, 1966. Among his pallbearers and honorary pallbearers were Kirk Kerkorian, three of the Binions (owners of the Horseshoe), Jackie Gaughan, and the governor and the governor-elect of the state of Nevada.

(Jimmy the Greek, Las Vegas's professional odds maker, and colorful in his own right, bears no relation to the late, great Nick.)

Amarillo Slim

"Amarillo Slim" Preston was among the elite of big-time poker. At the third World Series of Poker at Binion's Horseshoe Casino in May 1972, Thomas Austin Preston, Jr., a Texan with a slow drawl, loped off with $60,000. (Eight players had started in the poker series five days earlier, each with $10,000 in the pot, but one player dropped out with $20,000.)

Preston played in Europe and Australia, "wherever there's a big one." Before turning professionally to poker, Preston was a professional billiards player.

When he won the series, Amarillo Slim's final opponent in the game was Walter Clyde "Pug" Pearson. (What would gamblers do without nicknames?) Another player in the match, Adrian "Texas Dolly" Doyle, withdrew from the game after four days because of fatigue, nausea, and dizziness.

At one high point during the series, Slim's eye was taken by a blonde waitress with a small tattoo on her thigh. "Lordy me!" purred Slim. "What a purty sight!" He ordered a cup of java from the woman, but added that he'd like to talk about that tattoo "later."

Ken Uston

The newest of the Vegas glamorous gambler legends is Harvard Business School graduate Ken Uston, the head of a card-counting ring that is the bane of casino officials. After a few disillusioning years in the business world ("I'd been earning $2,700 a month in this straitlaced job that was boring as hell," said Uston), he became intrigued by cards. In his first six months, working with partners, he won about $150,000. He won $27,600 in 45 minutes one day at the Fremont Hotel. He and his cronies have officially been declared persona non grata in Vegas ("inimical to the interests of the state of Nevada") for several years now, and Uston has retaliated with discrimination suits. Meanwhile he still gambles occasionally with the aid of makeup and disguises. He also has trained a team of counters, some of whom play with his money and give him a cut. And he's been gambling in Atlantic City, where casinos tried to bar him but were unsuccessful. They're currently planning new ways to foil card counters with extra shuffling and more decks. Although he claims that "anyone with an IQ of 110 who passed high school algebra can be a counter" (a promotion for his book, *I Won Three Million at Blackjack*), Uston is a Phi Beta Kappa with a degree in economics.

---

3. What to Pack

As a western town, Las Vegas is casual. You won't see as many cowboys in high-heeled boots and Levis as you might have a few years back, but dress in Las Vegas runs the gamut of resort informality. Sports clothes are predominant during the summer—with open shirts and washable cottons—when the temperature climbs over the 100° mark. Only the more elegant restaurants suggest that anything as formal as a tie and jacket be worn by men. In the spring, fall, and winter, suits and woolens are comfortable, especially at night, although it's often warm enough for light cottons during the day.

A 19-year average showed bright sunshine 85% of the time.

Keep in mind that Las Vegas is in the desert. Humidity averages a low 22%. That's dry! And because it's a desert place, plan on daytime/nighttime variations of 20° or more. When it's hot, it's very hot, but the night chill can set in quickly. Women sometimes wear furs at night over light dresses.

Another fact about desert vacationing must be considered— dehydration. If you come from an area where the climate is humid, you'll shortly begin to notice that your lips, nostrils, and mouth become drier after the first couple of days. It's natural in the desert, where you also perspire more freely (quick, the cologne!).

Definitely, you should consume more liquids—about eight glasses of water, orange juice, lemonade, or whatever is the minimum liquid intake you'll need daily. That amount of liquid won't distress you in the least, either, because you'll have a powerful thirst. If you avoid taking at least this amount of liquid, you'll undoubtedly experience discomfort with cracked lips and other such problems. Big glasses of ice water are served in most dining places the moment you sit down, and don't be afraid to ask for more. Waiters and waitresses are used to the request; they get thirsty in Las Vegas, too.

A Closer Look at the Weather
(in degrees Fahrenheit)

	High	Average	Low
January	55	44	33
February	62	50	39
March	69	57	44
April	79	66	53
May	88	74	60
June	99	84	68
July	105	91	76
August	103	88	74
September	96	81	65
October	82	67	53
November	67	54	41
December	58	47	36

4. Trips to the Altar

Because of the liberality of marriage laws—no blood tests, no waiting periods, and no fuss—Nevada always has been popular with couples in a hurry.

More than 500 persons in the state are licensed to perform marriages. Until a few years ago, pastors of churches with congregations of five or more were qualified for the sanctifying trade. This has given rise to a special class of ministers known as Marryin' Sams or Lady Marryin' Sams, who operate out of a lineup of 20 or so quaintly named chapels along the Strip. Recently the legislature concluded that these gentlemen and gentlewomen have proliferated too fast, and a law has been passed stating that the performing of marriage ceremonies must be incidental to the pastor's main duties.

Probably the most famous of these marrying institutions is **The Little White Chapel.** As you'll see on the sign out front, Joan Collins was married there (to Peter Holm, in case you've forgotten). Although the cost of the ceremony was not publicized by the chapel's owner, Charlette Richards Sturgeon, the after-cost of the wedding received considerable coverage. Do not worry, however: The Little White Chapel will attend to marrying even the likes of thee and me, for a reasonable fee.

Marryin' Sams have a lucrative thing going. It's been estimated that they divide up about 56,000 marriages a year, with an average take of about $200 per couple. That includes $75 for the chapel, a bit for the minister, $20 each for witnesses, and a variety of optional extras such as corsages, photographs, recordings of the ceremony and recorded or live organ music. A cheapie no-frills hitching can cost as little as $100, sometimes less on a slow day.

Taxi drivers still compete at the airport for couples obviously in a marrying mood, hoping for and usually getting a tip from the chapel as well as some generous handouts from the couples, plus "a little extra" for witnessing the event.

Some Vegans are distressed that certain chapels make a mockery of marriage. A number of these chapels have little to do with houses of worship; they're little rooms to get married in, and that's it.

Marryin' Sams were outraged years ago when one of the hotels began to sponsor weddings performed onstage (couples were awarded free honeymoons in Hawaii) during the Don Ho show. They labeled it as unfair competition and vowed to work to stop the spread of this undignified practice.

Even if you go to a wedding chapel, by the way, you must have a marriage license. The county exacts its bounty. A license costs $27, and you must apply between 8am and midnight, Monday through Thursday, at the **Clark County Marriage License Bureau,** 200 S. Third St., (tel. 455-3156 or 455-4415 after 5pm and on weekends and holidays). If you can't fit the regular hours into your schedule, the bureau stays open continuously from 8am Friday until midnight Sunday. The Courthouse, 200 S. Third Street (tel. 455-4011), also doles out information on requirements for divorces—which are fairly easy to obtain, providing that the residence requirements are observed.

This neat little supermarket for tying and untying matrimonial knots is very big in Reno, but the same liberal laws are equally effective in Las Vegas, where you can get married in a helicopter, under water, or just plain on the ground.

II

GETTING TO KNOW LAS VEGAS

1. ORIENTATION
2. GETTING AROUND
3. FAST FACTS

Las Vegas is an oasis in a sparse and arid desert, the biggest city in the state of Nevada. It's located in the southernmost precincts of a wide, pancake-flat valley known as Las Vegas Valley and is hemmed in by treeless mountains. These mountains reach a height of 11,912 feet and glow in the distance with changing earthen hues at sunrise, as low mists burn off in a dance of rainbows—dramatic and lovely.

The city is 2,162 feet above sea level and hugs close to the California and Arizona borders. Las Vegas is closer to Los Angeles, California (298 miles southwest); to Phoenix, Arizona (294 miles southeast); and to Salt Lake City, Utah (442 miles northeast), than it is to Nevada's second-largest city, Reno (448 miles northwest). San Francisco is 620 miles to the west and slightly north.

Las Vegas got its name in the 16th century, when the Spanish Trail was hewn to link Santa Fe with the missions of California. Spaniards called the region Las Vegas, meaning "the meadows," for the grassy fields that abounded there because of natural springs. Very little of the architecture in Las Vegas relates to its Spanish heritage, however, which is surprising when you compare the city with many in Florida and California.

1. Orientation

You'll find practically none of the legacies of the past in Las Vegas. It's a contemporary place, where the look is Now—or, at least, barely yesterday. It's ablaze at night with miles of neon twisting around hotels and garishly touted little chapels doing an any-hour business in weddings, with formalities completed in a fast 15 minutes ("Payroll Checks and Personal Checks Accepted").

You can't wander through the gambling casinos of Las Vegas

for long before you notice the clocks—or, more significantly, the lack of clocks. Because you're there to gamble (aren't you?), why do you need to be distracted by knowing what time it is? Windows in the casinos are practically nonexistent, too. The 29th-floor casino at the Landmark Hotel, where day and night views of the Strip and surrounding desert were a happy distraction, didn't work out. Gamblers, apparently, would rather not know what time it is.

Gambling is the raison d'être for this town, and its pervasive presence will tempt you everywhere, from the provocatively mini-skirted keno girls who help you to play the game while you're eating breakfast in the coffee shop, to the system of establishing credit and cashing checks or changing bills in the casinos rather than at the hotel cashier's desk. There's always the possibility that you'll spend some on the way out.

At one time, Las Vegas hotel people were in a dither about whether or not to allow television sets in rooms (they ultimately did). But over the years, it's been realized that more distractions simply keep customers in town longer. Odds are *always* in favor of the house—that's what the gambling business is all about—and there's no way the house can lose in the long run, as long as you stay and enjoy yourself.

One of the things that most helped the mobility of visitors to Las Vegas in recent years has been the wide adoption of the European Plan. Meals seldom are included in hotel tariffs now, and you can dine anywhere you wish. So you can hit one place for an early lounge show, another for a dinner show, another for a midnight show, and yet another for gambling and imbibing and more lounge entertainment, and then you can go back to your hotel for more of the same. After-midnight buffets and chuck wagons are common; entertainers do their thing to as late as 5am; and big, low-priced breakfasts are served at any hour of the day or night.

Some of the hotels have added so many wining and dining services that now only about 50% of their income is from gambling. (It once accounted for 90% of their income.) That doesn't worry too many hotel people: Las Vegas's visitors have been leaving behind a fortune in gambling losses. (Gross taxable revenue from gambling was a staggering $3 billion in 1988.)

Maybe this has nothing to do with the considerable fortunes spent in Las Vegas . . . but a downtown souvenir shop that used to offer newspaper headlines bearing your name coupled with some catchy phrases, such as "————Wanted Dead or Alive" and "————Weds Vegas Showgirl," eliminated the headline that read "————Breaks Bank in Las Vegas." I've never known anyone who has, but you'll always hear about how somebody just missed it.

THE LAYOUT

Las Vegas doesn't seem large, unless you're trying to cover it on foot in the midday sun. The sections of town of most interest to you as a tourist are contained in a fairly compact triangle.

The Strip (its real name is Las Vegas Boulevard South) comes in from the southwest and heads northeast, intersecting with Fremont Street in the downtown Casino Center area. Because Fremont runs southeast (becoming Boulder Highway), these two major streets form two sides of a triangle, each about six miles in length. And inside this triangle (bounded on the south end by Hacienda Avenue) are the airport and nearly all the major hotels, casinos, golf courses, and shopping centers.

---

2. Getting Around

You can walk from the southernmost hotel on the Strip (the Hacienda) to the northernmost (the Sahara), but it's a considerable hike. At night it can be enjoyable if you have lots of time; during the day the farther you walk, the hotter it seems to get. And if you wish to go downtown to the spread of hotels on Fremont Street, add another three miles or so and several hours.

The following are some good alternatives to foot power.

PUBLIC TRANSPORTATION

The **Strip Bus** goes from the Hacienda Hotel at the southernmost end of the Strip, stops at all the major hotels, and turns into the Casino Center. If you get off at Fremont, you can pick up a bus back to the Strip at the corner of Fremont and Third. Bus fares are a uniform $1.10, exact change only. If you plan on using the bus several times, purchase a ten-ride commuter card from the driver for $7.30. Buses run about every 15 minutes from 6am to 12:45am, and every half hour from 2:45am to 6am. For further transit information, phone 384-3540.

There's now a new/old mode of transport up and down the Strip. It's the **Las Vegas Strip Trolley** (tel. 382-1404), a classic trolley replica that stops at the main entrance of Strip hotels as well as at the Las Vegas Hilton and the Convention Center. The ride is climate-controlled and really quite pleasant. Trolleys run about every 30 minutes from 9:30am to 2am daily. You can't miss seeing them because they look like the old-fashioned trolleys. The fare is $1; exact fare is required.

TAXIS

The easiest, most leisurely approach to transportation in Las Vegas is the taxi. Cabs charge $1.70 for the first fraction of a mile and 20¢ for each additional one-seventh mile—that is, $1.40 for each additional mile. Roughly speaking, a taxi ride between Strip hotels and downtown will be about $10. That's not cheap, but by using a cab you avoid the bother of parking and the cost of tipping for valet service. And you can save money by sharing the fare with someone interested in trying his or her luck at the same place that you wish to visit.

There are plenty of taxis, particularly at the entrances of the larger hotels. If you want to arrange for a taxi at a particular time, any one of the following companies will provide the service: **Desert Cab Company** (tel. 736-1702), **Whittlesea Blue Cab** (tel. 384-6111), or **Yellow and Checker Cab Companies** (tel. 873-2227).

As I've also mentioned in "The ABCs of Las Vegas" section, below, the limousine from the airport to Strip hotels costs $4 per person and to downtown Las Vegas costs $5.50 per person.

CAR RENTALS

Plan ahead. If you intend to rent a car during your vacation, before you leave home check your policy or call your insurance agent to determine the limits of your coverage. Does your insurance cover theft, vandalism, or collision damage to the rented car? Does your credit card cover these risks if you use it for the rental? If not, you may want to pay the added cost for the collision-damage, theft, and vandalism waiver. As of this writing, most rental firms make customers liable for damage up to the total value of the car. The waiver currently averages $10 to $12 per day.

If you rent from one of the well-established companies, large or small, the odds are that the car won't be a clunker. Check the cost, daily or weekly, and the charge for mileage as well as optional insurance and taxes. And since not all rental companies are located at the airport, ask about pickup and delivery—you may need to take a taxi from the terminal.

If you plan to pick up the car at one location and return it to another, ask about the drop-off charge, if any. And if you rent the car at a weekly rate and decide to return it early, you may be charged at the much-higher daily rate. Ask!

Before you drive away, check the registration—make certain that it's still in effect. Finally, find out if the company has a phone number for emergency road service.

Quite a few of the major companies—Hertz, Avis, Budget, and Nationwide—have offices at the airport and/or along the Strip. An alternative to the majors is **Brooks Rent-a-Car,** 3039 Las Vegas Blvd. South at Convention Center Drive (tel. 735-3344, or toll free 800/634-6721). Rates for all sorts of cars—they try to maintain the lowest in Las Vegas—start at $22 a day with 100 miles

---

Miles to/from Las Vegas
(to the nearest 5 miles)

Bakersfield	285 miles	Palm Springs	275 miles
Barstow	155	Reno	440
Bishop	275	Sacramento	595
Fresno	385	San Bernardino	225
Hoover Dam/Lake Mead	30	San Diego	340
Lake Tahoe	445	San Francisco	620
Laughlin	100	San Luis Obispo	417
		Santa Barbara	345

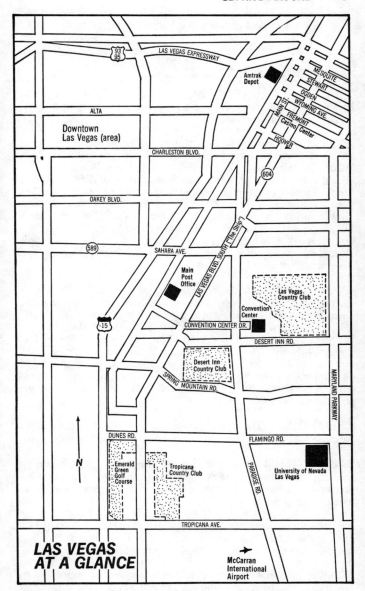

LAS VEGAS
AT A GLANCE

free, then 25¢ per mile, or $40 per day with unlimited mileage.
Weekly rates begin at $140, with 700 miles free; thereafter the mile-
age charge is 25¢ per mile. Minivans are $50 a day with 150 miles
free, then 25¢ per mile. All cars and minivans are late-model Fords.

Brooks is open from 6am to 1am and can arrange for pickup and drop-off at the airport or at any hotel until 11:30pm.

---

3. Fast Facts

Here's an alphabetical guide to certain basic (and some not so basic) information intended to help make your trip as enjoyable and frustration-free as possible.

AIRLINES: Nonstop flights connect Las Vegas with a number of cities in California: Bakersfield (Delta Air Lines); Burbank (America West, US Air); Fresno (Delta Air Lines); Long Beach (America West); Los Angeles (American Airlines, America West, Delta Air Lines, US Air); Ontario (America West); Orange County (America West, Southwest Airlines, US Air); San Francisco (America West, United Airlines, US Air); San Jose (America West, Delta Air Lines, US Air), Santa Barbara (Delta Air Lines); and Santa Maria (American Airlines). Major carriers also offer nonstop service from New York City area airports: Continental flies direct from Newark, and American West flies direct from JFK.

AIRPORT: The $7.50 surcharge on your ticket to Las Vegas pays for the city's main airport, ultramodern McCarran International, where you can begin gambling at the slots as soon as you disembark.

It takes about 15 minutes and $8 to $10 to get to the middle of the Strip by taxi. In addition to the base fare of $1.90 for the first one-seventh mile and 20¢ for each additional one-seventh mile, there is also a 20¢ tax per group for pickups at the airport and a 20¢ charge for each passenger over three. The limousine (or minibus) from the airport to Strip hotels costs $4 per person; it's $5.50 per person to downtown Las Vegas.

AREA CODE: The area code for Las Vegas—in fact, for all of Nevada—is 702.

BABY-SITTERS: If you're staying at one of the large hotels on the Strip or downtown, the concierge can make arrangements for you or recommend organizations to call. Two sitter agencies are listed in Chapter IX.

The Las Vegas Hilton has a unique Youth Hotel within the premises for children aged 3 through 18. However, you must be a guest at the hotel to take advantage of the facilities. See the details in the Hilton entry in "The Top Hotels" section, Chapter III.

BANKS: As in most cities, the banks are generally open from 10am to 3pm. However, if you need to cash a check, your hotel may be your best resource, depending on the amount involved. See also the "Cash and Credit" entry, below.

BUSES: The Greyhound Trailways depot is on 200 South Main

St. (tel. 384-9561). There are two drop-off/pickup stops on the Strip—at the Tropicana Hotel and at the Riviera. Tickets must be purchased at the downtown terminal before you board.

CASH AND CREDIT: You can readily cash traveler's checks at the cashier's cage in the casinos. If you intend to gamble, cash the checks first—they're not negotiable at the tables.

Establishing credit for a short-term stay in Las Vegas is accomplished more often through the casinos than through the banks. Bring credit cards, a driver's license, and other identification, and you can usually be "cleared" within 24 hours to cash personal checks up to the limit you've arranged with the casino. Once you've established credit with a casino, it remains in effect for repeat visits to the city. It's also possible to write to a casino in advance and establish credit before you arrive.

CASINO PROTOCOL: You can wear, or not wear, almost anything at a casino. And at a craps table, you can whoop and holler to your heart's content. Smoking is permitted at the majority of tables, but you may now notice some nonsmoking tables. There is one strict prohibition in all casinos—no cameras are allowed.

CHARGE CARDS: All major credit cards are generally accepted in lieu of cash at hotels, restaurants, and shopping and sports facilities in this town. However, it's always wise to check ahead if you're considering an exceptionally large purchase.

CHIPS: Casino chips were once as good as cash anywhere in Las Vegas. Nowadays they are accepted only in the casinos where they're issued—and in church; some people still drop them into collection boxes, an old Las Vegas tradition. The reason for the change in use as currency is that a rash of counterfeit chips began to show up. So cash in your chips before you leave any casino, unless you're planning to return there.

CRIME: In any city where as much money changes hands as in Las Vegas, you will also find crime. To avoid an unhappy incident, use discretion and common sense. If you're carrying a handbag, don't, for example, put it on the ledge just beneath the craps table where players rest their drinks. It's out of view and a tempting target. Always keep your handbag close to you and in plain sight.

DENTISTS AND DOCTORS: Hotels usually have a list of dentists and doctors, should you need one; in addition, they are listed in the Centel Yellow Pages. For dentist referrals, call the **Clark County Dental Society** (tel. 435-7767): for a doctor, call the **Clark County Medical Society** (tel. 739-9989).

DRIVING: Any trip to Las Vegas from California involves desert driving. Take basic precautions at all times but especially during the summer. Before leaving, check your tires, water, and oil. Take about five gallons of water in a clean container so that it can be used for drinking or for the radiator. Pay attention to those road signs suggesting when to turn off your car's air conditioner. Slow but continuous climbs through the mountains can cause overheating before you notice it on your gauge. And don't push your luck with gas. It may be 35 miles, or more, between gas stations, so fill up before you begin to run low.

If your car overheats, *do not* remove the radiator cap until the engine has cooled, and then remove it only very slowly. Add water to within an inch of the top of the radiator.

FESTIVALS AND EVENTS: The best and most comprehensive source for this information is the **Las Vegas Chamber of Commerce,** 2301 E. Sahara Ave., Las Vegas 89104 (tel. 457-4664), open weekdays from 8am to 5pm.

You'll also find weekly information in the Friday edition of the *Las Vegas Review-Journal* and in *Today in Las Vegas;* see the "Information" entry, below.

FOOD: Prices range from 89¢ to $70, with lots of choices in between. The bargain meals are usually breakfast and lunch; dinner tends to run higher. One of the city's main draws has always been its good food at moderate prices, calculated to bring in the gambling customers. Not only the downtown hotels but also most of the Strip establishments have all kinds of gimmicks, such as 89¢ breakfasts and all-you-can-eat buffet tables (which, for the most part, are no bargain). However, around town there are a number of restaurants serving superb food at reasonable prices. Many are not on the Strip. Some are franchise restaurants; most are not, and they are discussed later.

At the dinner shows in the larger hotels, the quality of the food is reasonable, and dinner plus a top-notch show for around $40 to $60 per person is not a bad buy—or at least it doesn't seem so in a city where visitors tend to let money flow like water.

Unlike the casinos, not all restaurants are open daily. If you have your heart set on a special place for dinner, be sure to check when it's open and if it requires reservations.

HAIR SALONS: First, ask at the hotel if there's a hair salon on the premises. If the hotel does not have one, ask for a recommendation. As a last measure, try a blackjack dealer with a desirable hair style for a referral. (Need I suggest that you ask when she's not busy?)

HOSPITALS: A 24-hour emergency service with outpatient and trauma-care facilities is available at the **University Medical Center of Southern Nevada Memorial Hospital,** 1800 W. Charleston Blvd., at Shadow Lane (tel. 383-2000); the emergency room entrance is on Rose Street. **Humana Hospital Sunrise,** 3186 Maryland Pkwy., near Desert Inn Road (tel. 731-8080), the largest proprietary hospital west of the Mississippi, also has emergency facilities.

Note: Humana has a **Poison Information Center** (tel. 732-4989) open around the clock.

INFORMATION: For brochures, maps, and information on accommodations, stop at the Las Vegas Chamber of Commerce—a very helpful center for visitors. The address, phone number, and hours are given above in the "Festivals and Events" entry. For Nevada tourism information, including that for Las Vegas, call toll free 800/638-2328 (a 24-hour line). For Las Vegas reservations and show information, call 800/423-4745.

One of the best sources of information on what's doing in Las Vegas is *Today in Las Vegas*—a free weekly publication that you'll find at almost any bell desk in a large hotel as well as at the airport. It includes up-to-the-minute reviews, listings, and times of all shows and events.

INSOMNIACS: Insomnia is not a problem in Las Vegas— everything moves around the clock. You need never know what time it is, whether it's day or night, or what the weather's like outside.

LIQUOR LAWS: There are no restrictions on the hours when liquor can be sold or served, but you must be 21 to imbibe legally in town.

NEWSPAPERS: The *Las Vegas Sun* is the town's morning paper. The Friday edition of the afternoon paper, the *Las Vegas Review-Journal,* offers a rundown of the shows in town as well as an overview of most other forms of entertainment, restaurants, and happenings in nearby resorts.

PETS: Hotels and motels generally will not accept pets. If you're traveling with Bowser the dog or Boneypart the cat, ask before making the reservations. Motel 6 does accept a pet (within reason) but will not permit the animal to be left unattended.

If you travel via RV, motor home, trailer, or van and take pets with you, an ideal location next to the Strip is the Circusland RV Park, adjacent to the Circus Circus Hotel and Casino. Circusland has family and pet sections with dog runs.

POLICE: For emergency help, dial 911. The nonemergency Police Department number is 795-3111; the number for the Nevada Highway Patrol is 486-4100. For road conditions, call 486-3116.

RELIGIOUS SERVICES: The Las Vegas area has hundreds of churches and synagogues (at last count about 380), representing virtually every denomination. It's been said that on a per-capita basis there are more houses of worship in Las Vegas than in any other metropolitan area in the nation, and we all know what everyone's praying for. The breakdown is 49% Protestant, 24% Roman Catholic, 23% Mormon, and 3% Jewish.

The houses of worship listed below are located along the Strip and downtown (for other denominations and locations, consult the Centel Yellow Pages):

First Baptist, 300 S. Ninth St., at Bridger Ave., downtown (tel. 382-6177); **First Southern Baptist,** 700 E. St. Louis Ave., on the Strip (tel. 732-3100); **Guardian Angel Cathedral** (Roman Catholic), 302 E. Desert Inn Rd., on the Strip (tel. 735-5241); **St. Joan of Arc** (Roman Catholic), 315 S. Casino Center Blvd., downtown (tel. 382-9909); **Reformation Lutheran,** 580 E. St. Louis Ave., near the Strip (tel. 732-2052); **First United Methodist,** 231 S. Third St., downtown (tel. 382-9939); **Temple Beth Sholom,** 1600 E. Oakey Blvd., near the Strip (tel. 384-5070).

STORE HOURS: Stores are usually open from 10am to 9pm Monday through Friday, to 6pm Saturday, and from 11am to 5pm Sunday.

TAXES: Sales tax in Las Vegas is 6%.

TIPPING: Those over 21 undoubtedly already know about tipping the usual 15% in restaurants. However, when you're at a table in a casino, be it craps, blackjack, roulette, baccarat, or whatever, a cocktail waitress will be around to ask if you want anything to drink. There is no charge for the drink, hard or soft, but it is appropriate for you to tip (or "toke") the waitress—$1 (or a comparable chip) is about right, more if you wish.

At the gaming tables, it's perfectly acceptable to tip the dealer or croupier in proportion to the service you've been getting and the size of your winnings.

When checking into a hotel with several bags, a tip of $5 is par for the course.

Valet parking is a great convenience at any of the Las Vegas hotels. A tip of $1 is appropriate, and it's not much to pay for the service.

When you leave the hotel, a tip of $1 per day for the period of your stay, left with the maid or in the room, is a most reasonable amount and will be appreciated.

If you want a better-than-average seat at any one of the shows, tip the maître d'. The usual donation is $5, but if it's a "big name" show, you might up the ante to $20 for the seating *you* want, although the top of the range is optional.

TRAINS: The **Amtrak** station is at 1 N. Main St., at the Union Plaza Hotel (tel. 386-6896, or toll free 800/872-7245).

USEFUL NUMBERS: You can obtain **weather information** for Las Vegas at 736-6404, 8am to 5pm; **information on highway conditions** at 486-3116; and **the time of day** at 118 (a three-digit number, similar to directory information, 411).

III

LAS VEGAS ACCOMMODATIONS

1. THE TOP HOTELS
2. MODERATELY PRICED HOTELS
3. INEXPENSIVE HOTELS

A statistician could be kept busy full time just turning out figures on accommodations in Las Vegas. At last count, the city had over 51,000 hotel rooms, and motel rooms added another 21,000. Because most rooms in Las Vegas are doubles, that's enough space to sleep every resident in a small city—plus a town or two.

Still, new accommodations are forever being built. A few hundred additional rooms are under construction at this writing, and many more are on the planning boards—with money already allocated to begin work.

The builders apparently know what they're doing. On busy weekends, you'll see *Sold Out* and *No Vacancy* signs all over town. So the city keeps booming, mushrooming up and out, straining to keep up with demands.

If it takes a data-processing machine to keep up with new hotel projects, you can imagine what it's like in personnel departments. Some hotels have 2,000 or more employees. Every time a new hotel opens, there's a scramble for top jobs, which makes tidal waves in other hotels, casinos, restaurants, beauty parlors, and boutiques and in every service that fits into hotels. But even though job-hopping in Vegas sometimes reaches frantic proportions, tough competition keeps people on their toes. Service is amazingly good.

THE THREE LOCATIONS

As a tourist in Las Vegas, you'll be concerned mostly with hotels in three locations—along the **Strip,** in the **downtown** area on Fremont Street, and in a sort of amendment to the Strip along **Convention Center Drive.** Centers of activity on the Strip and on Fremont Street intersect, and Convention Center Drive runs into the Strip between the Riviera Hotel and the Desert Inn, almost directly opposite the Stardust. It's difficult to get lost in Las Vegas, and there's no such thing as being far away.

Generally prices along the Strip are higher than those downtown. But the rule gets twisted often. You'll find bargains on the Strip too. Some visitors also characterize the Strip as formal, dressy, straitlaced (a perspective, I suspect, that results from a visit to Caesars Palace or the Las Vegas Hilton). Downtown, they say, they have an opportunity to rub elbows and talk with more people because of the small-town friendliness in such hostelries as the California and the Golden Nugget. But a similar downtown ambience can be found at the Hacienda at the southern extremity of the Strip and at Circus Circus in the center of the Strip.

Most of the Fremont Street crowd is casual indeed, dressed more for shopping than for gambling. Same goes for the downtown casino and hotel habitués—a far cry from the black-tie sedateness of the classic European casinos. Although gambling in the more elegant and grandly chandeliered hotel casinos along the Strip isn't quite so shirtsleeve (understated garb and jackets and ties tend to be more common, especially during the cooler spring, fall, and winter months), there's no rule that states that you can't wear just about what you please in the casino, in the hotel, even at the show.

The Strip is nearest to the McCarran International Airport, where you'll debark from your flight. From there, you should anticipate about $10 in taxi fare to most Strip locations, although many hotels provide complimentary limousine service to the airport. The airport limousine (tel. 739-7990) to the Strip hotels costs $4 per person; the limousine to downtown costs $5.50 per person.

Caution

You're taking a chance if you arrive in Las Vegas without a reservation. The airlines alone carried 11 million passengers into the city last year, and the largest numbers arrive on weekends. Besides this, considerable traffic floods the highways from Los Angeles, 289 miles away, and from lots of other points within closer range. And for several years, Vegas hotels have been developing and extending their convention arrangements, making the city one of the top convention cities in the United States. So hotel space gets tight, very tight, especially on crowded weekends, when looking for a room without reservations may be a big gamble.

Hotels, however, generally maintain an excellent record in meeting the needs of the fantastic weekend invasion of visitors. Most stick to their quoted rates and will provide you with reasonably priced accommodations whenever possible.

On the other hand, a number of motels (fortunately, a small number) *do not* have available rate sheets, and many of these are known to jack up prices to the level of highway banditry on busy weekends. It's not uncommon for unwary visitors to pay $50 or more for a motel room for the night, when they should be getting a lot more for a lot less.

So protect yourself by comparing prices and making a reserva-

Package Plans For Savings

If you're planning only a short stay in Las Vegas, look into the hotel package plans. They grant considerable price reductions. Dining, cocktails, big shows, and other extras are built into the offerings. Some are for golfers, too, and provide opportunities to play on more than one good golf course, usually with greens fees and other costs included. Inquire when you reserve a room whether packages are available.

tion in advance at one of the hostelries recommended in this book. Of course, if you should arrive without an advance reservation, avoid those places that won't show you a rate sheet. When prices climb very much above the ones listed here, you can be assured that there's something awry.

A NOTE ABOUT LISTINGS

To sectionalize this chapter in easy-to-follow form, I have covered deluxe accommodations first, rooms in the moderate-price range second, and rooms in the budget-price category last. In each section, hotels on and near the Strip precede downtown locations. Motels are listed at the chapter's end.

Also, since in Vegas the hotel/casino complex is not only a place to stay but also the reason for coming, many tourists barely leave their hotels. This is just the way the hotels want it; each offers a full complement of dining choices, nightlife, gambling, and so forth. Although a chapter on restaurants follows this one, so many excellent restaurants are right in the hotels that I'm going to list many notable ones here. Nightlife options, however, will all be dealt with in a separate chapter.

1. The Top Hotels

The Mirage, 3400 Las Vegas Blvd. South, Las Vegas, NV 89125 (tel. 702/791-7111, or toll free 800/627-6667).

With all of its neon and glitter, Las Vegas finally came up with a real $630-million showstopper that halts traffic on the Strip without a spec of neon. Totally spectacular! After all, how can you possibly ignore a magnificent volcano that erupts every 15 minutes (it used to erupt every 5 minutes but caused too many traffic backups by viewers) in a setting of lush tropical landscaping and a five-story waterfall. You can gape at the volcano in all its glory from 6pm to 1am. And that's only for openers at The Mirage.

Somehow you know that Steve Wynn, formerly of the Golden Nugget downtown, has his hand in this beauty with its brilliantly white-and-gold-banded finish, which first graced the Strip in November 1989. Wynn has a remarkable talent for crossing the flamboyant with the elegant to create what Las Vegas always strives to be.

Entrance to The Mirage is via a palm-lined causeway over a lagoon up to a white porte cochere. Every detail has been attended to for the convenience and the comfort of the guests. Valet attendants move vehicles to parking areas via tunnels under the lagoon. Baggage is unloaded and moved via an automated conveyor system. Should all this elegance and attention overwhelm you, a stop at the Lagoon Saloon, near the registration area, may be in order.

The Mirage resort is a Y-shaped hotel on 100 acres (some of the most expensive real estate in the West). It features five international restaurants, a spa, a salon, elegant designer-name shops, tennis courts, world-famous entertainment, and, of course, a superb Polynesian-themed casino. There are two natural habitats other than those for the guests—one for the dolphins (to come soon) and another for one or two of the white tigers used in the Siegfried and Roy show. (Tigers are rotated weekly in their white grotto paradise.) The bottlenose dolphins' 1.5-million-gallon habitat will serve as an educational center also open for public viewing.

The sensational doesn't end with the exterior. Behind the check-in area is a wall-length 20,000-gallon aquarium with small sharks, stingrays, and over 30 varieties of tropical sea life. (Do not worry about the well-being of the inhabitants of the aquarium because Jane Onio, the former Director of Program for the National Aquarium in Washington, D.C., is the Director of Marine Operations at The Mirage.) The lobby is handsomely finished with bamboo, thatched ceilings, marble paving with inset carpeting, and rattan furnishings. Farther inside The Mirage is a lush tropical garden—within a 90-foot-high glass-enclosed atrium filled with palm trees, banana trees, tropical orchids, and waterfalls.

As to the accommodations, The Mirage has three 29-story towers with 3,049 rooms, including one- and two-bedroom suites. The six ultraelegant secluded lanai bungalows, each with its own private pool, have no price—they are reserved for big names, such as Michael Jackson. The prices are $89 to $159 for deluxe rooms and $365 and up for suites.

You wouldn't expect all the 3,049 guest rooms to be decorated in the same manner, and they are not. There are five different color schemes for deluxe rooms, super deluxe rooms, king parlors, tower suites, and penthouse suites. Bright tropical colors taken from exotic flowers, birds, and the jewels of undersea life have been used throughout the rooms to contrast with the soft, neutral backgrounds—creating a relaxed, restful mood. The décor beautifully combines color and taste. Whitewashed natural rattan and caning are used throughout. Floor-to-ceiling headboards of louvered white panels enhance the spaciousness of the rooms. And every room features either a pool, a mountain, or a Strip view. The suites are heaven—with the good looks, amenities, furnishings, colors, and everything else you might possibly want in an apartment (well, almost). The top five floors of The Mirage are exclusively tower and penthouse suites accessible only by private elevators. Rooms equipped for the handicapped and nonsmoking floors are available on request.

There simply is nothing commonplace about staying at The Mirage. The swimming area, if I can use a simplistic phrase, is a series of interconnected lagoons with tree-lined islands, waterfalls, grottoes, and inlets. Nonswimming guests (such as myself) can walk to the islands to bask gloriously in the sun. (Getting a tan at the tables is simply not possible, yet.) Cabanas are clustered around the area for sun, shade, or privacy. When hunger or thirst sets in, there is the **Paradise Café** and the **Dolphin Bar** for a lavish lunch or a cool drink. If swimming among the lagoons, the grottoes, and the inlets is not your preferred mode of exercise and relaxation, there are six championship tennis courts and a fully equipped spa with an exercise room and a sauna offering aerobics and massage to keep you in shape for the trials of the gaming tables. This paradise also includes a beauty salon and an elite collection of boutiques and shops (the distinction being one of name and price).

Of course, The Mirage has 24-hour room service (rapidly disappearing in many hotels) with guaranteed 20-minute service (found in only one other hotel I know of, which is not in Las Vegas).

Restaurants

Kokomo's at The Mirage is situated within the atrium's tropical rain forest and has its own interior lagoon. Given the proper day and hour, you may see Steve Wynn here at a very special table. Kokomo's specialties are steak and seafood flown in daily. Seafood choices range from Dungeness crabcakes to broiled lobster tail, with a lengthy list in between (from $17 to $36). On the other hand, the hearty meat eater can always opt for the 22-ounce T-bone steak or the extra-thick rib lamb chops from a select variety of steak, chop, and rib offerings (from $14 to $28). For lunch, if you've never had prime rib on a kaiser roll, this is where you'll find it, along with such tasty choices as a crock of chili, smoked trout filet, tostada salad, and seasonal fruits in the Caribbean fruit salad (from $5 to $12). Desserts from the bake shop are calorically impressive—for chocolate lovers, there's an outrageous chocolate raspberry mousse cake; for those who enjoy a tasty nip with dessert, there's a fresh fruit cobbler with Wild Turkey sauce. Kokomo's is open daily for lunch from 11am to 2:30pm and for dinner from 5:30 to 11:30pm.

The **Mikado** has the quiet elegance of a private Japanese home with placid streams, delicate gardens, and hand-painted murals. It offers dishes prepared in the Japanese teppanyaki style, as well as a sushi bar. Dinners include a shrimp or scallop appetizer, miso or tori soup, Mikado salad, vegetables, tea, and dessert. Entrees may be of thinly sliced New York steak, chicken, lobster, or vegetarian teppanyaki. Or you may decide on one of several combination dinners. Dinners range from $16 to $35. A la carte fare, served with rice and tea, costs $11 to $22. Sushi and sashimi and a selection of maki and hand rolls (California, tuna, and so on) are also available. For the indecisive, The Mikado has an excellent Udon pot of thick noodles with chicken, shellfish, and vegetables simmered in a delicious light broth for $20. The Mikado serves dinner nightly from 6 to 11:30pm.

The **Moongate** has the look of classical Chinese architecture surrounding an open courtyard. Sculpted panels form a backdrop for oriental murals. The Moongate serves the classic Cantonese and Szechuan cuisines of China, although the desserts are deliciously occidental creations of The Mirage chefs. Entrees include a variety of elegant poultry, meat, vegetable, and seafood dishes. The exceptional tea-smoked duck is marinated in Chinese spices and wine, slowly smoked, and cooked until crispy. You might prefer the black peppered beef, seasoned with crushed peppercorns and garlic, stir fried, and served on a bed of crispy rice vermicelli. Among the seafood dishes is Maine lobster steamed or stir fried with scallions and ginger, Szechuan style, or with black bean sauce. Ah, but what a dessert is the fried banana wonton—a crispy fried wonton filled with banana and white-chocolate chunks, dusted with brown sugar and cinnamon, and served with vanilla ice cream and walnuts. Definitely not for the dieter. The Moongate is open nightly from 5:30 to 11:30pm.

What would life be without an Italian restaurant? At The Mirage is **Ristorante Riva,** offering northern Italian cuisine—the classic regional dishes—in a simple but elegant setting. If you have a taste for farinacei, consider the homemade ravioli-shaped pasta stuffed with ricotta cheese, spinach, and herbs and served with a fresh marjoram cream sauce. For seafood, there's always a fine cioppino—the zuppa di pesce with shrimp, scallops, lobster, mussels, and clams in a light tomato-and-fish broth. The specialties of the day may include a broiled veal chop served with sautéed peppers. Hot and cold antipasti are on the menu at length. And then there are the desserts, from the tiramisu to my favorite (and most un-Italian), crème brûlée. Entrees range from $11 to $27.

The **Bistro** is carefree and romantic, a taste of Montparnasse, with handsome murals in the style of Lautrec and a touch of Degas here and there. The emphasis here is on gallic specialties, with delectable light sauces and not the weighty cream varieties. Entrees include elegant choices of poultry, veal, beef, lamb, and seafood. You may find the halibut filet topped with a shrimp mousse, baked, and served with a vegetable sauce; a filet mignon broiled and served with beaujolais sauce; and the ducksteak Madagascar—breast of duckling sautéed, sliced, and served with a peppercorn sauce. The appetizer list is fraught with temptation, but if you can make your way through both appetizer and entree, consider the wild seasonal mushrooms ("in crust") appetizer sautéed with shallots, flamed with brandy, reduced with white wine and cream, flavored with fresh herbs, then lovingly folded into filo dough and baked. Entrees range from $19 to $30; appetizers add $8 to $13 to the total; desserts, including "Sinful Chocolate," cost $4 to $6. The Bistro serves dinner nightly from 6 to 11:30pm.

The selection of restaurants is no less diverse for family dining. There are few restaurants where I've dined as often and as consistently well at a modest price as at the **California Pizza Kitchen** in The Mirage. As you might guess, the Pizza Kitchen offers a lengthy list of individually sized wood-fired gourmet pizzas—each one more delicious than the last—beginning with the Original BBQ Chicken pizza (with barbecued chicken, sliced red onion, cilantro, and smoked gouda cheese) and extending on through 23 more choices, including vegetarian and cheeseless pizzas. But unless you've dined at the California Pizza Kitchen before, you might not know that they also serve pasta, much less how delicious the pasta dishes are. The choices are numerous, including a delicious broccoli fusilli blessed with garlic, sun-dried tomatoes, and parmesan. The calzone is incredible—a full-size pizza dough folded over the filling before it is wood-fired to bake in the flavors. (Can you believe moo shu chicken prepared this way?) Salads range from a pleasant addition to the pizza or pasta on to choices more in the nature of an entree. Desserts are equally as impressive, as is the list of beverages. Wine and a selection of 15 beers, including nonalcoholic ones, are available. Pizzas range in price from $6 to $9, and pasta dishes range from $7 to $9. One other important factor: For those who don't want to leave the scene of the action, I should point out that the California Pizza Kitchen is handily situated right next to the Race and Sports Book. The Pizza Kitchen is open weekdays from 11am to 11pm and weekends to 2am.

The **Bermuda Buffet** has the relaxed, airy look of the English gardens of Bermuda. The Buffet offers a magnificent abundance of tempting all-you-can-eat choices (over 60 menu items each day) for breakfast (7 to 11am), lunch (11am to 3pm) and dinner (3 to 11pm). Dinner ranges from $6 to $13. On Sunday there's a champagne brunch.

The **Caribe Café** is the festive coffee shop of The Mirage. It's open 24 hours and offers a lengthy selection for the all-American breakfast, lunch, and dinner as you like it, plus exotic desserts and dishes for all hours in between.

For desserts of all delectable types, The Mirage offers the goodies in **Coconuts Ice Cream Shop.** This light, bright ice-cream parlor serves *freshly made* ice creams, frozen yogurts, and sorbets daily from 10am to 10pm.

And wait until you see the casino, which is magnificently designed to resemble a Polynesian village. The unique concept of putting gaming areas under wood canopies creates a feeling of intimacy unlike that in any other casino I've been in.

Not to be outdone in any respect, The Mirage's entertainment is outstanding. The 1,500-seat **Theatre Mirage** features the incredible illusionists Siegfried and Roy performing nightly three weeks of each month. (What better name than "mirage" for magic?) Members of the cast include the magnificent and extremely rare white tigers. If you haven't seen the Siegfried and Roy show and love being astounded and mystified, don't miss it. I guarantee that it's unlike anything you've ever seen staged before, even if you've seen the pre-Mirage show at an earlier time. Certainly it is one of the most expensive shows ever produced, with fabulous costumes and space-age staging and lighting. Siegfried and Roy perform the first three weeks of each month at 7:30 and 11pm, except Wednesdays. The show is $56 plus tax, including two drinks and tips. International celebrities such as Cher, Kenny Rogers, Dolly Parton, and Johnny Mathis create their own magic the fourth week of each month.

As to gaming activities, of course there are those that you will find elsewhere, even those at levels suitable for a travel writer. But then there are also $500 slots and baccarat tables with stakes to $5 thousand or to $15 thousand. For the truly exceptional, there is one private room where the smallest chip is $1,000.

Bally's–Las Vegas, 3645 Las Vegas Blvd. South, Las Vegas, NV 89109 (tel. 702/739-4111, or toll free 800/634-3434).

Many hotels claim to be resorts, but Bally's–Las Vegas fully qualifies as a complete and self-contained resort. It has a 75,000-square-foot shopping arcade; day and night activities galore; gambling; two major showrooms; complete health-club facilities for men and women; a youth center; a therapeutic pool; an Olympic-size swimming pool; ten tennis courts, with seven lit for night play (no charge for guests); six restaurants and snack bars; a comedy club; and numerous cocktail bars—the works. Not to mention golf privileges for guests at the Dunes' 18-hole course, just across the street. It's a spacious spa, a singular world under one roof. This property (and every Vegas hotel—they've all learned a lesson) has now installed the best available multimillion-dollar system to detect and control fires.

Although Bally's (even before rebuilding after the 1980 fire) cost a lot more than $100 million, the public relations staff sticks with that "modest" figure. "The figure is easiest to remember," they say. But everything at Bally's is on a colossal scale. They transported over 800 tons of marble from Italy just for the fountain at the front entrance; the furniture order was the largest ever placed for one hotel; for two years, sculptors in three Italian towns were kept busy just making marble columns and statues for the hotel; the plumbing fixtures are so numerous that they could be used to build a rest room every quarter mile between Las Vegas and Los Angeles; and each of the hotel's 600 chandeliers involves at least two tons of crystal!

Bally's is one of the two largest luxury resort hotels in the world. It ranks as a tourist attraction in its own right—such as Boulder Dam or Versailles—and people detour just to see it. Others spend their entire vacation there, never going anywhere else.

If I start describing the hotel's entrance floor and branch out, you'll be lost before I get halfway through the casino. It's bigger than a football field with both end zones. Within the casino's chandeliered precincts enclosed by an Italian marble balustrade, you'll find about 1,000 slot machines, 11 craps layouts, 84 blackjack tables, 9 roulette wheels, 2 baccarat tables, 20 poker set-ups, a sports and race book, and a 100-seat keno lounge with closed-circuit TV to other areas. That's just for openers. I'll skip now to the rooms and rates first. Then I'll return to the nearest thing to open Marlboro Country I've seen—indoors.

There are 2,832 basic, grand, and deluxe bedrooms; player's suites; and town-house suites—reachable via 24 high-speed elevators. Some sumptuous royal suites run $1,250 a night (double occupancy), but if the entire budget for your Las Vegas vacation is well below $1,000, there's hope.

Guest rooms for one or two with king-size beds or two double beds (often called double-doubles) are pegged at $85 to $135. Each has separate living-room space, color TV, a direct-dial phone with message light, an AM/FM clock radio, individually controlled air conditioning, and nightly turndown service. These rooms are decorated with flair. Some rooms have round beds and mirrored ceilings, and these go for $140 a night. Suites with one bedroom and a living room are priced from $190 to $225, ascending to a lofty $268 to $1,250 for a two-bedroom suite.

In a Technicolor aside, columnist Rex Reed referred to a suite that he occupied as having lime draperies, pink furniture, a Popsicle-orange bedspread, a butterscotch-and-tomato-red bar, and a passion-purple bath. Said he: "I trudged off to my 14-color banana-split bedroom."

Each individual room or suite has a brass star on the door, signifying that "every guest at Bally's is a star." There's also a peephole through the star so guests can see who's knocking before they open the door.

Now, back to the hotel's public areas. Facing the Strip but set back about a block from the boulevard, is the marqueed drive-up entrance—your first stop. It juts out over the double-lane roadway and is fronted by a bronze statuary grouping. From there, the check-in and registration counters are to your left, and the casino is to your right. Separating the casino and lobby segments are colonnades and white marble statuary.

Behind the hotel are the swimming pools. The smaller one is a therapy pool seating 50 people, where water flows through jets at 800 gallons a minute. The bigger pool has a 320,000-gallon capacity.

On the floor below the lobby is a 40-store shopping arcade that offers an old-fashioned candy store with décor as tempting as the candied delights, a barbershop, a beauty salon, a florist, a jewelry emporium, a furrier, a boutique, and so forth.

And, of course, an important facility for those traveling with kids is the Youth Center, offering video arcade games and an ice-cream parlor.

Restaurants

No fewer than six restaurants offer dining to suit your mood. Most are located along Restaurant Court, a movie re-creation of an old-world street. The food is international, running the gamut from pâté de foie gras to hot pastrami, with plentiful selections in between. These are more gee-whiz statistics: The hotel keeps shrimp on hand by the boxcar load, 10,000 pounds to be exact; the seven sparkling kitchens use about 12,000 eggs each day; and Bally's 350 cooks turn out about 18,000 meals a day.

The **Café Gigi** is the hotel's poshest haute-cuisine eatery, with décor designed to reflect the palace of Versailles. Intimate dining alcoves are framed by luxurious draperies. Walls and ceilings are a soft green, highlighted with gold leaf. The room is further enhanced by crystal chandeliers as well as by gold-detailed mural wall panels and mirrors from the movie *Marie Antoinette*. The booths themselves are beautifully upholstered in rose velvet.

Your meal at Gigi might begin with smoked Scottish salmon served with dark bread, coquilles St-Jacques—creamy scallops in wine—or marrow on toast with truffle sauce. Since this is the kind of place for leisurely European-style multicourse feasting, you might proceed to a soup course—it could be anything from lobster bisque with cognac to French onion soup au gratin, perhaps followed by a wilted-spinach or Caesar salad. There's a considerable choice of entrees in the $27 to $40 range, among them steak Diane, braised fresh salmon in champagne and grapes, filet mignon with sauce béarnaise, roast duckling in orange or cherry sauce, and baby rack of lamb with fresh vegetables. Side orders of ratatouille niçoise or asparagus in hollandaise sauce are available, and, of course, there's a fine list of wines to complement your meal. As for desserts, they range from flambé specialties, such as crêpes Suzette, to a platter of fresh fruits and imported cheeses. Although you may not want to order such a complete meal as the above, this is not a place for skimping; as with a yacht, if you have to worry about the price, you can't afford Gigi. Save it for a night when you've made a killing at the casinos. Café Gigi is open Wednesday through Sunday from 6 to 11pm.

Tracy's is named after Spencer Tracy (don't tell me you didn't guess it), who was nominated 11 times for an Academy Award. He insisted that he was an "unromantic type" despite the fact that he appeared with nearly every top female star in Hollywood. The escalator ride to the restaurant takes you through a wonderland of beveled glass, with reflections of a spectacular crystal chandelier glittering everywhere.

The interior is done in soft shades of coral, with large gold pillars and two-story-high windows dominating the room. Each round table is lit by a small white-shaded lamp and has comfortable chairs.

Dinner can begin with imported prosciutto and melon; creamy marinated herring; a cup of double chicken consommé with noodles or chilled borscht; or perhaps Tracy's salad bowl with Belgian endive, artichokes, fresh mushrooms, and watercress. Entrees include mignonette of prime beef sauté with goose liver and truffle sauce and broiled double-rib spring lamb chops with mint jelly. All dinners are served with soup or salad, potatoes, and vegetables; entrees are $15 to $25. A large selection of desserts (such as fresh strawberry shortcake and French pastries) is available, and there's a good wine list.

If all this is not enough, there is a special Chinese menu as well. Appetizers include paper-wrapped chicken; rumaki with water chestnuts; and a combination plate with barbecued spareribs, eggroll, paper-wrapped chicken, fried prawns, and fried wonton. Soups range from egg flower to chicken broth with noodles and pork. There's a spicy Szechuan chicken with sautéed Chinese vegetables as well as Mongolian beef and fresh shrimps with sautéed vegetables. Other selections include lemon chicken and lobster Cantonese. All entrees are served with steamed rice, Chinese tea, and fortune cookies. Desserts include fresh pineapple, Chinese kumquats and lichee nuts, and homemade almond cookies. Entrees range in price from $14 to $22. Dinner at Tracy's is served Friday through Tuesday from 5 to 11pm.

Venice is the theme of **Caruso's,** Bally's elegant Italian restaurant. Hand-painted murals of Venetian scenes frame the entrance of this unique rust-toned room with its marble entry; cobblestone-motif carpeted floors, antique iron ovens, brilliant chandeliers, and classical statuary complete the décor. The menu offers a wide variety of choices. A good beginning to your meal is an antipasto platter or an appetizer of shrimp cocktail. All entrees are served with garlic bread toasted with sharp cheeses and pasta or potato. There are several fish and seafood items—lobster tails sauté oreganata, mountain brook trout sauté amandine, Caruso shellfish stew—as well as Italian specialties such as veal (scaloppine or parmigiana), homemade Italian sausages with roasted green peppers, and eggplant parmigiana. Of course, you can also order a pasta dish—such as fettuccine in cream and butter with grated parmesan, spaghetti with meatballs or sausages, or lasagne—as an entree or a side order. Among the à la carte desserts are rum cake and an excellent strawberry cheesecake. Entrees at Caruso's range from $15 to $25. Caruso's is open from Friday through Tuesday from 6 to 11pm.

Barrymores' honors America's most famous theatrical family —John, Ethel, and Lionel (not to mention Drew)—who during their careers earned, collectively, over $10 million and managed to die penniless. The planked ceiling of hand-rubbed hardwoods is complemented by carpeting of planked design, combining with carved oak bas-relief panels and copper accents to create a warm and comfortable ambience.

The cuisine is gourmet quality, featuring steak and seafood for the most part. You can begin with such appetizers as escargots bourguignonne and bluepoint oysters or cherrystone clams on the halfshell. Specialties from the open hearth include French-cut lamb chops, roast prime rib of beef au jus, and filet mignon with sautéed mushrooms. Seafood entrees offer an excellent selection, ranging from blackened red fish New Orleans style, to sautéed orange roughy, to a 2½-pound lobster. All entrees are served with potato and vegetable du jour; they range in price from $18 to $45. For dessert, you might select one of the assorted French pastries, a plate of assorted homemade ice creams and sherberts, or chocolate twist torte. Barrymore's is open nightly from 6 to 11pm.

The **Deli** is a New York–style eatery. Its immense menu offers an astounding number of choices. Combination sandwiches include salami, Swiss cheese, turkey breast, coleslaw, and Russian dressing. And among the traditional favorites are cream cheese and Nova Scotia salmon on a bagel; pastrami on rye; a Reuben with corned beef, Swiss cheese, and sauerkraut, grilled on rye; matzoh ball soup; and brisket on rye—all for $5 to $12. For dessert, try the deep-dish fruit pies with vanilla ice cream. The Deli is open daily from 8am to midnight.

The **Orleans Coffee House** is open around the clock and features a French Quarter décor. Most of the above-mentioned Deli fare is available here, too, but you can also get hot entrees, such as fried prawns with a choice of soup or salad, fresh vegetable, potato du jour, and rolls and butter.

Finally, there's a snack bar by the pool and a **Swensen's** ice-cream parlor in the shopping arcade.

Caesars Palace, 3570 Las Vegas Blvd. South, Las Vegas, NV 89109 (tel. 702/731-7110, or toll free 800/634-6001, 800/634-6661 for reservations).

From the day it opened, Caesars Palace has purveyed Lucullan luxuries under the name of the Caesars. The big hotel can no longer claim to be the biggest, but the invitation to lounge while being fed grapes by an adoring and nubile slavery is the image the Palace has continued to maintain.

At night, Caesars Palace bathes itself in a blue-green light, which glows from behind the grillwork that sheathes the hotel. Out front, the towering row of fountains puts on a magnificent display and takes up a couple of city blocks of valuable land. When the wind blusters across the desert, however, the fountains are liable to douse anything within a hundred feet. That's given rise to the quip that the Palace is "the biggest Italian car wash in town."

Alongside the beautiful fountains are 50-foot-high cypresses in double rows, slim and green. Reproductions of classic statuary—*The Rape of the Sabines, Winged Victory of Samothrace, Venus de Milo*

An Invitation to Readers

In researching this book, I have come across many wonderful establishments, the best of which I have included here. I'm sure that many of you will also come across wonderful hotels, inns, restaurants, guesthouses, shops, and attractions. Please don't keep them to yourself. Share your experiences, especially if you want to comment on places that I have covered in this edition that have changed for the worse. You can address your letters to me:

Mary Rakauskas
Frommer's Las Vegas
c/o Prentice Hall Press
Travel Books
15 Columbus Circle
New York, NY 10023

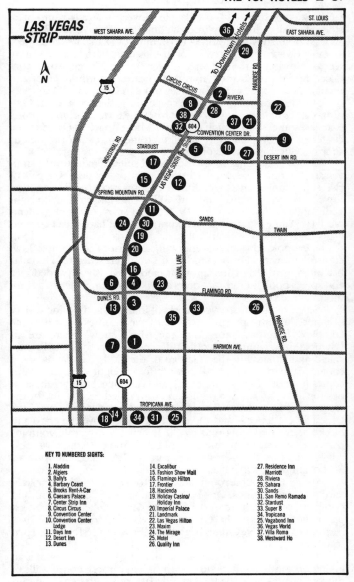

LAS VEGAS STRIP

KEY TO NUMBERED SIGHTS:

1. Aladdin
2. Algiers
3. Bally's
4. Barbary Coast
5. Brooks Rent-A-Car
6. Caesars Palace
7. Center Strip Inn
8. Circus Circus
9. Convention Center
10. Convention Center Lodge
11. Days Inn
12. Desert Inn
13. Dunes
14. Excalibur
15. Fashion Show Mall
16. Flamingo Hilton
17. Frontier
18. Hacienda
19. Holiday Casino/ Holiday Inn
20. Imperial Palace
21. Landmark
22. Las Vegas Hilton
23. Maxim
24. The Mirage
25. Motel
26. Quality Inn
27. Residence Inn Marriott
28. Riviera
29. Sahara
30. Sands
31. San Remo Ramada
32. Stardust
33. Super 8
34. Tropicana
25. Vagabond Inn
36. Vegas World
37. Villa Roma
38. Westward Ho

—complement the sweeping scene, and inside and outside the hotel has enough marble in balustrades, columns, statues, and gewgaws to have depleted Italy's Carrara marble quarries.

A few years ago, a dramatic innovation to the Caesars Palace façade was constructed—the People Mover, an arcaded automatic sidewalk facilitating entry into the hotel from the street, 240 feet away. It originates at a colonnaded Temple of Diana, its centerpiece an exact Carrara marble replica of that goddess of the hunt. A more recent addition is the Olympic Tower People Mover, which connects the Strip with the Omnimax Theatre, a thrilling entertainment center (about which I will say more in Chapter VII). Its geodesic-dome entrance mirrors the shape of the theater, and the Omnimax exterior light show is visible from the Strip. Within the hotel is an awesome 18-foot-high replica of Michelangelo's *David* in the center of the Appian Way, an elite arcade with such prestigious shops as Gucci and Ted Lapidus.

Caesars Palace has 1,600 rooms and suites. On its fourth anniversary the hotel opened a 14-story addition topped by a pair of two-story duplex suites with four bedrooms each. In 1974 another tower was added—this time with 375 rooms and suites with eight bedrooms. And in November 1979 the 24-story, 600-room Olympic Tower came into being. Its luxurious rooms have velvet-covered walls and sunken Roman tubs; its suites contain a seven-foot-diameter pool and Jacuzzi overlooking the Strip. The Olympic Tower also houses the above-mentioned Omnimax Theatre, a circular bar offering nightly entertainment, and a recently expanded race and sports book lounge that bears a striking resemblance to a commodities exchange.

Seven restaurants, several cocktail lounges, and a wide variety of entertainment options are some of the facilities piled into the complex. But that's not quite the whole show. There are an Olympic-size swimming pool and a pool shaped like a Roman shield and situated in the "Garden of the Gods," its landscaping copied from the Pompeii Baths of Rome; eight outdoor tennis courts (two of which are night-lit); and complete health-club facilities for men and women. Golf can be arranged nearby. As for the casino, it is lit by two majestic crystal-and-brass chandeliers—the largest in existence—and the domed ceiling above the craps and blackjack areas is supported by 20 Italian black marble columns trimmed with white marble and gold leaf. And then there's a cocktail lounge that floats in its own lagoon. It's called **Cleopatra's Barge,** and I'll get to it later.

Single and double room rates run from $125 to $170 for standard accommodations. One-bedroom suites are $230 to $560, and two-bedroom suites are in the $375 to $900 range. The most expensive of these are the Olympic Tower and Villa suites. Two-bedroom Villa duplex suites begin at $690. Add $15 for a third person in a standard room.

These prices are reasonable for what you get. Every room is an invitation to wallow in luxury, with sink-in carpets, entire walls of mirrors, chaises, some beds on raised platforms with steps, and mirrored ceilings—separated from the living area (cum sofas) by arched dividers. Even the drinking glasses in the baths are wrapped in gold metal foil rather than in the usual waxed paper. The décor is colorful (fuchsia, purple, and red); the entire effect is airy, plush-grand, and comfortable. Hallways in the towers are lined with niches exhibiting more statuary. The decorators certainly went wild, but their efforts succeeded. The rooms at Caesars Palace achieve luxury with a fun angle.

Restaurants

Most typical of Caesars Palace is the **Bacchanal.** A quotation from the menu says it all: "I, Caesar, welcome you to the most resplendent arena of gustatory delights . . . the BACCHANAL!

"My staff has in every way attempted to anticipate and satisfy your slightest wish . . . both in the magnificence of your surroundings and in the abundance and superlative quality of the cuisine. Here, you shall embark upon an adventure in gourmet dining unparalleled outside my empire . . . created and composed by my Master Chefs. Each component part of my dinner has been selected to complement each other item within that dinner. Three selected wines appropriate to the entrees are included in the price of the dinner." (Currently dinner at the Bacchanal is about $65 per person.)

Inside the menu are ostensible words of wisdom of the Roman emperors—Caligula's "Apud mensam plenam homini rostrum deliges" ("Tie the man by the beak to a well-filled table," or possibly more accurately, "Choose a well-stocked table as a rostrum for a man").

The setting is, of course, fittingly sumptuous. The entrance to the room is guarded by two golden lions, and the interior highlighted by a marble-walled lighted pool with a statue at its center; displayed around the pool are huge bowls of fruit, pastries, and ice-sculpture swans. Walls are white latticework or fluted columns interspersed with deep-purple swagged velvet curtains, the beamed blue ceiling suggests an open sky, and a grape arbor loops from beam to beam. Diners are comfortably ensconced in posh red-leather booths. Service is equally lavish; beautiful women in sexy harem outfits (known as the "Wine Goddesses") pour wine from shoulder height into ornate chalices. Only in Vegas! As for the meal itself, it's a veritable orgy of seven courses, lacking only a minion to feed you grapes: tidbits served with an aperitif; an hors d'oeuvres tray; tureens of soup; a "Roman piscatorian delight" (fish course); a "parade of gastronomical surprises fit for all of the twelve Caesars" (main course); vegetables; flambé desserts and pastries, cheeses, fruits, and coffee—and lots of wine to wash it all down. The menu is preselected with seasonal entrees. The Bacchanal is open for dinner Wednesday through Sunday. There are two seatings, 6 to 6:30pm and 9 to 9:30pm. Reservations are recommended.

Just as lavish but with a Venetian palazzo theme, the circular **Palace Court** is filled with art treasures. Reached via a crystal-and-bronze elevator, it is framed by a bronze-balustraded spiral staircase and illuminated by a Venini crystal chandelier; its white-latticed windows overlook the pool. The walls are hung with heroic paintings attributed to the School of Peter Paul Rubens and portraits of the 12 Caesars by a 17th-century painter, Camillo Procaccini (these used to hang in New York's posh Four Seasons restaurant). Tables are covered with Czechoslovakian lace cloths; set with gold-and-white Lenox china, vermeil flatware, and hand-blown crystal; and lit by silver candelabras. The centerpiece of the room is a domed stained-glass skylight (an orange-and-yellow sunburst), under which is a weeping fig tree shading a buffet display of fruits, cheeses, desserts, and ice sculpture. Around the tree are six terra-cotta pots of smaller trees and chrysanthemums, a lamppost with an exquisite glass glove in front of each. Statuary, faïence, and polished steel furnishings with velvet upholstery complete the picture. Adjoining the dining room is a piano bar with its own minicasino under a huge crystal chandelier. Gentlemen are required to wear jackets at the Palace Court.

Dinner offers a wider and, of course, pricier selection. Hors d'oeuvres range from pâté of goose liver Strasbourg to pike mousse and soups from lobster bisque flamed with Armagnac to chilled cream of cucumber topped with caviar. Among the entrees (which cost $25 to $45) are Maine lobster in tarragon butter with saffron rice, rock Cornish game hen in truffle sauce, steak Diane with wine sauce and mushrooms prepared tableside, and twin baby lamb chops with mint sauce. The sommelier will be happy to assist you in selecting the right wine to go with your entree. For dessert, perhaps try a flamed liqueur coffee with petit fours. The Palace Court is open for dinner nightly. There are two seatings, 6 to 6:30pm and 9 to 9:30pm. Reservations are necessary.

The newest culinary establishment attending to the dining needs of the high rollers in Caesars Palace is the **Empress Court,** where your palate is blessed with magnificent Chinese food prepared in the grand tradition by chefs from Hong Kong and served among elegant surroundings.

This is definitely not your chow mein and sweet-and-sour whatever restaurant; before you ever eat a bite, the stately columns and hand-rubbed woods will dispel that notion. The gourmet details are spelled out in Chinese on a magnificent menu (with accompanying English text). Dishes are primarily Cantonese, but there is a good selection of other regional specialties, including some Szechuan dishes. To simplify life, assorted delights are included in a choice between two complete prix-fixe dinners: the Empress selection is about $55, and the Emperor selection is about $40. Dishes vary weekly.

If you prefer to pick and choose among the many dishes, your choice of appetizers (from $6.50 to $14) might focus on the crispy crab claws or the minced squab in crystal wrap. A second course (from $9 to $28) might include such rarities as abalone and shark's fin soup, braised shark's fin in brown sauce, tender bamboo mushrooms in savory broth, or bird's nest soup with bamboo mushrooms. As to entrees (from $22 to $46), every category is represented. There are abalone dishes; fresh fish and other seafood, including exceptionally delicious gingered oysters prepared in a clay pot; vegetable and tofu dishes (from $14 to $22); poultry, including golden crisp squab and the ultimate Imperial Peking duck (accompanied by a white-gloved waiter); selections of pork and beef fried rice like none you have ever eaten before; and noodles. Top of the line are the Peking duck and the braised abalone with Chinese greens. The truly exceptional desserts include Beijing glazed apples and banana and the double-boiled bird's nest served in fresh coconut.

Dinner for two might easily approach $200, but it will be a spectacular event—one by which you will always remember Las Vegas. The Empress Court is open nightly. There are two seatings—6 to 6:30pm and 9 to 9:30pm. Reservations are necessary, and I suggest that you make them a few days in advance.

Primavera, overlooking the Garden of the Gods swimming pool and spa, offers gourmet Italian cuisine with specialties from the north and south of Italy. For a first course, the antipasti cart presents an outstanding array of cold appetizers. Or you might defer to a house speciality, such as the fried mozzarella or the elegant consommé garnished with egg flakes, spinach, and grated cheese.

The entree list begins with pasta, all homemade, including the chef's specialty of ravioli lightly filled with spinach and essence of veal and served with your choice of bolognese, marinara, or butter sauce. Several of the pasta entrees are also available as side dishes.

The many veal entrees range from the veal marsala to a simple veal with prosciutto and fresh sage. One of the unusual poultry choices features thin slices of sautéed breast of chicken with kiwi fruit and lemon butter, finished with rich sherry wine. Prime sirloin steak is served sautéed and topped with a tomato sauce or panfried with a touch of garlic. Maine Lobster is served in a spicy marinara sauce. And look for the chef's specialty each evening.

Primavera offers a pastry cart of Italian specialties as well as cheese with fresh fruit in season. Ice-cream desserts are meals in themselves—for example, the Cassata Caligula has layers of pistachio, zabaglione, and chocolate ice cream.

Meat or seafood entrees cost $24 to $45, pasta dishes are $12 to $18, and appetizers are $7 to $17. To help sustain your appetite, Primavera offers a good selection of still and sparkling Italian wines. Primavera is open daily for breakfast from 9 to 11am, for luncheon from noon to 3pm, and for dinner from 6 to 11pm.

A few steps from the Roman Forum Casino is the **Ah' So Steak House**–Caesars' Japanese-style restaurant, a Disney-esque creation of plastic trees, thousands of artificial flowers, arched bridges over pools and grottoes, bamboo paneling, Japanese paper lanterns, and grasslike carpeting. A waterfall cascading over lavalike rock embedded with colorful foliage takes up one entire wall, and there are even electric fireflies amid the delicate blossoms of Nipponese fruit trees. The six-course prix-fixe teppanyaki meal (about $45 per person) is served by waitresses appropriately attired in kimonos and obis. All cooking is done tableside. Dinner includes an appetizer; miso or clear soup; tempura seafood and vegetables; a salad of marinated cucumber and shredded crabmeat; an entree of boneless chicken breast, steak, or lobster tail; an assortment of Japanese vegetables; steamed rice; green tea; plenty of sake; fresh fruit; and dessert.

Apart from the teppanyaki dinner, the Ah' So also offers tuna sashimi and sushi prepared with salmon, tuna, sea vegetable roll, and shrimp. Steak House–Ah' So is open nightly from 6 to 11pm.

The **Spanish Steps** offers à la carte Spanish specialties, seafood, and steak. The restaurant is named for the 18th-century Piazza di Spagna in Rome. Designed in the style of Granada's Alhambra Palace, it has an imposing Moorish-design brass-and-copper entranceway; the geometric pattern is repeated in layered copper walls and ceiling, marquetry tables, and terra-cotta tile floors. Variations of copper and brass are the main colors; tables are set with copper plates and candle lamps; and the open kitchen is agleam with copperware. Waiters and waitresses are dressed in dramatic gaucho costumes.

A good way to begin your dinner is with the house special margarita, which you can sip while perusing the menu. Among the recommended appetizers are the ceviche and the scampi prepared tableside with red and green salsa flambé. An excellent soup course is the clear clam broth with a crown of sherry whipped cream. Among the Spanish entrees are paella Valenciana and zarzuela de mariscos—a mixture of lobster, shrimp, clams, and squid in a rich red sauce. Choices from the grill include a T-bone steak and double-thick broiled lamb chops. The price range for entrees at the Spanish Steps is $16 to $45. Desserts run the gamut from a traditional flan to assorted French pastries, and a pitcher of sangría is a good accompaniment to your meal. The Spanish Steps is open nightly from 5:30 to 10:30pm.

The **Palatium** is dedicated to serving lavish buffets for breakfast ($6.95), lunch ($7.95), and dinner ($10.95), with a fixed price for each. Saturday and Sunday brunch is $10.50. The restaurant is all etched glass, gold trim, and now and then Caesars statuary. Breakfast is served from 7:30 to 10:30am weekdays, and from 8:30am to 2:30pm Saturday and Sunday; lunch is served from 11 to 2:30pm daily; dinner is served from 4:30 to 10pm Sunday through Thursday, to 11pm Friday and Saturday.

La Piazza Food Court offers a vast selection of dishes from the most popular cuisines—Chinese, Italian, French, and Japanese. Your choices are mind-boggling—it's a market researcher's dream come true. La Piazza is open from 8am to 10pm Sunday through Thursday, to midnight Friday and Saturday.

And last, but by no means the least, there's an award-winning champagne brunch ($14.50; $9.50 for children under 12) every Sunday from 9:30am to 2pm in the **Circus Maximus** showroom, presented in the grand tradition of Roman feasts, with the added flair of the bubbly.

Food orgies are all well and good, but should you want lighter fare and more casual surroundings, there is the immense **Café Roma,** a 24-hour coffee shop. Done in warm colors—golds, oranges, reds, and yellows—the Café Roma has its share of fancy décor: classic columns and arches, etchings of ancient Roman scenes, and striped awnings over a colonnade; however, you can dine here comfortably in your jeans.

The fare ranges in price from $8 to $25 for a hot pastrami sandwich; lox and bagel; or filet mignon served with soup or salad, potatoes, and roll and butter; not to mention borscht with sour cream, crab Louie, and veal parmigiana. After 5pm, Café Roma also has an extensive Chinese menu, ranging from $6 to $9 for appetizers and from $12 to $30 for entrees.

There's one more option for daily sustenance—the **Post Time Deli.** The Deli is more for the convenience of the race and sports book fans who don't want to leave the area and will settle for a hamburger, a hot dog, or a delicious sandwich. Wine, beer, and soft drinks also are available. It's open seven days from 9am to midnight.

The Las Vegas Hilton, 3000 Paradise Rd. (adjacent to the Las Vegas Convention Center), Las Vegas, NV 89109 (tel. 702/732-5111, or toll free 800/732-7117).

Set on 63 acres, the Hilton is one of the largest resort hotels in the world, with 3,174 rooms, a reception desk that measures 100 feet, a core of international restaurants, an appropriately plush casino, shops, and much more. Its 375-foot tower dominates the desert horizon.

You'll need time to explore the Hilton, including the landscaped ten-acre outdoor recreation deck on the third-floor roof with six tennis courts, an 18-hole putting green, shuffleboard, and a huge swimming pool.

The Hilton is too sumptuous to be called rococo, too heady with the grandeur of Louis XIV, XV, XVI, and other unnumbered potentates to be reduced to ordinary narrative. I lost count of the chandeliers in the casino when I became absorbed with the Grecian-style frieze of bas-reliefs bordering the ceilings and the neon rainbows over the slot machines.

Your passport to stay at the Hilton is $80 to $165 a day, single or double; suites cost $350 to $1,100. At that rate for one or two (an extra person is $15; no charge for children sharing a room with their parents), you'll get a very large room facing outside. Each floor of rooms is decorated in the motif of a different country—Spain, France, China, and so forth. All have remote-control color TV with a special gaming-instruction channel. A dresser with nine deep drawers is placed beneath an embellished wood-framed mirror. Upholstered easy chairs, deep closets, a marble-topped dressing table with sink, and a completely separate tub-shower bath round out the layout. Colors are chosen with an eye for the elegant. Hallways are curved, and some of the room doors are recessed for a foyer effect. There are lanai suites on the third level near the pool at $350 a night.

Furthermore, in a town that has very few facilities for children, the Hilton has gone all out for family business. It has a completely self-contained $2-million **Youth Hotel** within the premises, a separate place with dormitories for girls and boys age 3 through 18. (Sleeping quarters are monitored by closed-circuit TV.) The Youth Hotel is supervised 24 hours a day by qualified educators and recreation specialists, meals and snacks are served, and rates and amounts for milkshakes and goodies are settled by parents in advance and added to their bill. It's like a summer camp. Fencing, boxing, tumbling, arts and crafts, table tennis, arcade games, teenage dances, an outdoor playground, basketball, volleyball, magic shows, desert field trips, and a stage where the children produce and mount their own skits and plays are among the many recreational outlets. Rates are $5 an hour for each child. Overnight stays are $30 per child. (This rate covers the hours of midnight to 8am.) The Youth Hotel is open from 8am to 10pm daily year round; kids can stay overnight seven days a week from mid-June until Labor Day and weekends and holidays during the rest of the year.

Adults will appreciate the health spa for men and women, with exercise rooms, sauna and steam rooms, and a whirlpool bath. The spa also offers all kinds of refreshing relief from those late hours of cigarettes and alcohol over the blackjack tables: massage; specially invigorating baths; hot packs; cosmetic beauty baths; and even oxygen pep-ups and a treatment in a wonder body machine called Panthermal, which is claimed to remove every form of weariness, increase muscular working capacity, clean skin, stimulate body functions, diminish weight, and eliminate cellulite!

Restaurants

Just about every dining mood can be accommodated at the Hilton. There are offerings from the delicate delights of Japan, the light pastas and veal dishes of Italy, the subtle and elegant cuisine of France, as well as the finest beef fare selected for Hilton steaks and prime ribs.

Le Montrachet, the pride of the Las Vegas Hilton, features continental cuisine and a wine cellar with over 400 wines from around the world. Le Montrachet was created to achieve the utmost in elegant dining. The dark walls, plush banquettes, and flattering light create a rich, relaxed atmosphere that is conducive to appreciation of the chef's superb creations.

Dinner at Le Montrachet was one of the finest I have had at any restaurant from New York to California. Ordering from the six-course, prix-fixe menu, I began my meal with chilled foie gras of duck on a checkerboard of miniature green beans. Then came poached oysters on the halfshell, topped with orange butter glaze, followed by a delicate sweet basil sorbet. Choice of entrees was between roast rack of lamb marinated with sweet basil, fresh dill, mint, shallots, and tarragon; or medallions of veal and morel mushrooms with Noilly cream sauce. (Are your salivary glands coming to life?) A salad of lamb lettuce, endive, and watercress—tossed with walnuts, Dijon mustard, and lemon juice—was next, and all of the above was capped by a hot apple tart topped with caramel ice cream. The prix-fixe dinner is $55—about $20 less than if each course is ordered individually.

Should you decide to order à la carte, I suggest that you try something a bit different—and then wait for a very pleasant surprise. You might choose the medallions of venison on a bed of steamed red cabbage, or the poached filet of sole with mousse of lobster. A first or second course might be the raviolis of fresh crabmeat and morel mushrooms topped with caviar.

Entrees also include seafood choices from Maine lobster to Dover sole either grilled or boned and filled with mousse of lobster and served with truffle slices. The broiled veal chop stuffed with wild mushrooms and served with Madeira sauce and truffles is excellent, too, as is the broiled filet mignon served with a puff pastry shell of wild mushrooms and a pinot noir and Sandeman port wine sauce.

Then by all means review the pastry cart. If by some quirk nothing catches your eye, scan the dessert list and consider the Swiss chocolate soufflé, the crème anglaise with Cointreau, or the Painter's Palette with sorbets and fresh fruits of the season. Hors d'oeuvres range from $10 to $23 and soup or salad ranges from $5 to $7. Entrees are about $23 to $38; desserts are about $6 to $10. Le Montrachet is open nightly from 6 to 11pm. Reservations are necessary, as are jacket and tie.

Most dramatic of the restaurants is **Benihana Village,** a complex of two dining areas and four cocktail lounges set in a Japanese village with lush foliage, a three-story palace, and running streams. There are a hibachi dining room and a robata (Japanese barbecue) room. Seating is under pagoda roofs and a giant umbrella, and special effects include thunder and lightning followed by pouring rain (not on diners, however), dancing waters bathed in colored lights, and electronic fireworks. An arched wooden bridge over a stream connects the dining areas. There are also several cocktail areas, including one in which you can enjoy cocktails in your own private rickshaw.

In the hibachi room, all cooking is done tableside by chefs who wield their carving knives with the expertise of samurai warriors. Full dinners include a hibachi shrimp appetizer, soup, salad, rice, vegetable, green tea, and ice cream or sherbet; they're priced at $15 to $40. Hibachi chicken, sukiyaki steak, hibachi steak, and filet mignon are also on the menu. You can order a carafe of sake with your meal. The meal in the robata room contains a choice of corn on the cob, skewer of mushrooms, or onions and green peppers instead of tempura vegetables. Entrees of barbecued chicken, New York–cut sirloin, filet mignon, and steak-and-chicken or steak-and-shrimp combination are available for $15 to $35. You can order à la carte from any of the menus, all of which also offer half-price dinners for children under 12. Benihana is open nightly for cocktails from 5pm to midnight and for dining from 6 to 11pm.

For light Italian fare, the lovely **Andiamo** features an open kitchen where guests can watch the chefs busily turning out delicious meals. Both the à la carte lunch and the dinner menus offer a remarkable selection. Lunch at Andiamo might begin with hot or cold antipasti, including such delectables as fresh asparagus with sweet pepper sauce and crisply fried squid with fresh tomato sauce. Pizzas are decidedly not those found at your local parlor—the Porcini e Salsiccia, for example, is composed of porcini mushrooms, Italian sausage, and tomato sauce with mozzarella, fontina, and provolone. For pasta, try the Ravioli Neri all' Aragosta with lobster, tarragon, and lobster sauce. An impressive list of entrees includes selections such as salmon, swordfish, sirloin minute steak, and osso buco Andiamo. Your tab for lunch, without antipasti, wine, dessert, or coffee, will be about $10 to $16.

Andiamo's dinner menu is expansive, and the antipasti include one of my favorites, Carpaccio di Manzo—wafer-thin slices of tenderloin of beef blessed with parmesan, olive oil, and lemon juice. From the pasta entrees, you might choose the Fettuccine Verdi al Pomodoro e Melanzane—spinach egg noodles with eggplant, tomatoes, and sweet basil. Other entrees are exceptional, too—a whole baby salmon sautéed in butter, a veal chop with morel mushrooms and marsala sauce, and a charcoal-broiled filet mignon with Barolo Riserva red wine sauce. Pasta entrees run $12 to $20; seafood and meat courses will set you back $14 to $24. Should you still have space for dessert and the patience to wait 30 minutes, the soufflés at $5 are heavenly—there's a choice of Amaretto, Galliano, or lemon. Or you might consider the Venetian Dream of white espresso ice cream in a chocolate gondola for $9. Andiamo is open daily for lunch from 11:30am to 2:30pm and for dinner from 6 to 11pm. Reservations are suggested.

Within the rustic western **Hilton Steak House,** there's an open charcoal kitchen, meat is displayed in a glass-doored refrigerator case, and rough-hewn barnwood or stucco walls are hung with farm implements and antlers. Railroad lamps and saddles are suspended from the log-beamed ceiling.

You can order a filet mignon, New York steak, or a 20-ounce T-bone or combination steak and lobster. Alternatives to steak are broiled whitefish and barbecued pork ribs. Entrees cost $18 to $30 and are served with salad, corn on the cob or baked potato, and cheese-topped sourdough bread. Side orders of baked potato, acorn squash, or fresh mushrooms are also available. Desserts are chocolate mousse cake, apple pie à la mode, and a less-than-traditional pecan-apple cheesecake. The Hilton Steak House is open nightly from 6 to 11:30pm.

Also western in décor is **Mamchen's Deli,** complete with swinging saloon doors, leaded-glass windows, mahogany paneling and beams, oak floors, and branding tools hanging over the old-fashioned marble bar. It's not totally western, though—Mamchen's is lettered in Hebrew-style characters, and the menu features the likes of smoked salmon, onions and cream cheese on a bagel, pastrami on homemade rye, chicken soup with kreplach, and chopped liver sandwiches—all in the $7 to $10 range. And of course there's strudel for dessert. Mamchen's is open daily from 11:30am to 10pm.

The **Barronshire Prime Rib Room** offers prime-rib dinners, with Yorkshire pudding, mousseline potatoes, and creamed horseradish, at $20 to $25, depending on the cut. It has a hushed library ambience, complete with book-lined walls and a desk with an antique typewriter and open dictionary. The Barronshire Prime Rib Room is open nightly from 6pm to 11pm.

The **Odyssey Buffet** is one of the best in town, displaying the Hilton's reputation for quality. The breakfast buffet ($6.50) is served from 7 to 9:30am, lunch ($7.75) is from 11am to 2:30pm, and dinner ($9.25) is from 6 to 10pm. On Saturday and Sunday there is a champagne brunch ($9.25) from 8am to 2pm.

The **Café Eclair,** an authentic Viennese café stube, offers such light fare as sandwiches, ice cream, pastries, and Viennese *torten* (cakes) to eat or take out. It's open daily from 7am to 9pm.

Socorro Springs, the Hilton's spacious coffee shop, is open round the clock and is conveniently located just off the main lobby next to the casino. You can get a quick continental breakfast or a variety of three-egg omelets there, depending on the size of your appetite. The Springs also offers fitness specialties, such as cholesterol-free eggs. Full breakfasts cost $6.50 to $9.25. Lunch and dinner menus offer a good array of salads, sandwiches, and burgers, as well as such more substantive choices as chicken piccata, fried prawns, and sirloin steak, in the range of $9.50 to $13.50. Lunch and late-night favorites also include thick Sicilian pizza.

Finally, there's the **Paddock Snack Bar,** located in the SuperBook. The Paddock offers sandwiches, light bites, pizza, and soft drinks. Inside information has it that the corned beef sandwich served here is "the best" and will last through an entire football game. The snack bar is open from 7am to 10pm Sunday through Thursday, to midnight Friday and Saturday.

Desert Inn, 3145 Las Vegas Blvd. South (directly opposite the Frontier Hotel), Las Vegas, NV 89109 (tel. 702/733-4444, or toll free 800/634-6906).

A Strip fixture since 1950, the Desert Inn opened with 225 rooms built on 200 acres. Today the resort has 821 rooms, including 95 suites. In 1952 an 18-hole, par-72, championship golf course was created—a course that has played host to some of the nation's most famous golf tournaments. The golf course is part of the Desert Inn Hotel. The clubhouse features a pro shop, men's and women's locker rooms, and a deli-style restaurant. Play is restricted to registered guests and those playing with them. The greens fee for registered guests is $75 weekdays, $100 weekends (including cart); for others it's $135 per round. Club rentals are available. As for tennis, there are ten tournament-class courts, five of which are night lit; rackets can be rented. Unlimited tennis is free to Desert Inn guests. Other facilities include an Olympic-size swimming pool, about a dozen whirlpool baths scattered throughout the property, 14,000 square feet of shops, five restaurants, and, of course, a fine casino.

This abundance of existent facilities notwithstanding, in 1975 the Desert Inn undertook a $55-million expansion program. In this project, the Desert Inn was transformed into one of the most desirable hotels in town. It certainly has the most class of any hotel on the Strip, the usual ostentatious opulence replaced here by an understated (for Vegas) elegance. It has been redesigned and rebuilt, inside and out, from the foundation up. It now has the most attractive façade in town—a modular effect combining sand-colored stone and bronze reflective glass. Most notable is the previously unheard-of-in-Vegas refined taste throughout. In 1986, the Desert Inn began a multiyear, multimillion-dollar refurbishment program that was completed in 1990. Each room was totally refurnished. All the public areas, including the casino and the hotel lobby, were redecorated in a Southwestern motif. The Desert Inn's buildings are situated on 200 acres of beautifully landscaped grounds, containing a lake, a waterfall, the pool, and sundecks. Considerable use of bronze glass is pleasantly dazzling, reflecting the brightly colored canvas patio awnings and expanses of water, grass, and palms.

To complete the total resort experience, the Desert Inn spent $3 million constructing a luxury health spa. It is second to none as a relaxation and fitness facility, including a gym, spas, saunas, massage, and skin care programs. The Desert Inn spa offers the ultimate total-care concept.

Golf- and tennis-themed buildings contain 821 beautiful rooms and suites. The least expensive rooms are in the Forest Hills wing, and they offer a light, bright, and cheerful Cote d'Azur look, befitting the poolside locale. Beds (queen- or king-size) have colorful striped canopies and tieback draperies. Furnishings are of imported rattan, including comfortable lounge chairs and ottomans. Exceptional amenities include terrycloth robes, phones in the bathrooms, and twice-daily maid service with evening turndown plus a mint. Particularly spectacular are the 95 suites, all decorated to reflect the classic to the exotic. Some of the suites even have their own private swimming pools, but all abound in luxury. Rooms at the Desert Inn are priced from $95 to $185, single or double; the higher rate is for a minisuite complete with wet bar, sunken marble tub, and other such luxuries. One-bedroom suites are $250 to $550; one- to four-bedroom private-pool suites are $550 to $1,500; ultraluxurious accommodations ascend to $2,000.

Last but not least of many changes is the casino, featuring a recently added race and sports book and sporting a plush décor dominated by 30 impressive circular brass chandeliers. And as you might expect, headliners play the Crystal Room Showplace.

Restaurants

I'll begin with **La Vie en Rose.** The striking décor, highlighted by hand-painted murals, establishes the romance and the theme of the restaurant and the song made famous by the French chanteuse Edith Piaf. Muted roses and rose hues are subtly in abundance in the murals and carpeting and upholstery fabrics. A fresh rose on every table adds the finishing touch. La Vie en Rose is elegant dining at its most pleasant.

You can get off to a lovely start with a choice of hors d'oeuvres that extends up to Beluga caviar. Entrees include such specialties as the tender white veal sautéed with demiglace and fresh cream, served with carmelized apples and flamed with apple brandy; the braised Cornish game hen stuffed with wild rice and pistachios and topped with truffle sauce; and the award-winning steak Diane flamed with cognac. Entree prices range from $26 to $45. For dessert, a selection from the pastry cart will add another $7. La Vie en Rose is open Thursday through Monday and offers four seatings—at 6pm, 6:30pm, 9pm and 9:30pm. Jackets and reservations are necessary.

The **Portofino,** situated on the mezzanine, overlooks the casino action below, which tends to lend an air of excitement. It's quite luxurious, with Carrara marble decking and carpeting in a baroque acanthus scroll pattern of deep burgundy, green, and gold. The walls are Mediterranean stucco, which is typical of the site of Portofino. The ceiling has heavy beams and a suspended arbor from which hang chandeliers of hand-blown glass globes.

The Portofino, which specializes in northern Italian cuisine, features tableside cooking. The menu offers so many tempting northern Italian and continental specialties that you may find the choosing hard. For openers, the smoked salmon is great—but so are the crab legs; the fresh poached salmon served with cucumber salad and mustard sauce; and the shrimp, lobster, tuna, and crab mixed with artichoke heart, anchovies, romaine, and dressing. That's just the appetizer dilemma, and I won't even go into the soups and salads. As for the entrees, there are veal scaloppine rolled around a mixture of seasoned meat and cheese, simmered in wine; whole trout stuffed with crabmeat and served with drawn butter and lemon; seared beef tenderloin with mushrooms, shallots, red wine sauce, and sour cream; and whole New England lobster with tomalley (a sauce of lobster livers); and, of course, osso buco. Entrees are priced from $13 to $27.50. Side orders of cannelloni, gnocchi, and fettuccine Alfredo are also available. And if after all that you're still up for a rich dessert, there's zabaglione with fruit or mousse pie. The Portofino is open Tuesday through Saturday from 6 to 11pm. Jackets and reservations are necessary.

The Desert Inn has the touch of Far Eastern elegance with **HoWan,** located on the casino level. At the entry, an aquarium of exotic fish sets forth the quiet and beauty of the classic Chinese décor within. The dining area is finely decorated and somewhat reminiscent of the balanced proportion and elegance of the Ming Dynasty. There are antique vases and ginger jars, replete with court scenes of the Tung Chin period of the Ching Dynasty. Court portraits of the Emperor and Empress, painted on clay, are in the style of the ancient cave paintings in the Hunan province. Subtle shades of gold, black, and burgundy, with mahogany moldings, complete the Far East ambience.

HoWan means "good fortune"—certainly for those who dine here. The menu offers a variety of soups and appetizers to start you off, including minced squab HoWan; shrimp wrapped in edible rice paper; shark's fin soup; and Eight Precious Soup with diced chicken, prawns, mushrooms, green peas, beaten eggs, winter melon, and abalone, in a rich chicken broth. For your main course there's a complete selection of Chinese dishes, including such specialties as fresh fish, Peking duck, beef with oyster sauce, lobster HoWan, and almond pressed duck. HoWan entrees range in price from $11 to $40. Chinese standards, such as egg foo yung, chow mein, and fried rice in a variety of flavors—all in the $7 to $12 range—can also be ordered. HoWan is open Wednesday through Sunday from 6 to 11pm.

The country-club restaurant is **Champions' Deli,** which serves breakfast, lunch, and drinks. It's located in the Desert Inn Country Club and is the ideal spot to sustain or refresh yourself before or after golf or tennis. The Deli serves breakfast and lunch, including spectacular salads and a dozen hot and cold favorite deli-style sandwiches. For those seeking a simpler nosh, there are hot dogs and pizza. Champions' Deli is open daily from 8am to 5pm.

La Promenade, on the casino floor, is the Desert Inn's 24-hour coffee shop, considerably more elegant than the usual of this genre with its velvet booths and teal-blue-upholstered chrome chairs under immense tasseled gold umbrellas. The umbrellas are supported by massive copper-and-gold columns, each with six very delicate chandelier lamps attached and flowers and plants at its base. Expansive tinted windows offer a view of the pool and gardens.

A complete dinner is offered for $14, including soup or salad, entree (perhaps a broiled half spring chicken, fresh fish, or a New York Steak), and vegetable. That's in addition to a wide choice of à la carte items available at all times. Breakfast options range from fresh-baked muffins to kippered herring and everything in between.

Residence Inn by Marriott, 3225 Paradise Rd. (across from the Las Vegas Convention Center), near Desert Inn Rd., Las Vegas, NV 89109 (tel. 702/796-9300, or toll free 800/331-3131).

Just when you thought you were finally getting used to bustling hotels/casinos/spectaculars, along comes the Residence Inn by Marriott. It's a breath of fresh air, with grass. The Strip may be 24-hour fun, but now and then a little laid-back peace in charming, spacious, and elegant surroundings can help revive you for the next round of whatever.

The Marriott is, as they say, a residence inn (nongaming). It's really much more than an all-suite hotel. For all practical purposes, you have your own very private living quarters—a sanctuary comfortably furnished and cleverly arranged with separate sleeping areas for nighttime privacy whether there are one, two, three, or four people. Each of the accommodations is basically a beautifully decorated apartment with a breakfast bar and full kitchen—a full-size refrigerator, range and oven, microwave, coffee maker, dishwasher, dishware, and glasses. Marriott thought of everything, including a complimentary shopping service for your groceries. Many of the living rooms have cozy wood-burning fireplaces; all have satellite color TV and a VCR (you can't tape, but you can play).

The penthouse suites are perfect for two or for a family. They are on two levels with two bedrooms, two full bathrooms, two closets, and even two TVs. All the beds are queen-size.

And with the complimentary continental breakfast, there's a complimentary daily newspaper. Maid service is weekdays (the Marriott feels that you should have weekends to yourself). Valet service is available, and there are laundry facilities. As far as I can see, Marriott thought of everything to make your stay comfortable and enjoyable. The Residence Inn is the sort of place where you'd like to be able to stay longer.

There is, of course, a swimming pool and a heated whirlpool adjacent to a Sports Court for racquetball. A canvas-covered relaxation space is located next to the pool; it can get beastly hot in the summer sun. The Inn also has a collection of board games for the use of the guests in their rooms. Thursday evenings from 5 to 6:30pm there's a complimentary barbecue. The hospitality hour is weekdays from 5 to 6:30pm.

The Residence Inn is a nongaming enclave that could have been plucked out of Beverly Hills or Palm Springs. The 192 suites are grouped into small two-story structures, around which are beautifully landscaped walkways. What's more, your private entrance is just steps away from the curbside parking—there's no waiting for a someone to deliver the car or searching for it in a parking lot.

The central building encloses the lobby and the hearth room, where complimentary breakfast is served and where evening social hours are held. It's quite handsome with pink tile floors at the entry, bleached-wood furnishings, rose-and-beige carpeting in the hearth room, a fireplace, love seats done in desert tones of rose and gray-blue, pastel-tone floral prints, and uncluttered ceiling fans. The staff here is very helpful and will arrange transportation and also recommend local activities and current attractions.

Rates for one to six nights in the studio suites (with one bed) are $89 to $109; the penthouse suites (with two beds and two baths) are $129 to $149. From 7 to 29 nights, the rates decrease by $10 per night. For two compatible couples, a penthouse suite is an attractive bargain even without all the complimentaries. And, bless Marriott's heart, pets are welcome.

Flamingo Hilton, 3555 Las Vegas Blvd. South, Las Vegas, NV 89109 (tel. 702/733-3111, or toll free 800/732-2111).

The Flamingo Hilton recently broke ground on what is to become a 728-room, 28-story luxury tower that will include an Italian restaurant, a lounge, a tour lobby, a VIP lounge, an outdoor plaza, and 20,000 square feet of additional casino space. The tower is scheduled for completion in early 1991.

The Flamingo has come a long way since it opened. Jimmy Durante was the opening headliner, and the wealthy and famous flocked to the beautifully landscaped resort festooned with lush palms and tropical plants.

Today the grounds are still lush. The original palms and sycamores are now complemented by Russian and Chinese elms and olive trees, cobblestoned pathways, fountains, and flower gardens. In the midst of it all are an Olympic-size swimming pool, a sundeck, and the Little Vienna outdoor restaurant of the Crown Room Buffet.

Past remodeling expanded the size of the casino; it now has 7 craps layouts, 60 blackjack tables, 6 roulette tables, a Big Six wheel, a 90-seat keno lounge, and an 1,150-machine slot arcade where a Pot-O-Gold Jackpot and progressive slots offer potential winnings up to $1 million. Although the Flamingo offers almost every imaginable amenity, guests are welcome to use the facilities of the nearby Las Vegas Hilton, including the above-mentioned Youth Hotel for children ages 3 to 18.

Both old and new rooms (the former completely refurbished) are extremely attractive. The present 800-room tower accommodations have coordinated drapes and wallpaper in one of five color schemes: rust, blue, green, beige/yellow, or peach. They're large and handsomely furnished, and they offer views of the Strip or garden. A gaming-instruction channel on your color TV is one of many extras. Rooms in the old building are storybook homey, with old-fashioned lamps and cotton quilts, and pretty paintings on the walls. The tower has a health club; an indoor/outdoor pool; tennis courts for day and night play; and a new gourmet restaurant, the Flamingo Room. Room rates are $70 to $118 a night, single or double, depending on location. There are a total of 2,920 rooms and suites.

Restaurants

The Flamingo Hilton has introduced a different restaurant concept to Las Vegas with its **Food Fantasy,** a "buffeteria" that allows you to select the items that you wish from large, attractive displays. Modeled after the restaurant of the same name at the Hilton Hawaiian Village in Honolulu, it has a light and airy garden décor with a brick floor, an abundance of plants, and a garden/pool view. A large salad bar is part of the offerings.

Breakfast fare ranges from $4 to $8 for cheese blintzes (three) with blueberries and sour cream to eggs Benedict. On weekends, early-morning breakfasters (midnight to 7am) can feast on two eggs with toast, hash browns, and bacon or sausage. There is a large selection of sandwiches—such as sliced breast of turkey, a hoagie (a French roll filled with ham, cheese, turkey, pickles, and salad), and a French-dip roast beef sandwich with french fries. Also available are salads—perhaps avocado or tomato stuffed with seafood or chicken salad—and hot entrees such as broiled lamb chops with mint jelly, southern fried chicken with biscuits and honey, and New York–cut sirloin steak with onion rings. Many luscious desserts are on glorious, tempting display.

Also on the premises is a **Beef Barron,** an institution throughout the Hilton Chain. The décor reflects the Old West, with fine western art displayed on the walls. A warm ambience is effected by a gold, rust, and brown color scheme; soft lighting emanates from steer-horn chandeliers, and western artifacts—guns, saddles, and the like—are on display.

It's a Beef Barron tradition to begin your dinner with the house specialty—black-bean soup with sherry. A full dinner—priced at $46 for two—includes soup, a salad, a sirloin steak carved tableside, corn on the cob, a baked potato, a fresh vegetable, a decanter of house wine, and a selection from the pastry cart. If you want to order à la carte, you might consider half a barbecued chicken on the spit, prime rib au jus with creamy horseradish, or the steak-and-lobster combination. All cost $13 to $27.50 and are served with salad, fresh vegetables, and home-baked ranch rye bread. The Beef Barron is open nightly from 5 to 11:30pm.

Just outside the Beef Barron is the hotel's **Promenade Bar,** a piano bar where you can sit, relax, and listen to some delightfully gentle music.

A red rickshaw sits outside the **Peking Market,** the interior of which is designed to suggest an open marketplace in a bustling Chinese city. Merchandise—foodstuffs, kites, tea, dishes, fans, and so on—is displayed in cases lining the walls. An open wood-burning brick oven adds a cozy note, overhead are bamboo and rattan fans, and Chinese music is played in the background.

A full dinner for two, priced at $15 per person, includes eggrolls, barbecued pork, fried wonton, egg flower soup, tender sautéed beef with green pepper, sweet-and-sour pork, fried rice with shrimp and pork, cashew chicken, fortune or almond cookies, ice cream, and tea. A la carte entrees cost $10 to $16. You might order crisp chicken with lemon sauce, boned duckling with toasted almonds served with sweet-and-sour sauce, or prawns and sautéed fresh tomatoes. The Peking Market is open nightly from 6 to 11pm.

Adjoining the restaurant is **The Spirits of Dr. Wu,** an exotic bar furnished with peacock chairs. A photomural of a real Chinese market adorns one wall. Dr. Wu specializes in potent drinks, such as the Mongolian Kick, a blend of coconut cream, pineapple juice, light rum, vodka, and cream.

Then there's **Lindy's,** patterned after the New York deli and featuring the cheesecake that made the deli famous. Its marble tables, bentwood chairs, white tile floors, ceiling fans, and canopy awnings evoke a turn-of-the-century marketplace.

Lindy's menu offers breakfast, lunch, and dinner, all in the $5 to $13 range. Waffles with whipped butter and maple-flavored syrup or two eggs with hash browns, juice, toast, and a beverage are offered for breakfast lovers. Sandwiches run the gamut from braunschweiger liverwurst to kosher-style salami to smoked beef tongue. Those with bigger appetites might enjoy the broiled New York minute steak. The deli platters provide some great alternatives, such as smoked salmon with Bermuda onion, sliced tomatoes, a bagel, and cream cheese. Burgers come smothered with onions and other goodies. There are also entrees of filet of sole, grilled beef liver with onions, and barbecued meaty beef rib bones. The fountain offers only superlatives, from "mammoth malts" to "gigantic banana splits." There are also beer and wine. Lindy's offers the classic New York deli beverage—Dr. Brown's soda, in several flavors, including black cherry. Lindy's is open 24 hours a day.

The **Flamingo Room** is a pleasant place to relax over breakfast, lunch, or dinner. The room is done in pastels and light woods, with soft recessed lighting and a large expanse of windows overlooking the pool. The salad bar for lunch has an appetizing array (one of the largest in town) of beautifully fresh choices, including large shrimp. Dinner entrees offer a good selection of fresh fish, steaks, and rack of lamb for $15 to $28, although an average is about $18. Among the specialties of the house are a delicious mixed grill and the Flamingo barbecue. The Flamingo Room is open daily from 7am to 11am for breakfast, 11:30am to 2pm for lunch, and 5 to 11pm for dinner.

Finally, there's the **Crown Room Buffet,** a bright area buffet dining room located next to the Little Venice pool terrace. The Crown Room features a breakfast buffet at $5 from 7 to 11:30am and a dinner buffet at $6.50 from 4:30 to 9:30pm.

The Tropicana Hotel & Casino, 3801 Las Vegas Blvd. South, Las Vegas, NV 89109 (tel. 702/739-2222, or toll free 800/634-4000, 24 hours).

A new era of luxury has begun at the Tropicana. When this resort hotel opened in 1957, it was one of the most lavish in the state and was known as "the Tiffany of the Strip." Two years later it added more rooms and brought in the *Folies Bergère* direct from Paris (it's still running). By 1961 the hotel had added an 18-hole golf course and a country club.

In 1979 Ramada Inns, Inc., acquired the property, marking that company's first venture into the luxury hotel field as well as its first gaming hotel. It set out to renew the image of the Tropicana. The first major change was the addition of a 22-story tower to increase the room count to 1,150. The casino was doubled in size and redecorated in a grand and very plush European style.

A second reconstruction began in 1984. By 1986 the Tropicana had completed a $70-million expansion to give the resort hotel a totally new image and to expand its casino. Another 22-story tower was added with 806 guest rooms, increasing the total number to 1,913. Four of the six elevators in the new Island Tower are glass-enclosed and run up the face of the building.

The focal point of the expansion is a spectacular five-acre water park and "island" within the resort hotel grounds. For all those who enjoy swimming, the Tropicana now has the largest indoor/outdoor swimming pool in the world, plus a water slide and three Jacuzzis. One end of the pool can be heated during winter months and (can you believe it?) has swim-up blackjack tables! Where you might choose to keep your money is something else again, but suffice it to say that the hotel has a money-drier should the bills get soaked. If you just want to watch, there are lagoons with penguins, swans, Koi fish in an array of colors, and flamingos. The "island" also features variety acts during the day.

With the expansion of the casino, a good deal of redesign has taken place. The Baccarat Room is now a thing of beauty to behold—remodeled with mirrors, wall sconces, and crystal chandeliers befitting the game's historically elegant image.

Rooms in the new Island Tower are light, airy, and spacious. Furnishings are bamboo trim, and the drapes, bedspreads, and carpeting are in pastel hues that carry through the tropical feeling. As with the other tower and lanai rooms in the wings, all offer every modern amenity.

One of the most talked-about features of the Tropicana is its tennis layout. For 24-hour play, the Tropicana Racquet Club has four outdoor tennis courts. They're beautiful to look at, and if you're a watcher, you can observe from the paneled Paradise Cove lounge on a mezzanine balcony overlooking the courts. No greater comfort has ever been installed for kibitzers.

Room rates are $79 to $135, single or double; suites are priced at either $260 or $525.

Restaurants

Seven restaurants offer sumptuous repasts.

The Tropicana's requisite 24-hour eatery is the **Java Java Coffee Room,** decorated in a cheerful, predominantly green-and-yellow tropical color scheme. In addition to a full range of breakfast items served at any hour, there's a menu of salads, soups, and so forth. You can order anything from a kosher frank with chili or sauerkraut to a full meal of fried chicken with soup or salad, vegetable, potato, and rolls and butter—all for $6 to $12.

El Gaucho is a steak-lover's delight. It's done in an Argentinian motif—beamed ceilings, hides on the walls, bits, branding irons, halters, cinches, stirrups, and woven shawls. Beef is the specialty of the house: steaks, ribs, and combination plates. Entrees range from $15 to $35; the top end of the range is a steak-and-seafood platter. El Gaucho has a select list of imported and domestic wines. El Gaucho is open only for dinner, from 6 to 11pm Friday through Tuesday.

The **Rhapsody** offers an excellent selection of entrees for all tastes. Whether you're moved toward Long Island duckling, veal piccata, filet mignon, rack of spring lamb, scampi, rainbow trout, Columbia River salmon, cioppino (San Francisco), or broiled Australian lobster tails, the Rhapsody will delight your appetite. And the desserts are not to be ignored: There's peach Melba, baked Alaska, French pastries, chocolate mousse—many of those wonderful things you never seem to have enough room for.

Most entrees cost $15 to $30 per person, but some of the dishes are priced for two—for example, the chateaubriand for $39.50. The menu is à la carte. The Rhapsody is open Wednesday through Sunday from 6 to 11pm. Sunday brunch is from 9am to 2pm.

The Tropics is just that—a Polynesian aura with beaded curtains, colorful banners, tiki figures, lighting glowing from large shells, and a waterfall running through the center of the restaurant. The view to the outside is lovely. The restaurant has three glassed-in tiers that overlook the "island" and all the activities and shows. The Tropics serves breakfast, lunch, and dinner Friday through Sunday from 7:30am to 10pm. For the rest of the week, hours are 7:30am to 2:30pm. Polynesian delights are the specialty of the house. Breakfast will cost $5 to $7.50; lunch, $7 to $13; and dinner, $12 to $19.

An additional dining option is the **Island Buffet,** a decadent display of irresistible delights laid out in a dramatic setting, the old multitiered pink-and-blue Tiffany Theatre. Buffet breakfasts, served from 7 to 11am, cost $2.50; lunches, served from 11:30am to 4pm, cost $3.25; and dinners served from 4 to 10pm, cost $4.50.

Rounding out the dining choices at the Tropicana is the Japanese **Mizuno's Teppan Dining.**

The Riviera Hotel, 2901 Las Vegas Blvd. South, Las Vegas, NV 89109 (tel. 702/734-5110, or toll free 800/634-6753).

Labeled one of the most refined hotels along the posh central

Strip, the Riviera is in a class almost by itself. Liberace, candelabra and all, was on hand for the gala opening on April 18, 1955. The front building is *T*-shaped, of 9 to 18 stories, wrapped partially around an Olympic-size swimming pool and gardens. Other rooms are located in the lanai wing. Under construction is a 43-story tower, with 1,600 minisuites, scheduled for completion by 1991.

You enter the lobby without having to weave your way through a maze of slot machines and casino crushes. (Games are discreetly off to one side.) An arcade of boutiques lines the hotel's promenade.

The addition of the Monaco Tower brought the Riviera's room capacity to 2,136. A third tower, under construction, will raise the room count to 3,720. Completion is scheduled for the end of 1990, at which time there will also be a total of ten restaurants, a deli, two pools, health clubs, and a jogging track.

The Monaco Tower is tastefully furnished, with bedroom and bath separated by a walk-through closet. Rooms cost $60 to $100 per night for double or single occupancy; suites run $130 to $600. All rooms have double or king-size beds.

The area surrounding the Riviera's pool is spacious, with manicured lawns, piped-in music, a sundeck, and a snack bar. Facilities also include ten championship tennis courts (free to guests), and baby-sitting services are available.

Although the new casino at the Riviera is big and grand, it has an intimate quality that makes it one of the most popular along the Strip.

Restaurants

Among the posh Riviera dining facilities is the very romantic **Ristorante Italiano,** where a talented chef carefully supervises the preparation of delectable pastas, veal dishes, and seafood. Kenny Rogers, Steve Martin, Steve Lawrence and Eydie Gorme, Paul Anka, and Barry Manilow are among the stars who have turned out to sample linguine under the stars, for the ceiling here is atwinkle with stars. The décor evokes Venice, with windows looking out on murals of St. Mark's Square, the Rialto, the Bridge of Sighs, and the canals. The Italiano is, in fact, a recreation of an actual open-air rooftop restaurant in Venice that overlooks those sights. Exposed brick walls are hung with copies of famous paintings, and furnishings are bright red; candlelight and Italian music complete the ambience.

A meal at the Italiano might get off to a hearty start with a soup of macaroni and beans, although the baked clams casino seems a more apt choice. Among the entrees, priced from $16 to $34, there's a choice of about ten veal preparations—ranging from saltimbocca (sautéed slices of veal with prosciutto and mozzarella) to osso buco (veal shank sautéed in olive oil with tomatoes, onions, celery, green peppers, and Italian herbs). Other options include broiled steak with fresh mushrooms; chicken parmigiana; and a platter of shrimp, scallops, and clams cooked in a light sauce with wine, butter, mushrooms, green peppers, and onions. All entrees are served with spaghetti, except for pasta dishes such as linguine with red or white clam sauce and lasagne. Desserts range from light fare, such as Italian ices and melon, to caloric delights, such as cannoli and Italian rum sponge cake. Ristorante Italiano is open nightly from 6pm to 11pm.

Recalling the charm of its namesake once in the Wall Street district of New York, the newly reopened and redecorated **Delmonico** offers a refined atmosphere in which the components are rich pearl-gray walls adorned with framed prints and paintings; tables set with exquisite china, gleaming silver, and sparkling crystal; soft lighting from magnificent cut-crystal chandeliers overhead; and dark wood chairs with gray cushioning.

Open your handsome leather-bound menu and you'll find an original continental listing. There's a large choice of hot and cold appetizers from escargots in mushrooms with a red wine garlic sauce to fresh pâtés created daily; or you might begin with a Caesar salad or a fresh spinach salad with bacon dressing. For the main course, priced at $17 to $35, some interesting options are roast boneless breast of chicken in champagne cream sauce with pink peppercorns and sautéed medallions of veal with fresh melon and port wine. A distinguished wine list is available. Leave room for a selection from the gleaming cart of pastries. Delmonico is open Wednesday through Sunday from 6pm to 11pm.

Kristopher's is a steak house located in the Monaco Tower. It's a relaxed pastel environment with wicker chairs, ceiling fans, ferns, and smoked-glass mirrors. There's also an elegant lounge that overlooks the pool area. The selection of entree on the prix-fixe menu is the only major decision you need make (everything is included—from wine to appetizer, salad, entree, and dessert). Kristopher's offers a number of entree choices, such as prime rib, T-bone steak, breast of turkey, jumbo shrimp specially marinated, chicken breast, baby-back ribs, blackened redfish and swordfish (although the seafood choices change seasonally). After making your choice, settle back with some crackers and cheese spread, then proceed to a Caesar-style salad, hot bread with your choice of a special seasoned butter, wine, and your entree. The prix-fixe dinner is $16.95. Breakfast will cost from $3 to $10, and the buffet brunch is $8.95. The restaurant is open daily for breakfast (from 7 to 11am), lunch (from noon to 4pm), and dinner (from 5:30 to 11pm).

Kady's Brasserie, is the Riviera's 24-hour poolside coffee shop. Its offerings range in price from $6.50 to $22.50 and include everything from deli fare, such as corned beef with potato salad, to a full meal of double-rib lamb chops with french fries, not to mention salads, sandwiches, and eggs and omelets.

If you should choose to enter the uncertain state of matrimony, it's all possible within the Riviera (tel. 794-9494) at the **Royale Wedding Chapel.** (What better place is there to take the gamble?)

Aladdin Hotel & Casino, 3667 Las Vegas Blvd. South, Las Vegas, NV 89109 (tel. 702/736-0111, or toll free 800/634-3424).

The Japanese seem convinced of Las Vegas's success in the high-stakes contest for top billing as the gambling, entertainment, and convention center of the country. After all, Las Vegas is just a short jump from the La Costa Resort in Carlsbad—purchased by the Japanese in 1987 for $250 million. And La Costa—or any one of several Japanese-owned hotels in San Francisco—is little more than a five-hour hop from Japanese holdings in Hawaii.

In January 1986, Ginji Yasuda, a Korean-born resident of Japan, bought the Aladdin Hotel & Casino (then in bankruptcy) for over $54 million. Yasuda became the first non–U.S. citizen to own a casino on the Strip and the first to be licensed to operate a casino in the United States.

The Aladdin has 1,100 modern, spacious rooms that are totally redecorated and refurnished. Furnishings are beige and gold and convey a luxury theme whether you choose to stay in one of the remodeled rooms or in a newly created duplex suite. Room rates are $70 to $130 per night, single or double occupancy. One- and two-bedroom suites are $375 to $600, and the duplex super-suite extravaganza is $2,500.

To keep you fit, comfortable, and relaxed, the Aladdin sports a rooftop recreation center with a pool, lighted tennis courts for night play, and a snack bar for the lounge lizards.

The Aladdin has three entertainment venues: the 700-seat Bagdad Showroom; the 100-seat Sinbad Lounge; and, topping all the hotels in Las Vegas, the 7,000-seat Aladdin Theatre for the Performing Arts—the largest theater in Las Vegas (apart from that at the University) and undoubtedly the one with the best acoustics. The theater has featured a remarkable range of performers—from Rudolf Nureyev to Anita Baker; Fleetwood Mac; Tina Turner; and, in a historic charity reunion, the Doobie Brothers.

And what would a Las Vegas hotel be without its own version of a perpetual-motion machine—the nonstop 24-hour casino. Among the usual games, the Aladdin also features a new poker room and a high-limit race and sports book.

Restaurants

The Aladdin has three excellent restaurants, a deli, and the usual 24-hour coffee shop so necessary to survival in Las Vegas. The most prestigious of the eateries is **The Florentine,** which offers French, Italian, and continental cuisine prepared tableside. This elegant restaurant, as its name suggests, is graced with Florentine frosted-glass panels, as well as floral murals and crystal chandeliers. House specialties are veal marsala and sumptuous braised sweetbreads. Entrees on the à la carte menu are priced from $22 to $48. Wines from cellars all over the world are available here. Open Wednesday through Sunday from 6 to 11pm; reservations are suggested.

Another handsomely designed restaurant is **Wellington's,** an American version of an English pub—very masculine, with dark woods, brick floors, wrought-iron chandeliers, hunting prints, and a central brass rotisserie. This beef house features certified black Angus aged beef, as well as first-rate steaks and barbecued selections. Wellington's prepares excellent salads tableside and offers an extensive wine list. Entrees range from $18 to $25. Open nightly from 6 to 12pm; reservations are suggested.

Fisherman's Port has been a hit with diners from the day it opened. The restaurant features fresh seafood flown in from the East Coast. Despite the Cajun character of much of its cuisine, Fisherman's Port looks more New England than New Orleans, with its board floors, stanchions, captain's chairs, netting, and seascapes. The menu features soups, bisques, and bouillabaisse, and entrees range from orange roughy to Alaskan king crab, crawfish étouffé, and blackened redfish, all accompanied by hush puppies and black-eyed peas; the popular Cajun dishes are served spicy or mild, to suit your taste. Entree prices range from $15 to $23. There is a special wine list to complement the unique cuisine. The Fisherman's Port is open Wednesday through Sunday from 6 to 11pm.

The Delicatessen looks like an old-time deli—dark wood chairs with red cushions, red-and-black carpeting, and a counter that looks like an old-fashioned bar. You can watch the specialties of the house being prepared in an open kitchen—everything from scrambled eggs with lox and onions to cheese blintzes with sour cream or blueberries. Combination sandwiches, in an incredible variety, are served on three slices of thin corn rye and accompanied by potato salad, relish bowl, and garnish. For dinner, you can order the likes of boiled chicken in the pot, pot roast, or linguine and clams or shrimp. If you feel that you have room for dessert, everything from cheesecake (five varieties) to a banana split can be enjoyed while watching the keno board. Prices for lunch or dinner range from $4 to $10; prices for breakfast run from $2 to $5. The Delicatessen is open daily from 10am to midnight.

And **The Oasis,** the Aladdin's 24-hour coffee shop, is ready whenever you are with sandwiches, salads, main dishes, desserts, and fountain selections. Prices go up to $10.

Last, but by no means least, is the **International Buffet.** Its oriental dishes make it one of the best buffets in town. This is where you'll find some of the better Chinese and Japanese dishes, plus an interesting array of other offerings. The International Buffet serves breakfast ($5) from 7 to 10:30am, lunch ($6) from 11:30am to 2pm, dinner ($8.25) from 4 to 10pm.

The Dunes Hotel and Country Club, 3650 Las Vegas Blvd. South, Las Vegas, NV 89109 (tel. 702/737-4110, or toll free 800/634-6971).

Opened in 1955 as a modest 194-room hotel, the Dunes today consists of a 24-story high-rise tower (actually 21 stories—there are no floors numbered 11, 12, or 13); the connecting Sea Horse and Olympic Wings; and a new 17-story, 400-room tower. Part of a $75-million expansion program, the tower wing brought the Dunes' room count to 1,285. The newest addition is a shiny black-glass building called the Oasis. A striking sidewalk of colored mosaic tile leads you to.

The Dunes is one of the many Las Vegas hotels acquired by Japanese investors. It was purchased in August 1987 for the tidy sum of $157.7 million, and it has been announced that the owners intend to spend $300 million more to double the hotel's capacity.

When it comes to facilities, the Dunes has always been well equipped. It has two immense swimming pools (both Olympic-size), an 18-hole golf course (greens fees are $50 to $65 for guests; $70 to $90 for others) and a country club, a large and opulent casino, a complete health club for men and women, and shops proffering everything from toys for children to fine furs.

As for the rooms, they're comfortable to a fault. Spacious and attractively color coordinated, they're furnished with king-size, twin, or double-double beds. Running ice water on tap and a make-up area with theatrical lighting are just a few of the extras, and, of course, all the modern amenities are as you'd expect. Rates are $50 to $100 per night, single or double occupancy. Suites, at $130 to $1,800, are particularly sumptuous.

Restaurants

There are four restaurants at the Dunes. The most prestigious is the **Sultan's Table,** serving gourmet continental cuisine. A year after it opened, it was awarded the title of "America's finest and most beautiful new restaurant" by Diners Club. Now, some two decades later, it is still winning laurels with its Kismet pleasure-palace theme. This exotic eatery has a tented entrance; an interior done in royal purple, plum, and rich blues; beveled bronze mirrors; dripping crystal chandeliers galore; and stained-glass windows from Germany designed after an illustration from an antique book of the original *Kismet.* The windows are flanked by 300 yards of hand-loomed draperies. Colored lights play on a waterfall, and a cocktail lounge off the entrance is adorned with imported marble tables and jewel-toned banquettes.

You can begin your haute-cuisine feast with such classy hors d'oeuvres as foie gras with truffles, escargots de Bourgogne, and Scottish smoked salmon. Among the entrees, priced at $20 to $27.50 (or, for some, $50 for two), are breast of capon Kiev with wild rice, frogs' legs provençal, tournedos sauce périgourdine, and chateaubriand with vegetables in sauce béarnaise. Vegetables— such as broccoli hollandaise and hearts of palm amandine—are à la carte, and desserts range from simple sherbets to sumptuous choices such as baked Alaska flambé and strawberries Romanoff. The wine list offers an excellent selection of imported and domestic vintages, reasonably priced. The Sultan's Table is open Wednesday through Sunday from 6 to 11pm. Jackets are required for men.

Another spectacularly designed restaurant is the **Dome of the Sea,** where you dine in a large seashell-shaped affair while a steady movement of flying fish is projected slowly around the walls. Vari-colored lights pour through a domed ceiling, the tablecloths are blue and green, and a mermaid in a gondola even plays the harp. You'll feel as if you're dining in a magical undersea kingdom.

Hot and cold seafood appetizers include chilled melon with prosciutto, imported smoked Scottish salmon, and scampi sauté Dijonese. There's a wide choice of entrees: seafood nouvelle cuisine with sautéed crabmeat, lobster, and shrimp; Maine lobster thermidor; a traditional bouillabaisse; and imported Dover sole, sautéed in lemon butter or lemon and capers. Non–seafood fanciers can get a New York–cut steak or filet mignon. All entrees are served with a vegetable and potato du jour and range in price from $25 to $35. Desserts once again feature flambé specialties, such as cherries jubilee, although you can also select a French pastry. The Dome of the Sea is open Friday through Tuesday from 6 to 11pm.

The **Chinese Kitchen,** located in the Savoy, offers typical Chinese fare, such as chow mein, sweet-and-sour shrimp, and pork or beef with mixed Chinese vegetables for $5 to $15. It's open nightly for dinner from 6pm to midnight.

The **Savoy** is the Dunes' 24-hour coffee shop. It offers the usual kind of menu for the genre: salads, sandwiches, and burgers for $6 to $11, and hot entrees for $6 to $16.

The Sands Hotel Casino, 3355 Las Vegas Blvd. South, Las Vegas, NV 89109 (tel. 702/733-5000, or toll free 800/446-4678).

Right in the middle of the action on the Strip is the Sands with its 18-story tower, 750 rooms and suites, and 10 garden buildings surrounded by beautifully manicured grounds. The Interface Group, Inc., purchased the Sands Hotel and Casino from Kirk Kerkorian in 1989. The buyers have since announced that $150 million will be spent in improvements to the property, including the addition of 1,200 rooms and 45,000 square feet to the casino.

Currently facilities include two swimming pools, six night-lit tennis courts, a shuffleboard court, a nine-hole putting green, a beauty salon and barbershop, and a tennis boutique. The fully equipped women's and men's health clubs are staffed by professionals and feature heated whirlpools, saunas, and weightlifting and exercise equipment.

The spacious rooms are color coordinated in lovely hues and come fully equipped with all the amenities. Rates, single or double, run from $70 to $105 for the outlying buildings ($10 for a third person in a room) and start at $150 for tower rooms. Suites are $150 to $310.

The Sands' 30,000-square-foot plush casino contains a wide variety of the latest in high-tech slot machines, keno, a complete race and sports book, craps, blackjack, roulette, baccarat, and oriental games.

Restaurants

The Sands boasts a prestigious restaurant: the opulent **Regency Room,** which serves French/continental cuisine. Among the fine array of specialties offered on the extensive menu are scampi provençal, filet of beef Wellington, quail, and roast duckling à l'orange. Entrees cost from $15.95 to $37.50. There are also complete dinners from $16. The Regency Room is open Tuesday through Saturday from 6pm to midnight. Reservations are suggested.

The 24-hour **Garden Terrace** features everything from snacks and a soup-and-salad bar to full-course meals with daily menu specials, including "Fish-by-the-Ounce" from $5.75. The light, airy dining room, overlooking a spacious outdoor pool and lush garden, is decorated in mauve, pinks, blues, and greens.

Breakfast, served around the clock, offers a variety of omelets; scrambled eggs with Nova Scotia salmon and onions; eggs "your way"; blintzes; griddle cakes; and the usual assortment of pastries, beverages, and fruit. For midday hunger pangs (whenever you might experience them), there is a fine selection of sandwiches, including "create-your-own" hamburgers. Dinner entrees range from tenderloin of pork or prime rib to stuffed snapper. For the incurable steak lover, the Garden Terrace has sirloin or filet mignon. Prices range from $4 to $19.

The attractively appointed **House of Szechwan** offers an excellent menu of Chinese specialties, with over 70 items from which to choose. All entrees are cooked to order and include a marvelous selection of Szechuan and Cantonese dishes from $9 to $17. Chinese beer and wine are available. House of Szechwan is open Wednesday through Monday from 5pm to midnight. Reservations are suggested.

David-Papchen's Deli may be small, but it assuredly makes sandwiches suitable for a Samson appetite. You'll know you're at the right spot by the dried sausages hanging from the ceiling, loaves of bread on display, and Kaiser rolls set for stuffing. Everything is larger than life and absolutely delicious—from the super sandwiches to the succulent sausage platters and the many specials featured on the menu. Open daily from 7am to 10:30pm.

Frontier Hotel, 3120 Las Vegas Blvd. South, Las Vegas, NV 89109 (tel. 702/734-0110, or toll free 800/634-6966).

The Frontier contains 600 rooms in a ring-shaped, seven-story building and a three-story lanai wing. It is horseshoed around beautiful garden acres of manicured grass and towering palms, an Olympic-size swimming pool, fountains, and little rustic bridges over reflecting pools.

You can't miss the Frontier. Its huge sign out near the street fairly blasts out its name in electric lights. A couple of hundred feet high, it is reputed to have cost more than a million dollars.

The 350 guest rooms, the suites, the lobbies, the casino, and the sports book are undergoing redecoration, enlargement, and refurbishing.

Two tennis courts at the Frontier are busy day and night (both are lit for night play); they're for hotel guests only. Guests at the Frontier may play golf at the Desert Inn. And rounding out the facilities are convention space, a putting green, a fine casino, a car-rental desk, a baby-sitting service, three restaurants, three cocktail lounges, a first-rate showroom, and 8,000 square feet of shops.

All rooms have color TVs with free ESPN sports and a closed-circuit gaming-instruction station and direct-dial phones with message lights. They're priced at $60 to $125, single or double, depending on the view and the location; poolside rooms are more expensive. One-bedroom suites begin at $210; two-bedroom suites begin at $300.

Restaurants

Justin's is Frontier's gourmet room, and it reflects its predecessor, Diamond Jim's. It's elegant and Victorian-styled, with such pleasant touches as crystal chandeliers, red carpeting, and comfortably plush booths. Justin's specializes in tableside service with appropriate flourish. The list of house specialties has something for everyone—rack of lamb, veal Oskar, duck à l'orange, steaks, chops, and seafood. A different full-course (prix-fixe) dinner is featured each night. Dinner is from $19 to $49. Elegance notwithstanding, Justin's is friendly, and the food is good. Justin's is open nightly from 6 to 11:30pm. Reservations are suggested.

As to the new **Margarita's**—this is a gem. It's a warm, inviting, attractive Mexican restaurant done with touches of the Southwest—wrought iron, a cobblestone floor, and ceiling fans. In the restaurant there's even a flour-tortilla machine that prepares the complimentary warm tortillas served with your meal with the accompaniments of guacamole, bean dip, and salsa. You also can buy the tortillas to take out.

Although Margarita's breakfast is more of a brunch, it still includes such excellent choices as scrambled eggs with Mexican sausage (huevos con chorizo), huevos rancheros to be sure, and Mexican variations on the omelet theme (for $2.95 to $3.95). Specialties of the house include sizzling fajita platters of tender marinated steak, chicken, pork, or shrimp ($6.50 to $9). The cantina feast platter (for two) is a nosher's delight—a bargain sampling (for two) of a quesadilla, beef burrito, chimichanga (a deep-fried burrito), and chicken enchilada (for $10). The menu is loaded with other tasty choices (from $2.50 to $6.50)—chicken, steak, and swordfish dishes; baby-back pork spareribs; tamales, enchiladas, and chimichangas. If you have a large appetite, you might want to review additions from the appetizer list, including fajita wings or, my favorite, tortilla soup. For light nibblers, Margarita's has a good selection of salads. The flambé olé (for two) is the ultimate dessert (at $6) prepared at your table with fresh strawberries, bananas, and kiwis sautéed with three different liqueurs and served over vanilla ice cream. If you suspect that Margarita's has a great selection of giant fresh-fruit Margaritas, you would be right. They also have Mexican beers, tequilas, and a respectable wine list. And just in case you were wondering, the service is attentive and friendly, a pleasant complement to the food. Margarita's is open from 11am to 10:30pm.

Holiday Casino/Holiday Inn, 3475 Las Vegas Blvd. South, Las Vegas, NV 89109 (tel. 702/369-5000, or toll free 800/634-6765).

This is another Las Vegas superlative, the largest Holiday Inn in this country, with 1,721 rooms. Except for the traditional Holiday Inn sign, the first thing you'll notice is not the size of the property but the fanciful façade of the casino facing the Strip. It's a reproduction of a sidewheel Mississippi River gambling boat, complete with mannequin passengers and even Tom Sawyer and Huck Finn on a raft.

When the Holiday Casino/Holiday Inn added some 721 rooms and a new tower, it did the addition in style. With the ground-floor expansion, the main-floor area is spacious, light, and now quite easy to navigate. It also has a new collection of shops. The second floor has the swimming pool and sun deck. The new tower rooms are beautifully done in floral tints of light green, pink, and soft beige. Room 2705 has a spectacular view of the mountains and canyons, as do a number of others. The finishing touches are table lamps and movable metal-frame garden chairs done in an aged bronze finish. The club chairs are good looking and very comfortable, and for your total lighting comfort there are adjustable floor lamps. Other nice amenities are remote-control TVs and full-length mirrors. What's more, if you forgot your toothbrush or your hair dryer when you packed, the hotel will supply one. Another unusually thoughtful touch is the provision of laundries on two floors. You'll also find a beauty salon and barber shop on the premises.

Singles and doubles run from $70 to $90, depending on the day of the week; suites are from $180 to $300. One lovely complimentary touch is the hotel's emphasis on pleasant, very helpful service. The hotel's security system has been designed so that it's virtually impossible to get up to a room after 9pm without showing your key or card.

Since this is a family hotel, the casino is actually separated from the lobby, and great care has been taken to ensure that children do not have to venture anywhere near the casino. Even the shopping and game arcade, swimming pool, and health spa are separated from the action.

The lobby area has also been completely redecorated with plants, skylights, and plenty of places to sit and enjoy the passing parade. The casino now features all your favorite slot machines, a keno lounge, Bingo parlor, poker room, and a 24-hour race and sports book.

Restaurants

The Holiday Casino/Holiday Inn's gourmet dining facility, **Claudine's Steakhouse,** is a candlelit room that seats only 80 and offers steaks and seafood. Dinner might begin with smoked salmon with horseradish-mustard sauce or fettuccine du chef. Entrees, ranging in price from $15 to $28, include a variety of steaks—T-bone, filet mignon, and roast prime rib—and such seafood as lobster tails, salmon steak, shrimp, and scallops. Each entree is served with potato or rice and Claudine's specialty bread. Dessert selections, including pastries and ice cream, change daily. Claudine's is open Thursday through Monday from 5:30 to 11pm.

The hotel's coffee shop, the **Veranda,** features sandwiches, full dinners, and breakfast. There's a daily breakfast special for $4.25, luncheon with soup or salad and sandwich for $5.50, and Sunday champagne brunch from 8am to 2pm. Dinner specials range from

$9 to $13, and the Pasta Pantry serves Italian specialties from 5pm to closing. The Veranda is open daily from 7am to 10:30pm.

New Orleans meets Las Vegas in the newest of the Holiday Inn restaurants, **Joe's Bayou.** A great selection of "starters," as well as high-quality gumbos, stews, salads, blackened fare, jambalaya, and bayou specialties, is available. Each of the starters is a meal in itself, but one of the most interesting is the "bayou sampler"—an array of tidbits, including a pork rib, prawn, chicken, frog's leg, and catfish, with Cajun dressing. Or you might order stew (red or white) with scallops, oysters, or clams, or a combination of all three served with plantation greens (otherwise known as salad) and a choice of baked yams, potatoes, rice, okra, or hush puppies.

Considering salad as your main course? Joe's Bayou serves a shrimp, barbecued chicken, or crab salad in a crisp pastry shell, accompanied by corn bread or baguette.

Blackened fare includes not only the usual redfish but also an interesting choice of scallops, shrimp, or catfish. Bayou specialties range from shrimp and ham jambalaya to fried catfish. If you're not in the mood for a big meal, some great sandwiches, such as deep-fried oysters and barbecued chicken breast on toasted French bread, are an option. If you make it through to dessert, there's southern pecan pie or banana fritters, among other thoroughly fattening choices. Entree prices are $12 to $18. Joe's Bayou is open daily from 5:30 to 11pm.

And there's the **Galley Buffet.** Here you can partake of a 24-hour breakfast buffet for $2.99, a lunch buffet for $3.50 from 11am to 5pm, and a dinner buffet for $4 from 5 to 11pm.

Golden Nugget Hotel and Casino, 129 E. Fremont St. (at the corner of Casino Center Boulevard), Las Vegas, NV 89101 (tel. 702/385-7111, or toll free 800/634-3454).

When you consider accommodations in Las Vegas, among the best and the most luxurious are at the Golden Nugget Hotel and Casino. Gone is the fantasy of the Wild West that once characterized the hotel. Today this extraordinary downtown establishment commands top rating among all hotel/casinos. A hint of its interior elegance is presented by a new façade of pure-white Grecian marble, cut, hand-carved, and polished by old-world artisans; by the white canopies, Tivoli lights, and beveled mirrors; and by a white-on-white motif subtly accented with brass. Hundreds of palm trees in planter beds surround the entire property.

As you enter the driveway, you arrive under a gleaming white portico. Oval etched-glass panels flank the doors, which lead directly to the hotel registration and lobby areas. (Happily, you do not have to work your way through a casino to arrive at the front desk.) Inside, the décor is opulent, from the verdi marble–inlaid floors inset with custom-woven wool carpet to the antique furnishings and stained-glass panels.

Oversize guest rooms have been decorated in soothing pastels, soft creams, and desert shades. All rooms are equipped with every modern amenity—direct-dial phones, AM/FM radios, color TVs, tub/shower baths, oversize terry towels, toilette articles, and more. Of course, the hotel affords the services of a concierge, 24-hour room service in addition to that of the coffee shop, same-day laundry and dry-cleaning service, car-rental desk, valet parking, and other comfortable touches. The Golden Nugget prides itself on attention to detail, whether in the hotel's elegant appointments or in the extra effort extended by the staff to make a guest's stay enjoyable.

Set among beds of flowers and palm trees is an outdoor pool (open May through October) with a whirlpool spa, a snack bar, and a poolside lounge area. If relaxing in the desert sun is too much of a good thing, there's always the spa—a health emporium geared for body building, exercise, and aerobics. There are separate men's and women's facilities for massages, steam rooms, sauna, and whirlpool spas. A full-service beauty salon provides services for men and women.

The 30,000-square-foot casino is handsomely styled and designed and well equipped for the total comfort of its customers. There are 47 blackjack tables, 6 craps layouts, 3 roulette wheels, 2 baccarat tables, 2 pai-gow tables, 1 red dog, and a luxurious keno lounge. A full assortment of more than 1,100 video and traditional slot machines, all brass-clad, add the finishing touch to the casino area.

In addition to fine restaurants, the Nugget offers two notably beautiful drinking establishments. The Canopy Bar, just off the casino, features a gleaming brass bar-top and richly colored stained glass depicting 19th-century saloon scenes; and the exquisite Victoria Bar contains overstuffed furnishings, marble-topped tables, a magnificent wood-and-mirrored bar, a 24-carat gold-plated espresso/cappuccino machine, and a bar rail made of onyx.

Rates for the hotel's rooms are $60 to $120, single or double; suites start at $220 and go up to $800. Children under 12 stay free in a room with their parents; extra adults pay $12 a night.

Restaurants

Top of the line at the Golden Nugget is **Elaine's,** on the second level of the Spa Suite Tower. As you approach the ebony entry, you won't expect the classic French décor inside. The dining room is elegant, and the effect is rich. Your eye is caught by the superb Venetian crystal chandelier and the impressionist-style paintings. There's a feeling of privacy you rarely find in a dining room, undoubtedly effected by the curtained booths and well-spaced tables.

The menu is à la carte. Among Elaine's excellent specialties are rack of lamb, chicken with wild mushrooms, bouillabaisse, and a fabulous quail with a mousse of veal. Entrees range from $25 to $35. The wine list is of the same fine quality as the food. Jackets are required for men, and reservations are suggested. Elaine's is open Thursday through Monday from 6 to 11pm.

Stefano's is the northern Italian restaurant in the Golden Nugget. As you enter, you will feel as if you're in an Italian garden. Stefano's has a varied menu with a wide range of choices among some dozen fresh pasta dishes, including an exceptional fettuccine with prosciutto, parmesan, and a silky cream sauce, as well as veal and fresh fish. A perennial search for the perfect veal piccata ended at Stefano's—delicate white veal, exquisitely tender, lightly touched with lemon, and served piping hot. It's the seemingly simple dishes that display the genius of the chef (this one is from Rome). If you've ever wanted to indulge a childlike urge to lick the plate, Stefano's will bring it on. Be sure to order the salad. It's light and so fresh that there's sure to be a garden by the kitchen; and it's touched with just the right amount of delicate dressing.

All this beauty and superb food isn't cheap, but it's worth the price. And the service is attentive. The menu is à la carte, and dinner entrees range from $18 to $35. Stefano's is open daily for dinner from 6 to 11pm. Reservations are suggested.

Reflecting the décor of the hotel, **Lillie Langtry's,** named for the famed British actress who stole the heart of the infamous Judge Roy Bean, is a masterpiece of Victoriana. The walls are richly paneled in oak and mahogany, the chairs are plushly upholstered in a lovely floral velvet, and the tables are handsomely set with wheat-colored linen. At the entrance is a stained-glass domed skylight and globe chandeliers with dangling crystal; potted palms, brass railings, swagged velvet-and-lace café curtains, flickering gaslamps, fine murals of the Old West, and pressed-tin ceilings are among the many other elements that help create this gorgeous setting. Like every other part of this fine hotel, it is done in perfect taste.

The dinner menu at Lillie's place is Cantonese. You might begin your meal with an order of golden-fried shrimp or crispy rumaki—broiled chicken liver and water chestnut wrapped in bacon. These are suggested entrees: lemon chicken; shrimp Cantonese (jumbo shrimp with minced pork, onion, garlic, bean sauce, and other spices); chicken sautéed with cashew nuts, water chestnuts, bamboo shoots, and peas; and ginger beef cooked in oyster sauce and onion. Entrees, which range from $12 to $22, are served with oolong tea, rice, and fortune cookies. Two American entrees are listed—prime rib with baked potato, salad, and vegetable and barbecued spareribs with corn on the cob and onion rings. Exotic drinks are also featured at Lillie's: the Rangoon Ruby (vodka and cranberry juice), the Oriental Devil (banana and rum), and the Great Wall of China (coconut, rum, and vodka). What I most appreciate, however, is the presence of Western desserts on a Chinese menu. Here, Lillie comes through with class, offering not only fresh-baked cakes but also Häagen-Dazs ice cream. Lillie Langtry's is open nightly from 5 to 11pm.

And then there's **The Buffet.** As with everything else at the Golden Nugget, The Buffet is done in style with a beige-and-gold setting, individual booths, chandeliers, greenery, and pleasantly subdued lighting. The choice and the quality of the food are excellent; also, the hot food is really hot, and the cold food is cold. Breakfast ($4.95) is served from 7 to 10:30am, brunch ($7.50) is served from 10:30am to 3pm, and dinner ($8.75) is served from 4 to 11pm.

The **Carson Street Café** is open 24 hours and serves a steak for $1.99 from 11pm to 6am.

Ramada Hotel San Remo and Casino, 115 E. Tropicana Ave. (just east of the Strip), Las Vegas, NV 89109-7304 (tel. 702/739-9000, or toll free 800/522-7366).

For those who don't feel the necessity to be right on the Strip, the San Remo is a very handsome, comfortable place to stay, with new and beautifully redone accommodations and some of the most pleasant hotel personnel in town.

The San Remo is not in the "how-many-rooms-are-there-today" competition. There are 324 spacious accommodations styled with attractive classic Italian furnishings—light walls and dark woods against dark leather—full-size baths with fluffy towels; and the necessary accoutrements needed to complete hotel life, including color TV and phones. All of these reflect the millions put into the San Remo when it was restyled and refurbished. As with any proper Las Vegas hotel, there is a swimming pool and sunning area for total relaxation and tanning.

The gaming area offers all sorts of possibilities for expending (or taking in) chips in the usual ways. One aspect of the casino I especially appreciate is that it is roomier than most, making it easier to get from one table to the next. What's more, it isn't necessary to elbow your way through the casino to get to the registration desk.

Room rates for a petite King, deluxe King, or a deluxe King with a pool view range from $50 to $60 Sunday through Thursday, $65 to $90 Friday and Saturday, and $95 to $120 on holidays and during special events. Petite suites are $75 to $100 but $130 on holidays; one- or two-bedroom suites are $150 to $400 but $260 to $600 on holidays.

Restaurants

The San Remo has a lovely restaurant in **La Panache,** which offers fine continental and American cuisine selections. La Panache is open Tuesday through Sunday from 5 to 11pm.

The **Ristorante del Fiori** is the hotel's 24-hour casual dining restaurant and buffet in a gardenlike setting. Breakfast buffet ($3) is served from 7 to 10am, luncheon buffet ($4) is served from 11am to 2pm, and dinner ($5) is served from 5 to 9pm.

---

2. Moderately Priced Hotels

Excalibur, 3850 Las Vegas Blvd. South, Las Vegas NV 89119-1050 (tel. 702/597-7777, or toll free 800/937-7777).

Once-upon-a-time has come to life just across the Strip from the Tropicana, and it's called **Excalibur.** The opening for Excalibur was in June 1990—complete with towers; turrets; battlements; a drawbridge; a moat; and a full staff of squires, ladies-in-waiting, troubadours, pages, and serfs as befits the namesake of King Arthur's sword. You do know, of course, that according to legend,

Excalibur was a magical sword embedded in stone. It was proclaimed that whoever could pull the sword from the stone would be crowned king of England. After all tried and failed, Arthur, then a mere squire, succeeded.

For the moment at least, Excalibur holds the title of "the world's largest hotel/casino" with over 4,000 rooms on its 117-acre site. It was brought into being by Circus Circus Enterprises at a cost of approximately $300 million. Room count is a highly competitive business among Las Vegas hotels: It seems not to be how big a hotel is but how many rooms it has, and a hotel's king-of-the-mountain position at the top of this heap is always being threatened.

As you might expect from Circus Circus Enterprises, the Excalibur merges theater, festival, and casino for an extraordinary entertainment experience. Entering Excalibur, you pass through the porte cochere into a cobblestone foyer and then into a 40-foot atrium with towering rock walls. Its centerpiece is a majestic fountain that rises three stories from the Fantasy Faire below to display a many-colored water-and-light show. The imposing 200-foot granite registration desk is ornamented with murals depicting castle life and set off by authentic suits of armor that prepare the guests for contests in the casino.

Gold velvet-and-satin heraldic banners point you toward the entrance to the casino. Its vast interior is illuminated with rows of iron-and-gold chandeliers. Stained-glass windows inspired by tales of the Knights of the Round Table surround the casino. There is a gaming area of more than 100,000 square feet where you can embark on your own competitive adventure at 2,630 slot machines; at tables for blackjack, craps, and roulette; in the keno lounge; or in the race and sports book.

Among the many nongaming games offered are Sherwood Forest Archery to test your aim with a crossbow and William Tell Darts (not to the accompaniment of the overture), where winning requires that you throw a jumbo dart into an apple, although not off the head of your child.

As to total entertainment, theaters with Merlin's Magic Motion machines will physically move you to watch the fascinating visual effects that you see on the screen in front of you (the first in North America).

Combining the delights of food with the ultimate in entertainment, Excalibur has an 890-seat amphitheater with two dinner shows per evening. This is where you'll see Merlin, King Arthur, Queen Guinevere, and mounted knights in an extravaganza of medieval games and spectacular pyrotechnics.

Not to deny anyone of the joys of shopping, the Excalibur has The Royal Village's 23 shops and booths on the Fantasy Faire level to indulge your buying-splurge fantasies. Shops include artisans and craftspeople, a coin maker, a glass blower, candle makers, and leathersmiths. There is also a beauty salon for the repair of damsels.

Those seeking a reprieve from entertainment, gaming, shopping, and dining can relax by night at a lounge with live entertainment or by day at one of Excalibur's two swimming pools.

For the ultimate game of chance, you can be married in a castle at Excalibur's **Canterbury Wedding Chapel.** The chapel is done in a rosy-hue especially for entry into matrimony, and it even has its own small apse for photography.

Guest rooms in this world of fantasy are colorfully done in rich red, forest green, and autumn gold set against beige wallcovering with the remarkable look of a stone finish. All the furnishings are quite comfortable, and the deluxe accommodations have a convenient sitting area. Each of the rooms has a full bath, phone, and color TV with pay-TV movies.

Accommodations for knights, princesses, kings, queens, lords, ladies, and all of us lesser beings are $45 to $65 for standard to deluxe oversize rooms, depending on the day and holiday (if any). Suites with Jacuzzis are $110. A charge of $7 per person is added for more than two persons per room. There is no charge for children under 12 years in rooms with their parents. Room rates (not including the suites) generally are reduced from late November through the first three weeks of December.

Restaurants

Seven themed restaurants grace the castle. There is **Lance-A-Lotta Pasta** for spaghetti, with an interior décor of whimsical treasures from Venice to Rome. Next door is **Oktoberfest,** a German hoffbrau beer garden (please don't ask if there was one in Camelot) complete with wooden trestle tables, beers from all nations, and Bavarian entertainment. On up Palace Lane is the **RoundTable Buffet** —the medieval fortress defined by barrel vaults and flying buttresses and decorated with paintings of the great knights of King Arthur's world. Past the sentry of 10-foot dragons who guard the castle gate is the **Sherwood Forest Café,** which is framed by a pair of friendly gargoyles. This is where you'll find a display of the king's cannons and armory. To top them all is **Sir Galahad's,** featuring prime roast beef carved tableside and served with Yorkshire pudding. A few tricks have been employed to effect the illusion of Galahad's ghost appearing several times daily in a large mirror next to a hand-carved gothic maître d'. And then there's **Robin Hood's Snack Bar,** a fascinating pavilion-type structure built around two large sycamore trees that extend through the roof. If the food doesn't hold your attention, the scene depicting the travels of Robin Hood is sure to. For intimate dining, the **Camelot Restaurant** is situated across from Excalibur's wedding chapel, which you may consider for appetizer or dessert.

Sahara Hotel and Casino, 2535 Las Vegas Blvd. South and Sahara Ave., Las Vegas, NV 89101 (tel. 702/737-2111, or toll free 800/634-6666).

With its 24-story tower, the Sahara is the tallest structure at the north end of the Strip, farthest from the airport. It's dominated by a huge lighted "S," and beneath that flash temperature and time signals. The 222-foot sign, spelling out S-A-H-A-R-A in letters 18 feet high and 10 feet wide, is the tallest free-standing sign in the world. Ten other buildings, including a second tower of 14 stories, tote up to a hotel plant of considerable proportions. The Sahara's come a long way since it opened in 1952 with just 200 rooms.

With a reputed 100% occupancy in its 1,500 rooms every weekend of the year, it holds its own as one of the most successful hotels in the United States.

Now under the management and ownership of Sahara Resorts, Inc., the Sahara has undergone extensive renovations.

Rates for rooms are $55 to $125, single or double occupancy; suites are $200 to $550. All rooms have wall-to-wall carpeting; neat and simple modern décor and furnishings; good drawer space; a separate dressing unit with a big, big mirror; and all modern amenities, including clock radios.

Facilities include two pools (one Olympic-size), a showroom, a huge convention hall called the Space Center, shops, and services. A parking lot with space for 2,200 cars is connected to the hotel by an air-conditioned, carpeted walkway.

Restaurants

The **House of Lords** is one of the premier gourmet restaurants in Las Vegas. Mostly steak and seafood à la carte specialties are offered here in an intimate English setting—an ambience composed of heavy wood beams, rich wood paneling, stained glass, pewter, and such.

The menu features old favorites as well as new, specially developed dishes from scallopine of veal Marsala or française, to lamb chops, beef, and seafood (including abalone almondine) at $17 to $35. The House of Lords is open nightly from 6 to 11pm.

For an exotic dining adventure, South Seas fare is at the Sahara's **Don the Beachcomber** restaurant, which is lavishly done up in the expected exotic Polynesian décor. It's a comfortable restaurant where guests can enjoy any number of different tropical cocktails. As to food choices, Don the Beachcomber offers a menu of Polynesian favorites, such as boned Mandarin duck and lobster in rice wine sauce, as well as steak and other seafood for $14 to $26. The restaurant is open Tuesday through Saturday from 5 to 11pm.

As you might anticipate, the Sahara also has a 24-hour coffee shop, the **Caravan Room,** which turns out (among other things) huge, heavenly banana splits. Then there's the **Garden Buffet** offering an all-you-can-eat lineup of favorites for breakfast from 7 to 11am, lunch 11:30am to 4pm, or dinner 4 to 11pm. Items run the gamut of buffet food, including omelets, waffles, soups, salads, and carved meats; choices change through the day. The **Turf Club Deli** provides guests with great deli food, some of the best in town. It's open daily from 8am to 6pm.

Hacienda Hotel, 3950 Las Vegas Blvd. South, Las Vegas, NV 89119 (tel. 702/739-8911, or toll free 800/634-6713).

The Hacienda Hotel is the southernmost on Las Vegas Boulevard. She and her sister hotel, the Sahara, are getting to be known as "The Strip's Bookends."

The Hacienda has always maintained a reputation as a friendly place, with a downtown Vegas approach to hospitality. It was part of the masterly touch of a couple named Bayley. When Mr. Bayley died in 1964, his wife, Judy, took over and ran the place with a Midas touch until 1972, when she died. These days it's owned and operated by Sahara Resorts, Inc.

Rates are $41 to $81, single or double, for the hotel's 810 rooms, plus $8 extra for each additional occupant. Suites are $135 to $375, accommodating up to four persons. Children under 12 can stay free in a room with their parents.

All rooms are nicely color coordinated with contemporary flair. They aren't the lavish, sometimes excessively decorated accommodations you can find in other hotels, but they're meticulously kept. All have been decorated in desert/earth tones. Baths are tiled and have glass-doored tub/showers. Furnishings throughout are simply stated pieces.

The Hacienda has a swimming pool and six tennis courts, including two for night play. Use of the courts is free to hotel guests.

An interesting innovation at the hotel is the **Hacienda Camperland.** A trailer-camper park covering 20 landscaped acres adjacent to the hotel, it has spaces for 451 recreational vehicles. In addition to complete hookups, it has a country store, a snack bar, laundry facilities, its own swimming pool and recreational hall, kiddie playground, picnic tables, barbecue pits, showers, and 24-hour security. This installation follows the successful pioneering efforts with similar parks at the Stardust and the Circus Circus, proving that there's a big market for such facilities. Camperland rates begin at $12 per vehicle per night, plus $1 per person and per pet.

Restaurants

The Hacienda's gourmet dining room is a steak house called the **Charcoal Room.** It's romantically candlelit, seating is in black-leather booths and chairs, and the walls are adorned with smoked mirrors and Spanish-motif oil paintings. It also features an exhibition kitchen.

The Charcoal Room offers fine seafood and steaks broiled over charcoal and mesquite. The menu is simple, including the queen's and king's cut filet mignon, New York sirloin steak, broiled spring chicken, porterhouse steak, roast prime rib of beef au jus, Australian lobster tail with drawn butter, and sirloin-and-lobster combination. All of the entrees are in the $21 to $35 range and are served with iced relishes, whipped cottage cheese and Cheddar cheese spread, mixed greens and tomato wedges, Lyonnaise potatoes, a tureen of black-bean soup, sorbet with champagne, and freshly baked black-raisin bread topped with whipped butter. For dessert there are petit fours. The Charcoal Room is open nightly from 6 to 10:30pm.

The **El Grande Buffet,** a large buffet area overlooking the pool, offers reasonably priced brunch and dinner buffets with 12 hot entrees. Breakfast is $4; brunch and dinner are $5 but $6 on holidays.

In addition, there is the **Cactus Room,** a 24-hour restaurant that offers a full breakfast and lunch and features specialties such as chicken Kiev, steak au poivre, and cheese tortellini, as well as a complete Mexican menu. All dinner entrees are in the $9 to $18 price range.

The Barbary Coast, 3595 Las Vegas Blvd. South (at the corner of Flamingo Road), Las Vegas, NV 89109 (tel. 702/737-7111, or toll free 800/634-6755).

Evoking the romantic image of turn-of-the-century San Francisco—in the days when Chinatown opium dens, saloons, and gambling parlors flourished—the Barbary Coast is an exciting addition to its rather sedate Strip corner. Opened in March 1979, it is a Michael Gaughan enterprise, and the Gaughans are noted for giving a great deal for the money.

Here they've created 200 beautiful period rooms, all with oversize canopied brass beds, floral-design carpeting, black-and-white-striped wallpaper with matching bedspreads, barn-red ceilings, and crocheted white lace curtains on the windows. A parlor area is separated from the bedroom by gold-fringed scarlet curtains. It all combines to create an Old West feeling. Facilities, however, are strictly up-to-date: tub/shower bath, direct-dial phone with message light, individually controlled heating and air conditioning, and color TV with in-room movies.

The plush and lively casino is decorated in the same motif, with dangling crystal-globe chandeliers overhead. It has a race book lounge that doubles as an entertainment lounge at night. Casino offerings include 700 slot machines, 32 blackjack tables, 4 craps layouts, minibaccarat, pai-gow poker, and keno.

Rates for one or two people are $55 Sunday to Thursday night, $75 Friday and Saturday night. Children 12 or under can stay free in a room with their parents; extra adults pay $5.

Restaurants

The 24-hour coffee shop, the **Victorian Room,** has multipaned beveled mirrors lining the walls, giving the room a windowed effect. It serves all the requisite Vegas fare—from a bagel with cream cheese and lox to a steak–and–crab legs dinner with soup or salad, potato, and rolls and butter. It specializes in Chinese cuisine, from eggroll to Szechuan, served from noon to 5am.

Breakfast and lighter fare generally run $4 to $9; hot entrees are priced in the $10 to $24 range. Chinese entrees, such as almond chicken and sweet-and-sour pork, are in the $6 to $10 range.

The newest addition to the Barbary Coast's dining facilities is a gourmet restaurant, **Michael's.** Located just across the casino from the front desk, it's entered via a frosted- and etched-glass door. Featuring a turn-of-the-century décor, Michael's has been designed for intimate dining; it seats just 70 people. The beautiful white-marble floor and brass accents are a cool contrast to the deep-burgundy walls lined with banquettes and booths. Elegant settings of hand-blown crystal and gold-rimmed white china are enhanced by single roses in silver bud vases on each burgundy-and-white-lace-clothed table. Over the center of the room is a large stained-glass dome with 40 small lights that add to the glittery, gemlike effect.

The menu includes a variety of appetizers, such as jumbo sea-food cocktails of either Maryland lump crab or shrimp. In addition there are hot appetizers and soups, as well as a selection of such salads as hearts of palm vinaigrette, beefsteak tomatoes with anchovies and pimentos, and Caesar salad for two. Entree selections include double-rib spring lamb chops with mint jelly, filet mignon, and chateaubriand for two—all prepared over charcoal. Other choices are imported Dover sole and veal sautéed in butter and lemon. Entrees at Michael's are priced from $23 to $45. A distinguished wine list and desserts of cherries jubilee, strawberries Romanoff, and pastries round out the meals. Michael's is open nightly from 6 to 11pm.

The Landmark, 364 Convention Center Dr., Las Vegas, NV 89109 (tel. 702/733-1110, or toll free 800/634-6777, 800/458-2946 in California).

At 31 stories and 346 feet in height, the Landmark is one of Las Vegas's tallest buildings. Opened in 1969, it was one of the many properties of the late Howard Hughes.

The main thrust of the Landmark is its hexagonal tower, which you can see from practically everywhere in town. It's capped by three glassed-in double floors in a round disk that cantilevers out over the main structure. These upper floors contain suites, cocktail lounges, a restaurant, and a place to dance. Topside may be reached by a glass-sided elevator for vertical rides with a view.

Since late 1983 the Landmark has been under new management, and many positive changes have been made. The 150 tower rooms and the 350 garden rooms have been completely remodeled. In every respect, the details of the rooms have been chosen with comfort in mind, but with a pleasant, contemporary simplicity.

During the high season, rates for single or double occupancy are $55 to $75. Suites range from $90 to $210. Rates are lower in the summer and during December.

The award-winning pool at the Landmark is whale-shaped, 240 feet long by 52 feet wide, with a tropical island and sundeck in the center. Bridges connect the island with the pool deck, and a waterfall cascades over black lava rocks at one end. Other facilities include an arcade of shops, service desks, a showroom, and a casino.

Restaurants

Looking out across the pool to the waterfall is the **Cascade Terrace Buffet.** The menu lists the usual breakfast fare served daily from 7am for $3. Lunch ($4) and dinner ($5) buffets feature Southern-style cooking with a wide array of specialties, plus carved ham and beef. Dinner is served from 5pm.

The **Carnival Café** is the 24-hour coffee shop offering omelets, salads, burgers, sandwiches, and steaks (from $3 to $12).

Up on the 27th floor is the elegant **Visko's of New Orleans,** where diners can feast on a glittering view of Las Vegas as well as on delicious seafood and steak entrees. The menu offers dishes with a

New Orleans flair. You might begin with deep-fried crab fingers or perhaps the jumbo mushroom caps stuffed with shrimp and crabmeat, brushed with butter, and broiled. Seafood entrees range from fried catfish filet to sautéed shrimp broiled in seasoned butter (from $10 to $15). Beef offerings include prime rib, a New York strip steak, and filet mignon with or without a side order of sautéed shrimp (from $10 to $16). A selection of chef specials changes daily (from $20 to $25). All entrees are served with house salad and baked potato.

Stardust Hotel, 3000 Las Vegas Blvd. South, Las Vegas, NV 89109 (tel. 702/732-6111, or toll free 800/634-6757).

Until the International (now the Hilton) was opened, the Stardust was the biggest hotel in Las Vegas, its 1,400 rooms located in six buildings and a tower. Currently under construction is another 1,500-room tower. The Stardust has an Olympic-size swimming pool and five restaurants; it's also the home of the ultra-extravagant *Lido de Paris* spectacular—a not-to-be-missed Vegas production. The 183-foot-high, multiprogrammed sign out front and the glittering neon tower with a whimsical star (among several different lighting combinations that illuminate the full length of the hotel's façade) are a longtime Vegas fixture. The location of the Stardust is excellent, too—at the most central point on the Strip, for easy access to other areas in all directions.

The big hotel opened in 1958 and has gone through a multi-million-dollar remodeling. Facilities include two-story château suites, with one or two bedrooms and a living room with wet bar. At poolside locations, they have sliding glass doors leading to small terraces. An internal circular staircase leads to the upstairs sleeping quarters, and furnishings are brightly contemporary, colorful, and handsome. They're priced from $40 a night. One-bedroom tower suites or poolside minisuites begin at $140 a night. Regular poolside rooms are $89 to $112 a night, single or double. The Stardust offers package plans to suit a wide variety of vacation needs; ask the hotel for details.

The Stardust has pioneered another accommodations approach: campsites on the Strip. The setup, called **Stardust RV Park,** has 225 spaces on grounds behind the hotel. The RV Park has two swimming pools, laundry and shower rooms, a dog run, and a small convenience store. Spaces begin at $10, which includes hookup. Use of the RV Park is on a first-come, first-served basis. It's open year round to campers, travel trailers, motor homes, and tent trailers.

The Stardust casino is one of the largest—and busiest—on the Strip. It includes a huge race and sports book lounge. All the other popular games of chance are represented here as well. There is lounge entertainment nightly, except Monday.

Restaurants
There's a **Tony Roma's** restaurant at the Stardust, one of the famous nationwide chain featuring barbecued ribs. It is open for

lunch and dinner to 11pm. Tony Roma's has another Las Vegas location, which I will cover in Chapter IV.

Ralph's Diner is the Stardust's contribution to memories of places where some of us ate in the 1950s and early 1960s. There are a black-and-white checkerboard tile floor, stainless-steel everything, an old juke box, tiered booths, and a snack bar/soda fountain. About the only items missing are pictures of James Dean, Marilyn Monroe, and Elvis Presley.

Can you guess what, besides nostalgia, is served in Ralph's Diner? Hamburgers, fries, steaks, and those fountain drinks that somehow don't taste quite the same now. Meals cost $3.75 to $10.95. The diner is open daily from 6:30am to 2am.

William B's is a toned-down version of a Texas steak house—dark, masculine, and woody. The prime attraction here is steak and more steak, with seafood running a strong second. Steaks range from the usual New York steak, filet, and rib eye to prime rib, all of which are offered at $14 to $25. William B's is open daily from 5pm to midnight.

Toucan Harry's only goes to prove that there's no shortage of dining suggestions at the Stardust. This is the 24-hour coffee shop that serves everything from snacks (I'm partial to the hot chicken wings) to a platter of lox and cream cheese, cold sandwiches, hot sandwiches, salads, seafood, steaks, vegetable plates, southern-fried chicken, and smoked pork chops from $4.50 to $12. You could spend two weeks in Las Vegas and never run out of ideas from the menu. Then, from 5pm to 2am, Toucan Harry's features Chinese cuisine, offering a lengthy list (over 40 choices) of appetizers, soups, entrees, and Szechuan-style dishes. Entrees from the Chinese menu cost $9 to $15.

The **Warehouse** is the Stardust's all-you-can-eat 450-seat buffet and one of the best in town. What's more, there are large, comfortable booths and tables with plenty of elbow room. Breakfast is $5, lunch is $6, and dinner is $8. The Warehouse is open from 7am to 10pm daily. Saturday and Sunday there's a champagne brunch from 7am to 3:30pm. Dinner begins at 4pm.

Next to the race and sports book in the Stardust is the **Short-stop Snack Bar,** where you can get a super sandwich from $3.50 to $6, with beer or soft drinks, and watch the games, fights, races, or whatever, without interruption.

Maxim, 160 E. Flamingo Rd., Las Vegas, NV 89109 (tel. 702/731-4300, or toll free 800/634-6987).

A relative newcomer to the part of the Strip known as the "Golden Corner" (locale of Bally's—Las Vegas, Caesars Palace, and other prestigious hostelries), the Maxim opened its doors in July 1977. Although somewhat more modest than its neighbors, it offers all the big-hotel features: a swimming pool and sundeck, a large attractive casino, a showroom, convention facilities, shops, three restaurants, and two cocktail lounges.

Its 800 rooms are housed in twin 17-story towers. They are attractively modernistic, done in a rust, brown, and blue color scheme. All have one wall covered in silver foil, upholstered chrome furnishings, and bed units that encompass a framed rug with a super-graphic design or a mural of the Strip at night; all are equipped with every amenity, including a closed-circuit gaming station on your color TV. They're priced at $70 per night, single or double, on weekends and $42 per night on weekdays.

Restaurants

The **Tree House,** off the casino, is the requisite 24-hour eatery. It has smoked-mirror panels interspaced with murals, oak butcher-block tables, and lots of hanging plants. The menu gets you through the day, from pancakes or eggs Benedict with Canadian bacon in the $5 to $9 range, to salads and hot or cold sandwiches for $6 to $11, to rainbow trout or a New York steak with all the trimmings for $9 to $17. And there are terrific specials available, such as roast chicken for $4.95, fish filet for $5.95, and prime rib for $6.95.

Maxim's gourmet restaurant, **Da Vinci's,** has likenesses of the great man in etched glass at the entrance but is otherwise similar in décor to the rest of the hotel. It has modernistic lighting, brown-velour-upholstered chairs and booths, mirrored panels and coppertone panes.

The menu is continental, and it starts things off with such delicious appetizers as giant prawns scampi and escargots bourguignonne. Appetizers are served with garlic bread. The French onion soup au gratin, served in an earthenware tureen, is also a recommendable beginning. However, a plate of fresh vegetables with dip is served gratis to all, so you might even skip over the appetizers. Among the entrees are roast prime rib with creamy horseradish sauce and Yorkshire pudding; chicken in a butter and mushroom sauce; and veal Oscar—with crabmeat and asparagus topped with a mushroom cap and béarnaise sauce. There's a fine variety of wines available to complement your meal. Entrees range in price from $15 to $28. Flambé desserts are featured, and pastries are also available. Da Vinci's is open nightly from 6 to 11pm.

Imperial Palace, 3535 Las Vegas Blvd. South, Las Vegas, NV 89109 (tel. 702/731-3311, or toll free 800/634-6441).

A blue pagoda-topped 19-story white stucco structure, the Imperial Palace is an only-in-Vegas, East-meets-West proposition. For instance, only in Vegas could the traditional Japanese sunken tub emerge as a marble Luv Tub with mirrored walls and ceilings. Cocktail waitresses are attired in shortened kimonos, and the Oriental theme is carried out throughout the hotel in many other ways as well. Actually, all this Eastern splendor works quite well in the middle of the Strip opposite Caesars Palace.

The hotel added another tower in 1989, bringing the total number of rooms to 2,700. All accommodations are equipped with color TVs, direct-dial phones, and air conditioning. The décor features bamboo furnishings, Oriental-motif wallpaper and drapes, and Oriental art prints. And 100 rooms feature the above-mentioned love tubs; these rooms also have canopied beds on platforms with mirrored ceilings. Should the urge for a wedding come over you, there is always a minister on call.

Rates for the standard tower and East Building rooms are $45 to $105 per night, single or double, $8 for an extra person in the room; the Luv Tub rooms are in the higher range. Suites are $160 to $500.

Facilities include 45,000 square feet of convention space. The 75,000-square-foot casino has blue neon-lit pagoda-topped slot carousels and Oriental-design overhead beams decorated with dragons. In 1989 the Imperial added a state-of-the-art race and sports book. And since this is, after all, a desert, there are no fewer than six cocktail lounges, including a bar by the pool. The Sake Bar, Ginza Bar, Geisha Bar, and Mai Tai Lounge are convenient to the casino. All the bars offer a selection of Polynesian drinks in exotic settings. Dozens of specialty shops can be found on a main-floor arcade. Also on the premises are a large swimming pool and Jacuzzi, with a rock-walled waterfall and sundeck and a new health club for men and women. The Imperial Theater showroom, which seats 869, features dance extravaganzas as well as headliner entertainment.

The hotel offers two unique attractions in addition to the above: The management found that visitors were often reluctant to approach the tables for fear of being embarrassed by lack of knowledge, so it opened a **school of gaming** on the fourth floor, providing complimentary gaming classes to all Las Vegas visitors not just hotel guests. The classes are held four times a day and cover the basics of the games found on the casino floor.

The **Imperial Palace Auto Collection** is one of the largest in the country and was voted one of the ten best collections in the world by *Car and Driver* magazine. An elevator off the lobby whisks you up to the fifth floor of the display facility and years back in time. The cars, valued in the millions, include those owned by Adolf Hitler, Howard Hughes, Mrs. Henry Ford, and the King of Siam. Hitler's 1939 Mercedes Benz is complete with armor plating and a self-destruct mechanism that causes the gas tank to blow up. Howard Hughes's 1954 Chrysler was altered to include a specially engineered $15,000 air-purification system. For car buffs who appreciate rare examples of early models, over 200 antique, classic, and special-interest autos are on display daily from 9:30am to 11:30pm in a plush, gallerylike setting.

Restaurants

The Imperial Palace has two levels of dining for your enjoyment. The Dining Plaza on the fifth floor has the **Embers** for steak and lobster and the **Rib House** for ribs and a varied selection of barbecued entrees. Both are open nightly from 5pm to midnight. Also on the fifth floor are the **Ming Terrace** for Cantonese and Mandarin cuisine, the **Seahouse** for an array of seafood specialties, and the **Pizza Palace** for pizza and a lengthy list of pasta selections; all are open from 11am to midnight.

On the third floor, for more casual dining, are the **Emperor's Buffet** and the **Burger Palace.** The Emperor's Buffet is open for breakfast through dinner from 7am to 11pm, and it has an assortment of salads, entrees, and desserts at moderate prices. The Burger Palace serves the obvious, plus french fries and soft drinks, and is conveniently located next to the race and sports book.

As with all proper Las Vegas hotel/casinos there is the 24-hour coffee shop, the **Teahouse,** where the specialty of the evening is a prime rib dinner for $6.95 served from 5 to 11pm. The **Imperial Buffet** is served in the Teahouse and features roast beef from 8am to 3pm; a champagne brunch is also served Saturday and Sunday from 8am to 3pm.

California Hotel, 1st and Ogden Ave., Las Vegas, NV 89125-0630 (tel. 702/385-1222, or toll free 800/634-6255).

For those who seek exceptional accommodations downtown but would prefer rates somewhat less than the Golden Nugget's, there is Sam Boyd's California Hotel.

The rooms at the California are spacious and neatly assembled in subdued floral colors. Those in the older of the two towers (which are totally remodeled) are especially airy and attractive, even down to the small palm tree plaques that display your room number. The wallcovering is light, and the furnishings are reminiscent of Hawaiian décor—undoubtedly influenced by the fact that a large concentration of the California's guests are from Hawaii. For exercise other than picking up and putting down chips in the casino, on the 13th floor there is an outdoor pool that is open during warm weather.

Gaming at the California offers about 1,000 slot machines and a daily slot tournament—enough to keep anyone busy for days. Or you might try your hand at the blackjack tables, crap tables, roulette, keno, minibaccarat, or even pai-gow poker. The sports book is open from 9am until the start of the last game. Betting is available on all major sports and special events.

Just steps from the California Hotel is the **California RV facility**—the only RV park downtown. There are 222 spaces with full hookups, 24-hour security, a seasonally heated pool that is open 24 hours, full laundry facilities, and a dog run.

It's wise to do some advance planning for a stay at the California Hotel because it has 97% occupancy year round. Rooms at the California Hotel are $40, single or double, Sunday through Thursday; are $50 Friday and Saturday; and are $60 on holidays. There is a maximum of four persons per room, with an added $5 charge per night for an extra person. There is no charge for children 12 years and under staying in the room with their parents.

Restaurants

When hunger pangs strike, there's lots to choose from. California's **Market Street Café** has a prime rib dinner for less than $5; the **Redwood Bar and Grill** provides piano-bar entertainment with or without an 18-ounce porterhouse from 6pm to midnight; the **Pasta Pirate** features fresh pasta, seafood, and steaks; and the **Cal Club Snack Bar** has some great light meals and snacks.

A note about the Snack Bar: It's the only such eatery I've been in that offers chopsticks with other utensils, largely because it has some marvelous ultra-low-priced Chinese dishes, including the delicious Teri Bowl (teriyaki beef with rice) and shrimp tempura, as well as the usual hamburger, hot dog, and Philly steak sandwich.

Park Hotel & Casino, 300 N. Main St., Las Vegas, NV 89101 (tel. 702/387-5333, or toll free 800/782-9909).

The spacious green-and-sand-pink lobby with its wicker chairs, greenery, and terra-cotta floors leads you to believe that the rooms would be airy, light, and attractively simple in their décor, as indeed they are. The basic tones of the lobby are carried into the rooms— sand pink, tints of green, white lamps, and cream wallcoverings. Baths are small, but the basin is set in the adjoining area.

The entire hotel has a fresh, clean look. The Park represents itself as a "wonderful playground for adults who just want to have fun." True, but it's always nice to be able to come back to lovely quarters even if it's only for a brief rest before the next round at the slots or gaming tables.

The Park has 435 rooms and suites; for dining there's the 24-hour **Garden Room,** the **Patio Buffet,** and **Shady Nook Snack Bar.** The 50,000-square-foot casino offers the continuous entertainment of 700 slot machines, blackjack, craps, roulette, and poker and keno games. You'll find live entertainment in the Carousel Lounge. And, of course, what would a self-respecting Las Vegas hotel be without a pool. At the Park, it has an attractive freeform shape so that you never get bored with just paddling around.

The rooms at the Park, single or double, are $36 to $42 Sunday through Thursday and $52 to $60 Friday and Saturday. If you prefer a suite, those with one bedroom are $100 to $175; those with two bedrooms are $175 to $225.

Union Plaza Hotel, 1 Main St. (at Fremont Street), Las Vegas, NV 89101 (tel. 702/386-2110, or toll free 800/634-6575, 800/634-6821 in California).

Opened on August 1, 1971, the Union Plaza celebrated its first birthday with the "World's Biggest Birthday Cake." At the top of the brilliant Fremont Street light show on the site where the old Union Pacific Depot used to be, the building's double-towered, three-block-long frontage has permanently altered the Las Vegas downtown skyline. The 1,037-room, $100-million Union Plaza is one of the largest hotels in downtown Las Vegas.

Rooms have cable TV, direct-dial phones with message light, tub/shower bath, and two queen-size beds. There also are some rooms with king-size beds and a separate love seat that converts to a small bed; rooms with round beds; and a number of suites. The décor throughout the hotel is contemporary, with liberal use of walnut veneer and draperies and bedspreads in big, splashy patterns. The rooms are pretty and homey.

The Union Plaza's 650-seat showroom opened with *Fiddler on the Roof,* a smash hit, and it continues to feature Broadway-style musical productions or comedies, most recently World Class Ice Skating and *Nudes on Ice.* A 24-hour casino, an entertainment lounge, several dining rooms and bars, a shopping arcade, a sports deck with four lighted tennis courts and a quarter-mile jogging track, a pool, parking for 1,400 cars (including a five-story covered ramp), and a race and sports book lounge seating 300 complete the layout.

Rates for standard rooms at the Union Plaza are $30 to $60, single or double. Each additional person pays $8.

Here are a few facts about the Union Plaza: Adjacent to the hotel's parking ramps is the main Greyhound Terminal. . . . The Amtrack Railroad Station is right in the hotel . . . The Union Plaza is a joint venture of the Union Pacific Railroad and the Plaza Corporation of Las Vegas. So again a railroad has spurred new business in the West. . . . Shortly after the opening of the Union Plaza, Interstate 15 (linking Las Vegas with metropolitan Los Angeles, 289 miles to the southwest) was extended into the Casino Center, allowing drivers to go the entire distance from the Pacific Ocean to downtown Las Vegas without encountering a single traffic light.

Restaurants

The Union Plaza's restaurant is the **Center Stage.** It's located under a glass dome on the second floor of the hotel's north tower, with a spectacular nighttime view of the bright lights of downtown along Fremont Street. Adjacent to the Center Stage is a cocktail lounge. The restaurant's décor is soothing and attractive forest green and cream. You might begin dinner with an à la carte appetizer, such as smoked salmon or coquilles St-Jacques, or you can proceed directly to a complete dinner that begins with Act One—black-bean soup served with chopped egg, onions, and sherry. Act Two is a salad, Act Three is the entree, and Act Four is a fresh fruit basket with assorted nuts and tea or coffee. Entrees, which are priced at $14 to $35, include Rocky Mountain brook trout, grenadine of beef with either béarnaise or bordelaise sauce, and roast prime rib. In addition to all the Acts listed above, meals include a baked potato, fresh vegetable, and French or garlic bread. There's also an à la carte selection, and a nice wine list. The Center Stage is open daily for dinner from 5pm to midnight.

Another dining establishment at the Union Plaza is the **Kung Fu Plaza.** The foyer of this Chinese-Thai restaurant is Oriental indeed, with a Buddha, elephant statues, and dragon columns. Inside it resembles a garden, with leaf-print wallpaper, white latticework, and plants everywhere. The Kung Fu Plaza offers traditional Chinese fare: moo goo gai pan; beef with snow peas; Chinese soy sauce duck (unlike with Peking duck, the skin is soft); and the expected array of appetizers, including barbecued spareribs, egg rolls, and wonton soup.

Recently the restaurant added a delicious selection of Thai entrees to its menu. Dishes may be ordered to whatever degree of spiciness you prefer. Specialties of the house include spicy, crispy catfish—a favorite of mine; chicken chili mint—cooked with garlic and ground chili and served with chopped mint for a marvelous flavor; barbecue pork satay—marinated with Thai curry and served with a peanut butter sauce for dipping as well as with a special house cucumber sauce. And if you enjoy noodle dishes as much as I do, Kung Fu Plaza is famous for its Pad Thai noodles prepared with Thai chili powder and panfried with bay shrimp, bean sprouts, and peanuts. If you've never tried Thai food, King Fu Plaza is a great place to begin. Entrees range from $6 to $25. The restaurant is open daily from 11am to 11pm.

The Union Plaza's 24-hour coffee shop is the **Plaza Diner,** located off the casino on the main floor. In addition to the usual fare, the Plaza Diner offers daily specials of soup or salad, vegetable, bread, entree, and beverage. Lunch specials, available from 11am to 5pm, include shrimp or pork chops and run $5 to $8. Dinner might be a delicacy such as New York steak, prime rib, or brook trout, for $6 to $14. The Plaza Diner also features a bargain breakfast around the clock.

Four Queens Hotel, 202 E. Fremont St. (at Casino Center Boulevard), Las Vegas, NV 89101 (tel. 702/385-4011, or toll free 800/634-6045).

When the Four Queens first opened in 1965, it was a casino operation; the hotel followed later. These days it's a major downtown property with 720 rooms, occupying an entire block and decorated in a turn-of-the-century New Orleans French Quarter motif. The Four Queens offers 24-hour gaming and continuous entertainment featuring jazz and Dixieland artists in addition to complete hotel services. There's also a Ripley's Believe It or Not Museum with over 1,000 exhibits.

With singles and doubles $48 Sunday through Thursday, $58 on Friday and Saturday, and $8 for each additional occupant in any room, this is an excellent choice. Rates decrease substantially during the summer and winter. The 720 rooms are attractively decorated in a contemporary mode, with wall-to-wall carpeting, good-sized closets with double sliding doors, and prettily coordinated draperies and bedspreads. They're equipped with color TVs, direct-dial phones, and baths with glass-walled tubs and/or showers.

Restaurants
Magnolia's Veranda offers excellent food in a plush garden setting overlooking the casino. It's a pleasant alternative to the usual 24-hour coffee shop. The food is nicely prepared, whether it's a full-course meal or a quick snack. The service is good, too.

Hugo's Cellar features an abundant tableside salad cart and entrees such as fresh fish, prime rib, lamb, and duckling. Full dinners cost $17.50 to $32 and come with salad-cart selections, fresh vegetables, baked lavash, bread and cheese, and sherbet in between courses to refresh your palate. The finishing touch is light- and dark-chocolate-dipped fruits served with fresh whipped cream. Hugo's Cellar is open nightly from 6 to 11pm.

In addition, guests can enjoy nightly entertainment (jazz is featured), not to mention shrimp cocktail, in the **French Quarter Lounge.** And for your sweet tooth, there's an old-fashioned **Ice Cream Shoppe,** which serves up delectable concoctions in a variety of flavors.

Fitzgerald's Hotel & Casino, at Third and Fremont streets, Las Vegas, NV 89101 (tel. 702/382-6111, or toll free 800/634-6519, or 800/274-5825).

This hotel is housed in a 34-story tan and reflective-glass building. The casino dominates the ground floor. It's decorated in earth tones and offers 45,000 square feet of gambling facilities, including 1,120 slot machines, 20 blackjack tables, 3 craps tables, keno, roulette, and red dog. Public areas of the hotel are situated on two levels, with the casino, lobby, and entertainment lounge on the ground floor and restaurants and a lounge on the upper level.

The hotel's 650 rooms are modern and attractive, equipped with direct-dial phones and color TVs. There's free indoor parking for guests. Rates are $36 to $46 Sunday through Thursday and $50 to $60 Friday and Saturday, single or double. An extra person in the room pays $10.

Restaurants

Cassidy's Steak House is a dim and intimate eatery with tufted booths and old cowboy photos on the walls. Beef dishes, such as filet mignon with mushrooms, are a specialty, but there are also seafood dishes, such as a combination of shrimp, scallops, oysters, and clams, and other special items, such as veal piccata. But the surprise specialty is real Mexican food prepared by a Mexican chef. Dinner entrees range in price from $10 to $24. For dessert, Cassidy's features flaming items, such as peaches or cherries flambé. Outside the restaurant there's a small lounge where you can enjoy a before-dinner cocktail or a postprandial liqueur. Cassidy's is open for breakfast from 8am, for lunch from 11am to 3pm, and for dinner 5 to 11pm.

Next to Cassidy's is **Chicago Joe's,** a small Italian restaurant with lace curtains, red carpeting, and small tables with upholstered chairs that match the wallpaper. The lunch menu features pasta dishes such as lasagne, spaghetti, and rigatoni, and sandwiches filled with roast beef or Italian meatballs—all in the $6 to $12 range. At dinner, such Italian specialties as veal or shrimp parmesan and chicken cooked in garlic butter are offered for $11 to $17. Chicago Joe's is open Monday through Saturday from 11:30am to 11pm.

There's also **Molly's** 24-hour coffee shop and a buffet offering all-you-can-eat meals. The breakfast buffet is available from 8 to 11am for $3.99, lunch is from 11am to 3:30pm for $4.50, and dinner is from 4 to 9pm (to 10pm on Friday and Saturday) for $6.50.

Showboat Hotel, 2800 E. Fremont St. (between Eastern and Boulder Highway), Las Vegas, NV 89104 (tel. 702/385-9123, or toll free 800/634-3484).

Situated east of the Strip and somewhat south of downtown, the Showboat is a self-contained attraction. More so than most hotels in Las Vegas, it's a family place, with plenty of diversions for all. As of the moment, the Showboat is undergoing an extensive renovation and expansion that is scheduled to be completed in 1991.

The 800 rooms are large and pleasant, equipped with color TVs, direct-dial phones, and tub/shower baths. Singles and doubles are $55 per night; an extra person pays $8. Suites are $110 to $165 for one to two bedrooms. A number of the rooms are located around the swimming pool.

The Showboat is a sportsman's delight. One of the biggest and busiest lures is its 106 bowling alleys, with a pro shop, open 24 hours. (They're the site of the Pro Bowlers' Association events twice a year.) There's a snack bar facing the alleys for candy and a playroom (with attendant) where you can leave kids aged 2 to 7 for up to three hours at no charge.

A recent addition is a 45,000-square-foot **Sports Pavilion** where professional wrestling and boxing matches are staged, and sometimes televised on the cable sports networks.

There's a game arcade for kids. The hotel also has a barbershop and beauty salon, a gift shop, free valet parking, and a shuttle bus to the airport.

The coffee shop is open around the clock for meals ranging from a burger and fries to prime filet mignon with mushroom caps, plus all the requisite breakfast fare, deli items, sandwiches, and salads. Breakfast ranges from $4.50 to $7.50; lunch and dinner range from $7 to $22.

Large buffets are set out weekdays from 10am to 3:30pm ($4.25), Sunday for brunch from 8:30am to 2:30pm ($5.25), and at dinner nightly from 4:30 to 10pm (from $6.25 to $7.25). Kids' meals cost less.

There's a hometown attitude at the Showboat, which makes it most agreeable to regular repeat guests, who find all the amusement they want here without ranging out into the downtown area or to the Strip.

---

3. Inexpensive Hotels

The Circus Circus Hotel, 2880 Las Vegas Blvd. South, Las Vegas, NV 89109 (tel. 702/734-0410, or toll free 800/634-3450).

The Circus Circus is the only hotel in town that caters as unabashedly to children as it does to adults. From the clown-shaped marquee to the Circus Sky Shuttle to the tent-shaped Big Top, the Circus Circus is a delight for kids of all ages.

The hotel, which is located behind the immense casino-circus complex, is 15 stories high and has 800 rooms and suites. Another 805 rooms are located across the street in five three-story buildings known as Circus Circus Manor.

Rooms are priced from just $29 to $45 a night, single or double (prices are lower during the summer and December). An extra adult is $5. A typical room has two double beds or one king-size bed, a big mirror above the dressing table, color TV, direct-dial phone, wall-to-wall carpeting, and pleasant décor. The bath is separated from the dressing room by a big walk-through closet.

The focus of the hotel is, of course, the Big Top. On the main floor, casino action includes all the popular table games, a large keno lounge, lots of slots, and video gaming machines (blackjack, poker, and so forth). Originally the circus acts were presented directly over the casino in full view of all, but the daring acrobats and tightrope walkers were a distraction for the gamblers, and that's a definite no-no in Las Vegas. Now a sound-cushion ceiling insulates the main body of the casino from the circus goings-on, although the action can still be seen from selected parts of the casino floor.

On the mezzanine, the circus proper is ringed by carnival games offering nice prizes, arcades of electronic games, and snack stands for grabbing a quick bite. There's even a booth where kids (and lighthearted grownups) can be painted up like clowns. The one concession to the adults on this level is a revolving carousel bar; there's no gambling up there at all.

And, of course, there are the circus acts. Thirteen hours a day, from 11am to midnight, on the hour, you can see tumblers, trained animals, jugglers, and magicians. Trapeze artists soar through space, and aerial ballerinas perform on swaying carousel ponies. The atmosphere is nothing short of electric, and the smiles are contagious.

Gift shops and boutiques, a swimming pool, and other fun things are tucked into the Circus Circus cornucopia of goodies, a sensational (to use one of those superlatives that really are necessary in this case) hotel/casino/circus/spa that has to be seen to be believed. There's even a wedding chapel, if you'd like to get married under the Big Top.

Restaurants

Dining at the Circus Circus can mean anything from a hot dog to a full veal scaloppine dinner.

The **Steak House** is located on the main floor near the elevators. The décor is traditional, with rich woods, gleaming brass, leather-upholstered chairs, and soft lighting.

There's an open-hearth charcoal grill in full view of the dining area so that you can watch your steak being cooked. All the steaks are from midwestern beef aged 21 days in a glassed-in area just to the side of the restaurant. Good choices for steak lovers are the sirloin tip and the filet mignon, but there are also prime rib and lobster tail. Entrees costing $12 to $28 are served with a loaf of sourdough dark sweet bread and a choice of a one-pound baked potato or potato wedges with cheese. There is an extensive list of domestic and imported wines. The room is open daily from 5pm to midnight. A bar and a lounge adjoin.

Another dining choice is the **Circus Pizzeria,** located on the mezzanine. It's decorated in cheery red, white, and green, with striped poles and red-and-white-checked tablecloths. The specialty is—of course—pizza, either traditional or deep-dish. The dough is made fresh daily, as is the pasta, another dining choice. Pizzas range in price from $7 to $14, depending on size (small, medium, or large) and number of toppings. Pasta, such as spaghetti, rigatoni, and linguine, runs $5 to $9. You can order sodas by the glass or pitcher, and beer and wine are available for those over 21. The pizzeria is open daily from 11am to 1am.

The **Circus Circus Buffet,** served in a room off the casino, is an all-you-can-eat affair with over 40 items of all kinds priced at $2.50 for breakfast (beverage extra), served from 6 to 11:30am. Lunch, served from noon to 4pm ($2.75), and dinner, served from 4:30 to 11pm ($3.95), include beverage. Dinner includes carved-to-order roast beef and baked ham.

The **Snack Train,** on the mezzanine level, offers fast-food service, and the plushly pink **Pink Pony** (off the casino) is the requisite Vegas 24-hour coffee shop.

On the second level of Circus Circus, the **Skyrise Dining Room** offers a way to fill the urge for a one-pound New York steak or prime rib dinner at a great price. It's not posh-décor dining, but then it's hard to beat $6.95 when the entree also comes with soup or salad, potato, vegetable, and bread. The Skyrise Dining Room is open nightly from 5 to 11pm. There's also the **Skyrise Snack Bar,** offering fast-food service on the second level.

A DELUXE MOTOR CAMP

A few years ago, Circus Circus opened the luxurious **Circusland RV Park** adjacent to the Circus Circus Hotel/Casino and just steps away from the Strip. The RV park has all the informality and economy that RVers look for, plus the resort luxury of Las Vegas. There are spaces for 421 vehicles, all with up to 50-amp full-utility hookups. Well lit and attractively landscaped, the Circusland offers swimming pools for adults and a wading pool for tots, a fenced playground, saunas, Jacuzzis, a community room, a games arcade, fenced pet runs, laundry facilities, a disposal station, and a 24-hour convenience store. A free minibus provides transportation to and from the hotel. Rates are $12 per vehicle per night.

Quality Inn, 377 E. Flamingo Rd. (at Paradise Rd.), Las Vegas, NV 89109 (tel. 702/733-7777, or toll free 800/634-6617).
The Quality Inn offers 320 modern rooms, each with color TV, tub/shower bath, direct-dial phone, wet bar, and refrigerator. There's a large outdoor swimming pool, a whirlpool spa, laundry rooms, beauty and gift shops, a 24-hour coffee shop, Speakeasy

Café, a cocktail lounge with entertainment, and a medium-size casino.

Rooms are housed in six three-story buildings set in a lush landscape amid waterfalls, fish ponds, and babbling brooks. Sunday through Thursday rates are $55, single or double occupancy. Friday, Saturday, and holiday rates rise to $75 per night. Children 16 and under can stay free in their parents' room, and extra adults pay $5.

Villa Roma, 220 Convention Center Dr., Las Vegas, NV 89109 (tel. 702/735-4151, or toll free 800/634-6535).

Although the two-story Villa Roma was opened in 1964, the attractive creamy white paint job outside has improved its image. It has 100 rooms, with walk-ups (no elevator) to the second floor.

The fairly big rooms are furnished with king-size beds or two doubles, sofas, tables, and two chairs. Closets have sliding doors, and baths have tub/showers with glass doors. There's a color TV in every room, and local calls are free on your direct-dial phone. In-room coffee and refrigerators are convenient extras. Out back there's also a big swimming pool surrounded by Astroturf. And for those so inclined, there's a wedding chapel on the premises.

Rooms are in the bargain category, and they are especially notable for their excellent location near mid-Strip. Single or double occupancy is $39. Shopping, several big hotels and showrooms, and Strip buses are within close walking distance. Limo service is available.

Algiers Hotel, 2845 Las Vegas Blvd. South, Las Vegas, NV 89109 (tel. 702/735-3311).

This is one place that is surprisingly different . . . it has no casino. The hotel is much nicer than you might expect from the array of shops in front. The barrage of lights announcing "Cocktails," "Coffeeshop," "Souvenirs," and "Gifts" dominates the façade to such a degree that you'll find the hotel sign barely noticeable. (It's across from Circus Circus.) But if you keep looking and take the underpass below the signs, you'll find yourself in a central court and pool area. And that's it. The two-story hotel is arranged in a U-shape around the pool; there are 105 rooms.

As you enter the court at the Algiers, the small and informal office is to your left. Off it is the cozy cocktail lounge with bar and leatherette seats in reds. The cocktail bar is open from 11am to 3am daily; the adjoining coffee shop is open daily from 7am to 11pm.

It's quite plush for a coffee shop, with gold-vinyl-upholstered chairs and horseshoe-shaped booths; red-and-gold-flocked wallpaper and smoked-glass mirrors on the walls; lighting emanating from candlelight, crystal chandeliers, and wall sconces; and a small waterfall in a copper-chimneyed fireplace. You can also dine on an enclosed patio café area overlooking the pool. Luncheon specials are an unbeatable bargain—such as fried chicken or ocean perch, served with soup or salad, rolls and butter, and dessert, for under $7. Steaks are $9.50 to $11.95.

Rooms at the Algiers are priced at $39 single, $44 double, $51 triple, and $56 for four persons. All rooms are the same, whether you wish twin beds or a double bed. Carpets and bedspreads are prettily colorful; walls are wood-paneled. Furniture is contemporary, painted white, with tables and chairs, double dressers, tiled baths with tub/showers, and big walk-in closets. The rooms are of adequate size and very pleasant, equipped with color TVs and direct-dial phones. All the rooms shine with good housekeeping, too, which is especially impressive.

The Algiers Hotel is an informal place without the fanfare and the fuss and bother associated with most hotels along the Strip. It definitely does not attract the frenetic crowds that most casinos do. If you're simply looking for a pleasant hotel with a swimming pool, a place to eat, and a nice room, the Algiers is worth checking into. Its superior location along the Strip is an advantage, too, for days and nights roaming the town.

Vagabond Inn and Casino, 4155 Koval Lane, Las Vegas, NV 89109 (tel. 702/731-2111, or toll free 800/634-6541).

Well located, immaculate, cheerful, and fully equipped to meet your travel needs, these no-frills hostelries are among the best things to happen to budget travel since Arthur Frommer.

The Koval Lane establishment, directly behind Bally's–Las Vegas, couldn't be better placed. A stucco and shingled three-story building, it houses 360 well-proportioned rooms that are quite pretty for the price, with attractive matching spreads and drapes, gray carpeting, and peach-colored walls. Rooms are air conditioned and equipped with shower baths, color TVs, and direct-dial phones. The rates during the week are $38, single or double. On weekends the rates are $50. An extra person is $6 per night.

Facilities include a swimming pool and sundeck, a Jacuzzi, a gift shop, and ample free parking. You pass through a small casino to register; a small restaurant and bar are off to one side. There are scores of restaurants in easy walking distance.

Super 8 Motel, 4250 Koval Lane, Las Vegas, NV 89109 (tel. 702/794-0888, or toll free 800/848-8888).

I simply can't remember the last time I stopped at a hotel or motel that had rooms with waterbeds. The Super 8 Motel has ten such rooms, among others, if waterbeds happen to be your thing.

This Super 8 Motel is conveniently located one block from the Strip; is newly redone; and adjoins the Ellis Island restaurant, which is open 24 hours daily. There is a roomy lobby with sofas and chairs. Rooms are comfortable, decorated with floral-pattern spreads in peaceful tones of beige and blue. All beds are queen-size, and all baths have tub/showers. Suites also have minirefrigerators. Super 8, bless its heart, also has laundry facilities. For the loungers and water sprites, there is a pool.

Weekday rates are $33 for one person and from $38 to $40 for two. Weekend rates are $10 higher for singles or doubles. There is a $2 charge for each additional person in the double. Suites are $64 but $74 on weekends. Given a choice, I'd reserve a room on the second or third floor; it's quite a bit lighter up there than on the ground floor.

Restaurant

Adjacent to the Super 8 is **Ellis Island Restaurant,** with a pleasant décor and a menu selection that is excellent for breakfast, lunch, Sunday brunch, or dinner—all at moderate prices.

Vegas World Hotel and Casino, 2000 Las Vegas Blvd. South (at St. Louis Blvd.), Las Vegas, NV 89104 (tel. 702/382-2000, or toll free 800/634-6277).

This hotel is different from the average Las Vegas hotel/casino complex. First, its position is neither on the Strip proper nor in downtown. It's somewhere in between, at the junction of Las Vegas Boulevard, Main Street, and St. Louis Boulevard. Second, the casino is always looking for new twists to the same old games. Vegas World claims that "Double Exposure 21" (the dealer's two first cards are dealt face up) got its start here, as well as "crapless craps" —you can't lose on the first throw of the dice simply because 2, 3, or 12 (on the first throw) are points. (See Chapter VI for the rules of the game.) Third, the hotel is not ablaze in neon. In fact, at night you have to look for it. Its exterior décor is positively Space Age: Peeping through red-painted archways on the original structure is a building-size portrait of the moon; the tower depicts a blue-and-white planet Earth. A realistic depiction of the solar system on the 40-foot ceiling of the main lobby is done with fiber optics. It's replete with a replica of the Apollo Skylab and life-size astronaut models shown against a planetary background.

Vegas World has 600 rooms, divided between the main building and the 24-story tower. The rooms are moderate in size, each containing one king-size bed or two double beds. The décor is cheerful; all the usual amenities are present—direct-dial phones, air conditioning, color TVs, and modern bathrooms. (These last are quite small in the older building.) Room rates range from $47 to $62, single or double; it is $10 for each extra person.

Other facilities at Vegas World are a shopping arcade, two lounges, a video arcade, a beauty salon, a fully equipped casino, and a 1,200-seat showroom.

Restaurants

Vegas World's 24-hour coffee shop is the **Copperhood Restaurant.** It's standard all the way, from the red leatherette booths lining the walls and the Formica tables to the menu. Breakfast (served around the clock) is everything from danish to steak and eggs, for $3 to $10. Light fare (also available 24 hours a day), in the $5 to $11 range, consists of sandwiches, burgers, and salads as well as Hobo Stew (beef chunks and vegetables in a tomato broth), Pop's Texas-style chili, and a daily chef's special. From 5pm to 1am, you can order hot entrees—such as prime rib, batter-fried shrimp, and barbecued pork ribs, complete with soup or salad, vegetable, potato, and rolls and butter—for $9 to $16.

Nearby is **Kelly and Cohen's Steakhouse.** It's a small, intimate place, decorated in ornate Victorian style with red tufted-velvet booths and an elaborate brass-and-red-globed chandelier. Overlooking the whole is a portrait of Kelly and Cohen, head to head. The steak house menu is presented on an easel; specialties include prime rib and broiled trout. Entrees range in price from $13 to $28.50. Kelly and Cohen's is open for dinner nightly from 6 to 11pm.

El Cortez Hotel, at Fremont and Sixth streets, P.O. Box 680, Las Vegas, NV 89125 (tel. 702/385-5200, or toll free 800/634-6703).

This is one of Las Vegas's smaller hotels, and it's a gem. Built around 1940, it was completely renovated a few years back. The result is what appears to be a pleasant five-story hotel, with a sparkling coffee shop, a lobby, a dining room, an expanded keno lounge, and 308 guest rooms.

Slots at the El Cortez are "extra liberal," according to the hotel's promotional material, and they pay more than 7,000 jackpots every 24 hours. On the ground floor there's a lounge that never closes and is always crowded and a round-the-clock coffee shop, the **Emerald Room.** Needless to say, the casino is an all-day/all-night operation, 365 days a year.

Because the gambling action is so concentrated, some individuals almost never use their rooms. That's a shame, for not only are they nicely arranged and decorated, but also they're outstanding bargains at $23 to $40, single or double; the rates are constant the year round. An extra person adds $3. Each room has individually controlled heat and air conditioning, too, so you can keep temperatures at levels you prefer. They're also equipped with color TVs, direct-dial phones, and tub/shower baths.

Restaurant

Local Las Vegans always mention the El Cortez for good dining at reasonable prices. **Roberta's Café** is a place popular with families. The room is so popular, in fact, that double lines during dinner hours extend through the entire casino. A 1¼-pound porterhouse steak with trimmings at $9.95 is the biggest draw, but whopping lobsters, really big enough for two at $12.95, and half-steak/half-lobster specials for $12.50 are other menu tantalizers. Dinner is served from 4 to 11pm.

The food at the El Cortez Hotel is famous in Las Vegas. But Jackie Gaughan, the hotel's dynamic owner, has adhered to old-line Las Vegas attitudes, really giving guests as much for their money as volume traffic will allow. He shaves prices to the bare minimum and resists the corporate trend to cut the extras that have attracted people to the city, and his approach has made him one of the most successful hotel/casino operators in Nevada.

Ogden House, 651 E. Ogden (at Sixth St.), Las Vegas, NV 89101 (tel. 702/385-5200), or toll free 800/634-6703).

The Ogden House is a five-story hostelry located directly behind the El Cortez. The 102 rooms, all of which open off interior corridors, are simply but comfortably furnished, with one queen-size bed or two twin beds, air conditioning, phones, and color TVs. Room rates are a bargain at $23, single or double occupancy. An extra person adds $3.

The hotel has no eating or gaming facilities of its own. In fact, it operates as a sort of an annex to the El Cortez, with which it shares it management and switchboard. And guests of the Ogden House have full access to all the amenities of the El Cortez.

Gold Spike, 400 E. Ogden (at Fourth St.), Las Vegas, NV 89101 (tel. 702/384-8444, or toll free 800/634-6703).

The Gold Spike is located just a couple of blocks from the El Cortez and the Ogden House, and it is also owned by Jackie Gaughan. The hotel has 110 rooms and suites, the latter with balconies. All accommodations have phones, color TVs, and air conditioning. Prices are a very reasonable $20, single or double, and include free breakfast at the El Cortez; a suite is $31. An extra person adds on $3.

The Gold Spike has a small snack bar that features hot roast beef or ham dinners for under $3, as well as reasonably priced soup, sandwiches, and chili. And there are Marie Callender pies on sale for dessert. There's also a casino in the hotel, perfect for the "budget" gambler, with penny slot machines, 5¢ electronic keno machines, 40¢ live keno, 10¢ roulette, and $1 blackjack, as well as higher-stakes machines and games.

Western Hotel, 889 E. Fremont St. (at Ninth St.), Las Vegas, NV 89101 (tel. 702/384-4620, or toll free 800/634-6703).

The Western has the largest free-standing marquee (77 feet) in the downtown area, and its bingo parlor is known as "the most comfortable, and the happiest in town." It certainly does attract a sizable crowd. So do the slots, live gaming, and keno lounge, the latter offering 40¢ keno with prizes up to $25,000.

The Western is three stories tall, with 115 rooms. It's about three short blocks from the most crowded casino area along Fremont Street, certainly within easy walking distance of all the downtown attractions.

Cozy and immaculate rooms of colorful contemporary design are located off central hallways or off an open central porch on the top floor. They're priced at a mere $20 for a room with one queen-size bed or two twin beds and $24 for two doubles. The hotel doesn't need a shill to tell anybody that it's one of the best price deals in Las Vegas. Rooms have mirrored dressing alcoves, and the baths have tubs or showers with glass doors. Closet space is abundant. Naturally every room is air conditioned and has direct-dial phone and color TV.

"Western Fun Books," which guests may receive daily at the desk, are *really* fun books. They entitle you to some free meals, drinks, souvenirs, gifts, and so on at this and other Vegas establishments.

Sam Boyd's Fremont Hotel & Casino, 200 E. Fremont St. (at Casino Center Boulevard), Las Vegas, NV 89101 (tel. 702/385-3232, or toll free 800/634-6182).

Sam Boyd's Fremont Hotel & Casino, a downtown landmark since 1956, has recently undergone a $15-million renovation. The 450 rooms have been refurbished with comfortable double or king-size beds, color TVs, direct-dial phones, tub/shower baths, and wall-to-wall carpeting. For guests' protection and convenience, each room is equipped with a safe. Midweek rates are $36 for a single or double, and weekend rates are $52 for a single or double; it is $8 a day for an additional person. Deluxe room rates are $75 to $100. Holiday rates are $60 to $100.

The hotel is located smack in the center of downtown Las Vegas, where all-hour gaming spills through the hotel casinos, out into the streets, and into the coffee shops and restaurants, keeping the nights day-bright. Time isn't measured by am or pm in these precincts. Casino activities at the Fremont keep the action going with blackjack, craps, keno, race and sports book, bingo, and lots of slots.

Restaurants

When the need for nourishment overwhelms you, there are three restaurants and a snack bar handy. The **Overland Stage Café** is open 24 hours and offers Chinese dishes in addition to a complete American menu. Dinner possibilities (from $9 to $17) range from lobster Cantonese to broiled Swiss steak.

The all-you-can-eat meals at the **Fremont Buffet** are among the best bargains in Vegas. Breakfast, served from 7 to 10:30am, is $2.95; lunch, from 11:30am to 3pm, is $3.95; and Sunday through Thursday dinner, from 4 to 10pm, goes for $5.95. Friday and Saturday dinner is served to 11pm. The buffet features fresh vegetables and fruits at its salad bar, a variety of delicious hot entrees, pastries, and mixed berry sorbets. All meals include unlimited beverages, of the soft variety. Saturday and Sunday brunch is served from 7am to 3pm ($3.95).

On the second floor of the Fremont is the **Hualapai,** a first-rate restaurant offering superb food in a warm, relaxed atmosphere. Specialties of the house are ribs; filet mignon; rib-eye steak; Australian lobster tail; and a great combination—"Shells and Bones," with crab legs or lobster plus a half-pound filet or half rack of ribs. And for dessert, if you've never had cheesecake with caramel sauce and spiced pecans, this is the place to go all out and order it.

Entrees average $12.50 to $19. The Hualapai is open from

5:30 to 11pm Sunday through Thursday, to midnight Friday and
Saturday. Reservations are suggested.

Roxy's Bar, in the main casino area, features live entertainment
daily from noon to 6am.

Horseshoe Hotel & Casino, 128 Fremont St. (at Casino Center Blvd.), Las Vegas, NV 89101 (tel. 702/382-1600, or toll free 800/622-6468).

Located in the heart of downtown Las Vegas, the Horseshoe is
often thought of simply as a casino, and most patrons never realize
that it's a hotel. Not a big one, however. It has the original 83 rooms
on three floors, plus the 256-room high-rise when the Horseshoe
took over the Mint. The hotel and casino are run by the Binion family (although patriarch "Benny" died in 1989), well known in
gambling circles.

As you might guess, the casino is done up in the style of the Old
West, with antique etched-glass chandeliers; there are even antique
slot machines.

The Horseshoe has some of the lowest-priced rooms in
Las Vegas: $26 to $55, depending on location and day of the week.
The rooms are pleasantly decorated with the appropriate amenities. It isn't glamorous, nor should you expect to find boutiques
and the sort of extras you pay for at some bigger establishments.
But the location can't be beat in downtown Las Vegas. What's
more, there's a rooftop outdoor pool open from April to November.

One of the biggest draws at the Horseshoe Casino is a display of
$1 million in cash, one hundred $10,000 bills. You can have your
picture taken with the money free, and it's printed and ready in
about two hours. One of the family who works at the casino told me
that "the free picture deal costs the casino about $100 a day." He
added: "It's so popular, it's worth it."

The Horseshoe is also the setting each spring for the World Series of Poker, in which all participants must begin with minimum
stakes of $10,000.

The casino also is unique for allowing craps table bets up to
$5,000, reputed to be the highest sum allowed in Nevada in any ca-
sino for a single bet at craps. However, it's been said that if you've
got a million to bet, the casino will take you on.

Restaurants

Although most Las Vegas bistros tend to turn into some deco-
rator's idea of the bad and bawdy splendors of the rollicking Old
West, the West that the Binions have created in their restaurants is a
civilized one indeed.

The **Skye Room** is at the top of the high-rise, where you can
enjoy a spectacular view of the Las Vegas valley while savoring your
entree. There's generally a choice of four cuts of steak, as well as
prime rib, broiled chicken, broiled fish, and sautéed shrimp at $12

to $25. This is one of those restaurants that offers a few items that are very well prepared. The wine list is small but good. The Skye Room is open nightly from 5 to 11pm.

Spaghetti Red's is a good choice for delicious Italian specialties that are reasonably priced. It's a great place for an affordable evening out, with entrees that average about $8 with a high of $12. Dinner is served nightly from 5 to 11pm.

There's also a **Buffet** on the second floor, where you can get breakfast from 7 to 11am ($3), lunch from 11:30am to 4pm ($5), dinner from 4:30 to 10pm ($7), and a night-owl special ($2) from 10pm to 3am.

The **coffee shop** is less elegant than the Mexican Bar and Steak House (below), but essentially the same décor prevails. Open 24 hours, it features such breakfast items as huevos rancheros and a large selection of omelets for $4 to $6. Lunch or dinner cost $6 to $17 for light fare such as soups, sandwiches, salads and chili, as well as fried chicken plate served with country gravy, potato, biscuits, and apple cobbler.

The **Steak House** features mesquite-broiled prime beef, such as New York steak and a 20-ounce porterhouse steak, prime rib, as well as lighter entrees such as rainbow trout and chicken. Dinners, which cost $12 to $25, include salad and baked potato. The Steak House is open nightly from 5 to 11pm.

Next door is the **Mexican Bar,** where tacos, burritos, chili, enchiladas, chiles rellenos, and combination platters may be had for $5 to $10. The Mexican Bar is open daily from 5 to 11pm.

Hotel Nevada and Casino, 235 S. Main St. (at Bridger Ave.), Las Vegas, NV 89101 (tel. 702/385-7311).

Among the hotels in downtown Las Vegas, with 165 rooms behind a plain and unimposing façade, the Nevada was opened on July 1, 1974. The casino has been remodeled, and the 155 rooms have been brightened up with wallpaper, carpeting, wood paneling, and furnishings.

Standard rooms at the Nevada cost $20 a night, single or double, Sunday to Thursday; they cost $26 Friday and Saturday. An extra person in a room pays $3.

The Nevada has a fairly small casino with 200 slots, keno, and gaming tables, and a small restaurant that is open 24 hours. It's directly across the street from the bus terminal adjacent to the Union Plaza.

You won't find entertainment at the Nevada. It's meant to fulfill modest needs. Around the corner on Fremont Street, within a block, are the Golden Nugget, the Horseshoe, and other hotels where guests can find plentiful entertainment.

Center Strip Inn, 3688 Las Vegas Blvd., South, Las Vegas, NV 89109 (tel. 702/739-6066, or toll free 800/777-7737 or 800/543-3902).

The Center Strip is directly between Flamingo Road and Tropicana Avenue. As its name indicates, it's situated in the center of the Strip; however, at the rate that new hotels are rising and expanding, this may not be a good designation for long.

The motel is long and narrow, extending back from the Strip with parking places alongside—a distinct convenience for any facility on the Strip. Rooms are spacious with furnishings that are comfortable. All accommodations have refrigerators, color TVs, and VCRs (the lobby has rental tapes if you don't travel with your own). There is also a pool with a sunning area. Other benefits are free local phone calls and a complimentary continental breakfast that is served daily.

The Sunday through Thursday rate for a room with one bed is $39, and the rate for a room with two beds is $49. Friday and Saturday rates are $69. Of the 92 rooms, the entry to one faces the ice machine, and so the room may not be as quiet as the others.

Westward Ho Motel & Casino, 2900 Las Vegas Blvd. South, Las Vegas, NV 89109 (tel. 702/731-2900, or toll free 800/634-6803, 800/634-6651 in California).

Westward Ho has 1,000 attractive air-conditioned rooms and, believe it or not, seven swimming pools and whirlpools. In spite of the motel's size, the staff is very friendly and helpful. The motel covers considerable acreage, and vans are provided to take you to your accommodations.

Every room has a color TV, a phone, a tub/shower bath, and a dressing area—and all are spotlessly clean. Special rooms for the handicapped are available. And the location, right in the heart of Strip activities, couldn't be better. Singles and doubles are $39 to $42 Sunday through Thursday and $49 to $52 Friday and Saturday. Also available are two-bedroom apartments that can sleep up to six, which cost $65 to $78 Sunday through Thursday and $75 to $88 on Friday and Saturday for four persons (there's a $2-per-night charge for each extra person up to six). They're ideal for families or large compatible groups traveling together.

The motel's casino has been expanded threefold and remodeled. The casino lounge has free nightly entertainment. In addition to the usual automatic teller machines and the other financial services offered in most casinos, Westward Ho has a foreign-exchange desk.

Restaurant

Le Café is Westward Ho's 24-hour eatery decorated with latticed walls, a green lattice-pattern carpet, attractive tilework, ceiling fans, and lots of ferns. Breakfast is served around the clock for $4 to $9. Lunch and dinner feature sandwiches and burgers, as well as hot food such as barbecued ribs, fried chicken, and filet of sole—in the $7 to $16 range. A special New York steak or trout amandine with soup or salad, potato, rolls, and beverage is $8. And if that's not enough of a bargain, there's a $4 luncheon buffet from 11am to 4pm, followed by a dinner buffet until 10pm for only $7.

Days Inn, 3265 Las Vegas Blvd. South, Las Vegas, NV 89109 (tel. 702/735-5102, or toll free 800/325-2525).

What once was the Imperial 400 Motor Inn is now part of the Days Inn chain. The motel is in the process of being renovated, and all is pleasant and tidy. The three stories of rooms are wrapped on three sides of a square around the swimming pool (heated to 80° in the winter), which is separated from the street by a cement-block barrier for privacy. A number of the rooms have balconies and face the Strip and mountains. Accommodations have been refurbished and decorated in earth tones—rust, brown, gold, and beige. All rooms have Formica-topped dressers with big mirrors, direct-dial phones, and color TVs.

Singles or doubles are $39 to $75; a king suite is $55 to $95. Pets are allowed. There's adequate free parking. The front desk is helpful with show reservations and tours.

Convention Center Lodge, 79 Convention Center Dr., Las Vegas, NV 89109 (tel. 702/735-1315, or toll free 800/634-6266).

Convention Center Lodge is right in the heart of the action, at "Stardust Corner." Its modern furnishings are comfortable and clean, all with private bath containing tub and/or shower, cable color TV, and direct-dial phone. Singles or doubles go for $28 to $38 on weeknights and $38 to $48 on weekends and holidays.

Motel 6, 195 E. Tropicana Ave. (at Koval Lane), Las Vegas, NV 89109 (tel. 702/798-0728).

Just two blocks off the Strip, this branch of the low-priced and well-located Motel 6 chain now has 877 units and is growing by the minute. It's the largest Motel 6 in the country. All rooms have air conditioning, free TV, phones in the rooms with free local calls, and a shower bath. There's even a swimming pool, plus a smaller pool in the Granada section. Room rates are $25.95 for one and $31.95 for two.

IV

LAS VEGAS DINING

1. STEAKS AND SEAFOOD
2. CONTINENTAL
3. SOUTHWESTERN AND MEXICAN
4. ITALIAN
5. GERMAN
6. JAPANESE AND CHINESE

Las Vegas is a super food town where you can find great American food in the most generous helpings available on the continent. The colossal buffet is a way of life. Along with noble efforts in American cooking, you'll also discover a wide selection of foreign and exotic cuisines.

The big hotels, glamour places to say the least, serve elaborate spreads, often at prices that make cooking at home almost unreasonable. The gambling halls do the same. While you're enjoying the casino games and slot machines, wandering hostesses in chorus-girl tights and miniskirts invite you to order any free drink you may wish—but don't forget the tip ("toke")—and many will even provide your favorite brand of cigarettes free. It's part of the game in Las Vegas—a "shill" at even the most renowned hotels and gaming places, to keep you from wandering from the tables. The house wins, and so do you—they get the business and you get some of the easiest-to-take wining and dining in the United States.

Topping the list of the Vegas food bargains are the buffets—amazingly low-priced all-you-can-eat breakfasts, lunches, brunches, and dinners. They're almost always in the $4 to $8 range, and at some the champagne flows freely. Among the hotels offering these sumptuous food orgies are the Aladdin, Bally's, Bourbon Street, Caesars Palace, Circus Circus, Dunes, Flamingo Hilton, Fremont, Golden Nugget, Hacienda, Holiday, Imperial Palace, Landmark, Maxim, Riviera, Sahara, Showboat, Silver Slipper, Stardust, Fitzgerald's, Tropicana, Union Plaza, and Westward Ho.

And signs all over town hawk 69¢ breakfasts, 99¢ shrimp cocktails, and the like.

In addition to the restaurant extravaganzas in the hotels, however, Vegas has plenty of good eating places. They have to offer a lot to compete with the hotel eateries and prices, and they also give you a chance to get away for a while from the razzle-dazzle, flashy neon ambience of the Strip and downtown. These are the places where the locals eat, and not only will you get an excellent meal at any of the upcoming listings, but also you will get to see another side of Vegas.

---

1. Steaks and Seafood

The Tillerman, 2245 E. Flamingo Rd., just west of Eastern Ave. (tel. 731-4036).

Ask anyone living in Las Vegas for a list of the best restaurants, and the list will almost invariably include The Tillerman. Behind this sort of recommendation is an exceptional restaurant with a consistently high quality of food and service.

It's all put forth in a handsome arboreal setting—a veritable forest of six ficus trees reaching up to a cathedral-height ceiling and skylight. All the trees, flowers, greenery are live (no *faux* for The Tillerman). Banquettes are forest colors—deep greens, rose, and mauve—on a terra-cotta floor. In keeping with the air of the restaurant, the tabletops are of highly polished wood; the burgundy napkins are rolled into candle shapes; and the dinnerware is a classic blue and white, complementing the fluted flatware. Chairs in the main dining area have high backs complementing the vertical lines of the room. Set apart from the central dining area are two cozy rooms perhaps designed for intimate chit-chat over dinner.

You might expect the waiters to be clad in forest green, but as befits the elegant tone of The Tillerman, they are sprucely garbed in black trousers, white shirts, burgundy ties, and burgundy braces.

First served are deliciously crisp crûdités accompanied by salad. Then there are delicious homemade baby loaves of bread (certainly the best I've ever tasted), from which one could make a complete meal. But on to the entrees. The specialty of the house is fresh ocean and freshwater seafood flown in daily. And to quote The Tillerman, "the beef is the finest available." I can attest to the former, but you simply can't believe the remarkable freshness of the accompanying vegetables. It's most unusual to be served vegetables other than a choice of potatoes, much less to have them presented fresh and cooked to perfection.

Fish specials of the evening may range from trout to swordfish. Other seafood entrees, depending on the season, may include Dungeness crab, lobster, select Alaskan king crab legs (cracked at the table by your waiter), or seafood brochette. Whatever the choices are, I've yet to have one that was not exceptional. As to meat alternatives, you might opt for the pan-sautéed chicken breast or the full cut of the bone-out prime rib (when available). In the absence of the prime rib, you can't possibly go wrong with the filet mignon or the New York strip steak. Entrees range from $15 to $34, the higher price for the Alaskan king crab legs.

The Tillerman has a full bar, so if you must spend a bit of time waiting for your table, this is a consoling factor. The drinks are very amply sized, and even the house wine is above reproach. The Tillerman does not take reservations. If you would rather not wait for a table, it's wise to come by 6:30pm because the restaurant generally is full by 6:45pm. The Tillerman is open nightly from 5 to 11pm.

The Golden Steer, 308 W. Sahara Ave., just west of the Strip (tel. 384-4470 or 387-9236).

(*Note:* Directly after heading west on Sahara, turn into the lot after the Texaco sign on your right.)

The bar on your left as you enter the Golden Steer has an Old West look and feel—red leather, a forest-green ceiling, steer horns, antique guns, western paintings, framed silver dollars, and red velvet curtains. To one side there's a beautiful old glass-encased slot machine that's never had the opportunity to gobble up a single coin.

Among the excellent entrees offered, there are a number that you would expect to find (and some that you would not) in a restaurant called the Golden Steer. Choices range from one-half of a broiled spring chicken at $12 to the prime rib (called a Diamond Lil or a Diamond Jim) at $21 to $27.50. But then you may prefer either the moist and delicious rack of lamb or the chateaubriand for two at $24 per person.

You can also enjoy a somewhat more unusual and sumptuous meal of Bob White quail—a pair for $24 per person. A Beef and Bird entree offers some of the best of both worlds, with quail and a petit filet mignon accompanied by wild rice for $21.

There is nothing commonplace about the veal or chicken specialties, although you may have seen them listed on other restaurant menus. The quality is exceptional, whether you choose the veal française—dipped in egg batter and sautéed with mushrooms and lemon—or the Chicken of the Angels—a boneless breast sautéed with mushrooms and hearts of artichokes. Chicken and veal specialties, served with spaghetti or toasted ravioli, go for $16.50 to $17.50.

As for the seafood, the highlight of the menu is an extra-large imported Dover sole for $22, served à la carte with a baked potato. Other specialties from the sea include Australian lobster tail and Alaskan king crab legs priced according to market.

One of the pleasant surprises here: Without a doubt, the Golden Steer has the best baked potato that I've ever eaten in any restaurant at any time; it's indicative of the quality that you may expect, whatever you order. I also hear from a good source that the restaurant has the best Caesar salad, bar none. I simply did not have room to try it.

The house offers a good selection of imported and domestic wines at reasonable prices. The Golden Steer menu identifies what it pours when you order your booze by its generic name—the quality, as you might expect, matches that of the food.

If you have room for dessert, there are several varieties of delicious cheesecake, or if you're a chocolate freak, the chocolate bomba ice cream may be just what it takes to hit the spot. Desserts range in price from $3 to $3.85.

You don't want to join the crowd at the Golden Steer if you plan to eat and run back to the baccarat table. Service here is appropriately paced for dining not for gulping. The Golden Steer is open daily from 5pm to midnight but closed on Thanksgiving and Christmas. Reservations are suggested.

Famous Pacific Fish Co. at 3925 Paradise Rd., between Flamingo and Sands (tel. 796-9676).

This is, without a doubt, one of the best seafood restaurants in Las Vegas. I counted at least seven *fresh* fish entrees on the menu — not fresh frozen or frozen fresh.

From Paradise Road, the Famous Pacific Fish Co. (FPFC) has the look of a large, white, barnlike structure; the entry is at the rear of the building. The interior is a delightful surprise — a vast, handsomely designed space with a high-pitched roof, white ceiling, white walls, dark woods, attractive industrial hanging lamps, trusses and beams, and much exposed piping and ductwork painted an unobtrusive battleship gray. Red-brick pillars hold the beams and crossmembers. Overhead are all things that speak of the sea — lines, lobster traps, swordfish shapes, diving equipment, two small skiffs, and so forth. Even the carpeting pattern appears to be a sea of brown kelp.

It's a relaxed, fun place with good food and good looks. There are charts on the walls and black-and-white photos of boats, more traps, nets, and models of ships above the bar. The tables are wood with captain's chairs. The booths are bleached wood, with cushioning in sea colors. As you enter, the comfortable and attractive bar area to the left is centerlit from the top and the bottom to highlight the ship models and the hanging array of glasses. If you're seated at a table or a booth near the entry at night, look behind and you'll see a spectacular view of the Strip (until they build something in between).

The Famous Pacific Fish Co. has a fine selection of luncheon choices from a lengthy list of cold appetizers, salads, sandwiches, fin fish, shellfish, and seasonal fresh fish specials. The Dungeness Crab cocktail (as in dungeoness) with grapefruit mayonnaise is a great choice for a cold appetizer. As to the hot first courses, the tried-and-true Oysters Rockefeller prepared in the classic New Orleans style are excellent, but be sure to ask about the special soup of the day that is prepared fresh by the Sous Chef.

Sauces, seasonings, and dressings are exceptional at the FPFC, and that's the finishing touch that makes the Fish Company Marine Salad so good. This is the salad with lobster, crab, shrimp, and scallops tossed with a homemade sour-cream-and-cheese dressing. And if you especially enjoy tasty salads with your meal, the Famous Pacific Fish Co. thoughtfully offers half-salad portions. Sandwiches, available only at lunch, obviously include seafood combinations, but the FPFC also has other interesting choices — such as the club-style croissant with smoked turkey and Monterey Jack cheese and the choice center-cut sirloin, broiled and served open face with garlic toast and onion rings.

At lunch, fresh fish specials are served with a fresh garden salad or homemade coleslaw (the very best I've ever had), steamed vegetables, rice, and warm bread. During dinner, a baked potato is an added option. Flights from both coasts bring in the seafood. On the menu you may find Hawaiian Ahi tuna, Pacific snapper, Louisiana catfish, Washington coho salmon, or even East Coast monkfish. Among the shellfish choices there's a delicious shrimp or scallop sizzling stirfry with fresh vegetables. For the incorrigible beef eater, there are three excellent choices—the filet mignon from choice Iowa-fed beef, mesquite broiled and topped with sautéed mushrooms and onion rings; the blackened top sirloin lightly dusted in Cajun spices; and the tenderloin kabob filet. Should you be of an indecisive bent, dine at the Famous Pacific Fish Co. on the weekend because every Friday and Saturday night there's a Maine lobster and prime rib combination.

Desserts change daily. If you have room, ask for the selection. The wine list is limited but good (most are from California wineries). There is also a nice selection by the glass.

Service is mixed, depending on the experience of the waiters. If you're the least bit fussy, simply indicate the amount of time you prefer to allow between courses. All the servers are young, very helpful, pleasant, and nicely attired in black slacks, blue shirts, and black ties.

Luncheon entrees cost $6 to $10, and sandwiches and salads cost $5 to $9. Dinner entrees are $13 to $20, salads are $7.50 to $9.50, and appetizers at lunch or dinner are $5 to $8.25. Alaskan King Crab legs and lobster entrees are priced according to market.

The Famous Pacific Fish Co. is open from 11am to 10pm Monday through Thursday, to 11pm Friday and Saturday, from noon to 10pm on Sunday. Lunch is served to 4pm daily. It's always wise to make reservations.

Tony Roma's A Place for Ribs, 620 E. Sahara Ave., near the Strip at Sixth St. (tel. 733-9914).

Tony Roma's is a popular place for ribs in Nevada, California, or any of its many other locations throughout the country. It's undoubtedly the most popular place for ribs in Las Vegas. The restaurant is simple yet pleasant, its wood-paneled walls hung with paintings. There's plenty of seating at booths and tables.

My favorite meal at Tony Roma's consists of their famous onion rings served in a half or full loaf, barbecued chicken, and babyback ribs with french fries and coleslaw. Selections are not limited to ribs and chicken, however. There's choice charbroiled rib-eye steak, London broil, and grilled swordfish steak brushed with lemon, as well as a half-pound Roma burger and salads—all for $6 to $15. In addition, each day brings a special, such as baked meatloaf on Monday, roast loin of pork on Wednesday, and sliced breast of turkey on Friday. Domestic and imported beer is served, wine is sold by the glass, and a variety of liqueur-laced coffees is available to finish your meal. At lunch a similar menu is offered, with smaller portions at lower prices—from $6 to $11.

Tony Roma's is open daily: Monday through Thursday from 11am to midnight, Friday to 1am, Saturday from noon to 1am, and Sunday from 3pm to midnight.

The Starboard Tack, 2601 Atlantic Ave., off Sahara Ave. one block east of Eastern (tel. 457-8794).

Ruggedly nautical in décor, the Starboard Tack has unpainted or white-brick walls covered with seagoing-theme photos and prints; tables made of highly polished, rough-hewn ship hatch covers; captain's chairs; lots of mast rope about; and a number of artifacts, such as a big ship's steering wheel. It's dimly lit (mostly by candlelight)—very atmospheric in a rustic-funky way. An oversize TV screen in the cocktail lounge is always tuned to sporting events, the action duplicated on a TV over the bar. The Starboard Tack has been a popular Vegas hangout for over 15 years.

The Tack features "reef, beef, and booze"—steak and seafood dinners with entrees such as sirloin teriyaki, roast prime rib with creamed horseradish, Alaskan king crab legs, and jumbo prawns sautéed in garlic butter. Included in the $12 to $30 price of your entree are offerings from the salad bar and fresh-baked bread and butter; a baked potato and corn on the cob are available as side dishes.

At lunch the menu concentrates on sandwiches, ranging from cold turkey to a bacon cheeseburger, as well as a few daily specials, and selections from the salad bar—all for $5 to $9. Homemade desserts are available throughout the day.

The Tack is open Monday through Friday for lunch and dinner from 11:30am to 6am, on Saturday and Sunday for dinner only from 5 to 11pm.

Alias Smith & Jones, 541 E. Twain Ave., between Maryland Pkwy. and Paradise Rd., in the corner of the Twain Plaza Shopping Center (tel. 732-7401).

Like the Starboard Tack, Alias Smith & Jones is of the rough-hewn genre, a multilevel, woody (diagonal cedar paneling here, too) setting filled with lots of flourishing plants and ferns (among the few nonplastic ones in town). Turn-of-the-century-style chandeliers attached to rotating fans, stained-glass panels, antique cabinets, and spindle-backed oak chairs (interspersed with booths and an occasional comfy upholstered wing chair) complete the picture. A big stone fireplace makes things especially cozy. The bar, down a few steps from the main floor, has an oversize TV screen.

It's a relaxed, "civilized," easygoing kind of place, with long, uncivilized hours (11am to 6am) and wide variety of victuals. The entire menu is available all day. You can design your own omelet by choosing from a possible 22 items; my favorite is the one stuffed with avocado, sautéed mushrooms, chopped tomato, bacon, and assorted cheeses. Omelets are served with cornbread and home fries. They're available, along with sandwiches, burgers, soups, and salads, for $5 to $12. More serious entrees, such as fried jumbo shrimp, beef ribs, and steak or chicken teriyaki are available for dinner for $10 to $20, complete with soup or salad, corn on the cob, and bread. Alias Smith & Jones also serves up a brunch on Sunday from 11am to 2pm. Entrees such as eggs Benedict, steak and eggs, omelets, and strawberry french toast cost $7 to $12 and come with an unlimited flow of Bloody Marys, tequila sunrises, margaritas, or champagne. Desserts range from carrot cake to hot fudge sundaes.

---

2. Continental

Marie Callender's, 600 E. Sahara Ave., at Sixth St. (tel. 734-6572).

The Callender family began making pies in 1948 when they sold their car for $700 and used the proceeds to start a small pie bakery. At first Marie baked about ten pies a day, but after two years she was baking 200 a day. When the orders reached into the thousands, the family opened their first pie shop in Orange, California. Today there are some 100 Marie Callender restaurants in the West, two of them in Las Vegas. They serve not only pies but also wholesome, home-style food.

The restaurant is now open for breakfast with a heartwarming array of all-American favorites—ham and eggs, french toast, pancakes, Belgian waffles with fruit, and a delicious quiche Lorraine. Breakfast is served until 11am on weekdays, until 1pm on weekends.

Different soups—potato cheese, clam chowder, and so on— are featured each day by the bowl or tureen; they're accompanied by croissants or home-baked cornbread. Also available are selections from the salad bar, a Frisco burger (served on toasted sourdough bread and sprinkled with parmesan cheese), a tuna stack sandwich piled high with white albacore tuna salad, and an avocado and alfalfa sprout creation sprinkled with walnuts. All these delights fall in the $6 to $8 price range.

The menu is in effect all day. Dinner (or lunch) favorites range from shrimp linguine (served with salad and bread); to seafood pot pie; to a hamburger steak (with a trip to the salad bar); to chicken topped with cream, cheese sauce, and parmesan and served with egg noodles. The restaurant grinds its own meat and makes its own pasta. Prices range from $7 to $10.

Leave room for some pie. Apple, rhubarb, cream cheese, lemon, peanut butter, coconut, custard, banana, black bottom, blueberry, sour cream/apple, German chocolate, fresh strawberry, and peach pies, among others, are baked fresh daily, and all can be ordered with ice cream, whipped cream, or heavy cream.

Marie Callender's is open daily from 7am to midnight. I recommend it highly.

Pamplemousse, 400 E. Sahara Ave., one block east of the Strip (tel. 733-2066).

Step inside, and you're no longer in Vegas but on the Côte d'Azur. Pamplemousse is an intimate and elegant restaurant decorated in subtle shades of pink and wine, with candles and flowers and ceiling fans. Classical music or light jazz plays softly in the background. There's a wood-burning fireplace that's used on cool evenings and an outdoor garden area under a bit of tenting. For small private parties, there's a dining area secluded from the main dining room. It's all extremely charming and un-Vegasy.

The restaurant's name, by the way, which means grapefruit, was suggested by the late singer Bobby Darin; it just appealed to him for some reason. Darin was one of French owner Georges La Forge's numerous celebrity friends and patrons.

Pamplemousse has no fixed menu. The restaurant's talented chef prepares four entrees every evening from the freshest ingredients available. The house specialty is duck, served with one of four sauces—kiwi, orange, cherry, or banana rum. There are also fresh fish selections and a beef or veal dish. But if there's something you're particularly craving, Pamplemousse will prepare a meal to order with 24 hours' notice. The price of your entree includes fresh breads, fresh boiled eggs, and a basket of fresh raw vegetables served with a dip. Entrees are $20 to $24. And to accompany your meal, you can select from perhaps the most extensive wine list in Las Vegas, chosen personally by Georges La Forge with great care. Beer is also available; no hard liquor is served. You can round out your meal with a delectable dessert—perhaps a tarte, a mousse, crème caramel, homemade ice cream, or a flambé.

Pamplemousse is open Tuesday through Sunday from 6 to 11pm. Reservations are essential. It has my highest recommendation.

The Savoia, 455 E. Harmon, near Paradise Rd. and next to the St. Tropez Hotel (tel. 731-5446).

This is truly a beauty and by no means a duplication of Georges La Forge's other success—Pamplemousse. The Savoia has an elegant outdoors look—light and airy and done in pink, rose, pearl gray, and cream, with much bleached wood. The restaurant is rife with greenery: healthy tall plants in dividers and wicker baskets. Overhead lighting in the main room is diffused against a pearl-gray ceiling and into pink, green, blue, and white abstract skate shapes.

Savoia is divided into several interesting dining and drinking areas designed for different styles of dining—from the formally casual to the totally relaxed. You enter into a main dining area with cream fabric booths trimmed in black, black *faux* marble–topped tables with bleached-wood trim, and bleached-wood chairs with pink-and-gray fabric cushioning. In the evening, the tables are covered with rose cloths over black. Table lamps bathe everything in a soft flattering glow.

To one side of the main room, pillars surround a pizza oven, as does a semicircular counter—another choice for seating. Or you might prefer the lounge area for dining; it is a beauty in black with a spectacular ceiling that looks like the night sky.

To the right and quite apart from the main room is a small, long dining area. Recessed lighting here casts a lovely glow through frosted seagreen collars. Paintings throughout have the desert sand tones and touches of a desert spring.

Savoia offers a very diverse selection for light dining. The more substantial entrees are found on the evening menu. Choices from the Savoia Deli include some remarkable and plentiful platters—from the assortment of smoked fish, cheese, and meats to the vegetarian antipasto (from $9 to $16). The Fish Smokehouse platter (cream cheese, bagels, and all) was more than I could finish in a single sitting. (I suspect that doggie bags are not uncommon.)

There are a number of fine pasta choices (from $7 to $14), including an exceptional black lobster ravioli served with lobster saffron sauce and the shells Sorentina with roasted eggplant, fresh basil, parmesan, mozzarella, and a final touch of fresh tomato sauce.

Gourmet pizzas (from $5.75 to $9.50) are a perfect size for almost any appetite. There's a classic cheese pizza, to be sure, but don't overlook others—including the Cajun with andouille sausage, red onion, and Cajun sauce and the seafood pizza with shrimps, clams, and mussels.

The choice of hot appetizers (from $4 to $7.25) includes several delicious seafood choices, plus escargots with garlic and parsley-butter garnish with a spritz of Pernod. Cold appetizers of carpaccio, roasted peppers, and buffalo mozzarella are also served midday, as are the soups and cold salads.

Evening entrees of veal, fowl, seafood, lamb, and beef present splendid and distinctive choices. If osso bucco is a favorite of yours, you won't be disappointed. For the less intense appetites, medallions of veal can be ordered sautéed in a white wine butter sauce with capers and fresh basil (San Remo) or garnished with wild mushrooms and sauce Marsala (St. Tropez). Among the fowl choices are duckling, capon, and roast Kosher chicken. But I especially enjoy the braised quails Dodine served on a bed of spaghetti squash (a delicious texture) and blessed with port wine. Among the seafood entrees, as you might expect, there is a hearty bouillabaisse with saffron-flavored broth. And for those who appreciate the beauties of salmon, Savoia offers it perfectly poached or grilled. Noisettes of baby lamb are served with their natural juices and herbs. Beef choices offer a petit filet mignon with sautéed shrimp scampi and a broiled New York sirloin steak. All specialty entrees (from $10 to $20) are served with fresh vegetables and the potato of the day.

The midday menu excludes evening entrees, but otherwise it duplicates most of the offerings. Some added choices are in the antipasti, which afford mix-and-match possibilities. I love the grilled Japanese eggplant with the jumbo prawns or the pasta salad.

Savoia also serves a famous and delicious French Riviera specialty—the Pain Bagnat—a round, crusty French bread abounding with albacore tuna, olives, lettuce, anchovies, hard-boiled eggs, and Savoia dressing.

However much you may order for the midday or evening meal, save space for dessert. The list is extraordinary, and each dessert is a small spectacular (from $2.50 to $4.25). Two stand-outs are the cappuccino cup—a fresh waffle cup edged with chocolate, garnished with Giandula ice cream, Frangelico, Chantilly, and assorted roasted candied nuts—and the Tartufo St. Tropez—white Belgian chocolate ice cream covered with a hard shell of white chocolate, presented on a bed of Grand Marnier strawberry coulis, and garnished with strawberries and whipped cream. If you don't have quite that much room left, you can always opt for the crème caramel Portugese flavored with expresso beans or a fresh fruit tart.

As you might expect, Savoia has an excellent wine list, including a good selection of wines by the glass.

The Savoia is open daily from 10am to 11pm. It is always worth the short hop from the Strip.

Art's Place, 532 E. Sahara, near Sixth St. (tel. 737-1466).

Art's Place is an eatery almost everyone will love every bit as much as the locals do. There's nothing chi-chi about Art's Place—it's simply a great place to go for good food and conversation. Art's is pleasant and relaxed, with lots of wood and hanging greenery, maroon vinyl table covers, maroon chairs, maroon carpeting, and wood-plank flooring around the bar. TV sets are strategically placed just about everywhere for coverage of whatever sport is going on at the moment. Walls are decorated with pictures of fighters and other athletes, fight posters, and many awards of note to Art.

If there's no space for seating in the back room, small tables and stools at the bar handle the overflow. Or you can sit up front where there's an "atrium"—slanted windows overhead give a pleasant outdoor dining look. Of course there are slots, not in casino numbers but enough to keep you busy while you're waiting for breakfast, lunch, or dinner.

The food at Art's Place is first-rate, and there's lots of it at great prices. I didn't quite make my way through the big bowl of chili I ordered, plus the fresh roll, but it made a great late-afternoon snack from the take-it-with-you container. Service is good, and you'll even get a glass of water nicely presented with a thin slice of lemon. The kitchen may be a bit slower than you expect, but the food is prepared from scratch, so you won't regret the wait.

Art's Place serves the usual choices for breakfast (from $2 to $6) with hash browns and toast, as well as a steak and eggs combination. Lunch offers delicious chili; some great burgers served with french fries (from $3.25 to $5); and a Philly steak sandwich ($6) with steak, onions, peppers, mushrooms, and melted cheese on a fresh roll plus fries. A specialty of the house is Art's famous chicken soup by the cup, bowl, or take-home quart.

The list of appetizers (from $4 to $5) is varied and includes some delicious chicken wings or chicken fingers; a shrimp basket; and a quesadilla that amounts to a whole meal—a flour tortilla with tomatoes and melted cheese, served with salsa.

Regular dinner entrees (from $5 to $12), served 24 hours, are half of a barbecued chicken, delicious baby-back ribs (full or ½ rack), and a combination of a ½ rack of ribs and ½ of a barbecued chicken. The combination is served with your choice of baked beans, cole slaw, or corn on the cob; other dinners are accompanied by french fries or a baked potato. The top of the price line is the combination dinner. And then there are some great specials served from 5 to 10pm. On Monday, Wednesday, Friday, and Sunday, Art's has an all-you-can-eat fish and chips dinner for $5.95. On Tuesday from 5 to 10pm, Art's special is a 12-ounce prime rib served with potato and vegetable for $5.95.

The collection of desserts rotates in a glass case to make picking and choosing easy. But if sweet alcoholic beverages are more your notion of a dessert (or an appetizer), check out the house's "Rebel A Rouser" for $4.75—a fascinating mix of Southern Comfort, Bols amaretto, and Martell brandy topped with chocolate truffle. There is a full bar with a good assortment of beers and wine by the glass.

Art's Place is open 24 hours daily. And, in case you're wondering, Art is the father of the present mayor of Las Vegas, Ron Lurie.

Peppermill, 2985 Las Vegas Blvd. South, directly across from the Stardust Hotel (tel. 735-4177).

There are many things that make dining a delight at the Peppermill. The interior is pleasant, attractive, and comfortable—it puts you at ease and prepares you for an exceptional meal. The décor ranges from purple to rose, lavender, and black. The tucked booths are vinyl, trimmed with lavender velvet. There is a gathering of flowering dogwood trees with branches that rise to a mirrored ceiling with recessed spots for lighting. Greenery is everywhere and—although it is not from nature—adds to the warmth of the room.

As to the food, everything is as it should be. The service is first-rate. The small loaves of bread served with your meal arrive hot enough to melt the butter. And all is fresh as can be from the tomatoes and vegetables in the soup to the spinach in the salad. The presentation of the food is exceptional—certainly more than I expected. I did not see a dish brought to table that did not look like a Las Vegas extravaganza. The portions are enormous; the fresh fruit salad was large enough for two with some left over for Carmen Miranda.

The Peppermill serves breakfast, lunch, and dinner (as you might expect from a restaurant that is open 24 hours daily) plus all sorts of fountain specialties. The list of dishes is lengthy, whether you're in the mood for an omelet, pancakes, waffles, a burger, a sandwich, snacks, a fruit plate, a salad, pasta, a steak with shrimp or fettuccine, a hearty T-bone, ribs, chicken, or one of several varieties of seafood.

If your appetite is light, consider ordering a couple of items from the appetizer list with the soup, salad, and bread or the fiery hot chicken wings with a salad. In the sandwich department, I especially enjoy the breast of chicken Cordon Bleu—sautéed and layered with sliced ham, Swiss cheese, lettuce, and tomato and served open-face on a grilled roll. Among the entrees, it's hard to resist the rack of delicious baby-back pork ribs.

Breakfast ranges from $4.50 to $8; sandwiches are from $6.50 to $8; salads are from $8 to $11; and entrees are from $8.50 to $17.

A cocktail lounge adjoins the dining area and offers the services of a full bar and, of course, wine or beer.

And should you manage room for dessert, you simply will not believe your eyes. The size of Peppermill's ice cream soda, with all the goodies that go into it, is incredible—it's a work of art. If you think that's extraordinary, order the banana split (perhaps at another sitting)—two whole bananas; three humongous scoops of ice cream; strawberry, marshmallow, and chocolate toppings; and whipped topping and nuts. Desserts cost $3 to $5.

The Peppermill also has a children's menu (under 12 years of age) for breakfast, lunch, and dinner (from $3.25 to $5.50) as well as a choice of children's beverages (95¢).

The Garden Eatery/Omelet House, 2150 W. Charleston, near Rancho Dr. (tel. 384-6868).

This eatery, a little bit away from the Strip, has to be one of the best breakfast/lunch establishments in Las Vegas in terms of quality, quantity, and price. As you walk up to the restaurant, you may feel that you're about to enter the neighborhood sports book—there are no windows and a rather simple, down-home exterior. The interior is very rustic, with a bare ranch-house feeling: simple, unpolished wooden booths and tables; wall lights; and simple hanging lamps. But let's get down to the basics. You can just have eggs with the usual accompaniments, or you can have them with Vienna/Polish sausage. But why? There are 32 omelets to choose from, three varieties of quiche, all from $2.75 to $5.75—including a real barn-burner, the Rio Grande Surfer, with chorizo sausage, onion, and Cheddar plus 16 available add-ons. Those with a strong stomach and a sense of humor should look for the Flatlanders Special.

You're a traditionalist? Try the old-fashioned buttermilk pancakes; you can even have them with apples, bananas, or blueberries and whipped cream (so much for tradition). For the super-hearty eater, there's a Flap Special with two pieces of bacon or sausage, pancakes, and two eggs—all for $3.75.

On the other hand, if you arrive just in time for lunch, there's an assortment of absolutely delicious hamburgers served on fresh onion rolls (with pickle and fruit garnish), salads, homemade soups (with pumpkin-nut bread or another of your choice), chicken fingers, and homemade chili. The chili size contains over a third of a pound of lean ground chuck sprinkled with mixed cheeses and onions for $4.50; a cup is also available for $2. The big Italian beef sandwich for $5 is a winner: tender roast beef chunks simmered in Italian sauce (gravy, to you purists) and served on Italian bread and sprinkled with Jack cheese. The top price on the menu for any single item is $6 (with the exception of the Flatlanders Special). All drinks are of the "soft" variety, including a good selection of teas. For a great refresher, have their Freshen-Up, a delectable combination of orange juice, Fresca, and "special secret ingredients."

The Garden Eatery/Omelet House is open daily (except Thanksgiving and Christmas) from 7am to 3pm.

---

3. Southwestern and Mexican

Chili's, 2590 S. Maryland Pkwy., near Sahara (tel. 733-6402).

I love Chili's, and not just this one. What more can you ask of a restaurant than delicious food (every bite of it); fine presentation; friendly, prompt service; sizable drinks; and perfection in every little detail? And all of this is in a relaxed, fun setting of family and nonfamily photos and a collection of interesting odds and ends on a shelf that runs throughout the restaurant.

In a world fraught with mediocrity, you will find nothing average at Chili's. Let's say that you order the marinated and grilled southwestern shrimp, as I did. First, the shrimp is done to perfection. It's served on a bed of rice deliciously seasoned with chopped scallions and bits of tomato and is accompanied by cole slaw that you could eat by the bowlful, plus slices of cinnamon apples, each in its own compact dish. The lemonade I ordered arrived in a large, chilled glass mug with a slice of fresh lemon. The margaritas looked just as good and seemed to be among the most popular beverages in the house. Wine, beer, and a big selection of soft drinks also are available.

The menu is a delight because there's something for everyone. You don't want shrimp today? Then how about a full rack of charbroiled baby-back ribs topped with Chili's own barbecue sauce, or fajitas, or Chili's strip steak? For those more in the mood for light noshes or serious snacking, there are homemade soups; chili; excellent salads; a variety of burgers, tacos, and sandwiches; and such goodies as Buffalo wings and quesadillas filled with spicy chicken. The top price on the menu is $10 for the full rack of barbecued baby-back ribs and the strip steak. Sandwiches, burgers, salads, and the like average from $4 to $6. For the kids 12 and under, there's a selection of hamburgers and hot dogs, and a grilled-cheese sandwich for $2.

Chili's doesn't take reservations, but things seem to move right along when you put your name on the list. You might even choose to eat in the bar and watch the Rebels on TV (given the right season). Chili's is open Monday through Thursday from 11am to 10pm, Friday and Saturday to 11pm, and Sunday from 11:30am to 10pm.

Café Santa Fe, 1213 Las Vegas Blvd. South, near Charleston (tel. 384-4444).

Should you call the café, you will first reach the adjacent Thunderbird Hotel. As a matter of fact, you can dine, nap, get married, and drink in the café's all-night bar (although not necessarily in that order) within the same enclave, since the hotel has a wedding chapel.

The Café Santa Fe is just a bit away from the main action on the Strip, but it's well worth the visit. The Karamanos family has tried, by way of its southwestern menu and handsome restaurant design, to capture the feeling of the true Southwest. The pink stucco walls, wooden pillars, beamed ceiling, Native American rugs, straight-backed Spanish chairs, cacti, and tiled floors all reflect the unique combination of Native American, Spanish, Mexican, and south-western traditions found in the restaurant's cuisine.

If you arrive for breakfast, there are the usual gringo offerings, as well as those with a southwestern flair. Among the "Omelettes Grandes" are the Santa Fe Joe, with ground beef, panfried onions, mushrooms, spinach, and Swiss cheese; and the South of the Bor-der, with shredded beef chili, onions, and Monterey Jack cheese. The caballero with a hearty appetite might also order three fresh eggs served with medallions of beef tenderloin, chili relleno, and casera potatoes. All egg orders come with casera potatoes, butter-milk biscuits, and preserves. Breakfast ranges from $2.95 to $5.75; the eggs with beef tenderloin is $7.95.

Highlights of the luncheon menu are two freshly made beef patties with chili and cheese, the barbecued sliced pork in a zesty sauce, and the Santa Fe filet sandwich broiled and served open-faced with onion rings. The choices range from $4.75 to $5.75. Salads "from the pantry" include one with freshly cut greens topped with chili con carne, shredded cheese, diced tomato, sour cream, and guacamole; it is served with salsa and tostados. Salads, served with bread and butter, are $5.95 and $6.95.

Ah, but dinner's my favorite, and I simply could not resist the barbecued baby-back ribs—absolutely delicious and served with fri-joles covered with cheese and chunky french fries. What I could not finish I took home, and it was just as good the next day. Conserva-tive types might choose the boneless breast of plump chicken Mexicaine, marinated and topped with mushrooms, green chile salsa, diced tomato, and glazed Monterey Jack cheese.

Vegetarian customers will enjoy the café's beautifully fresh vegetables, steamed and served with Cheddar cheese. Guayamas jumbo shrimps, Veracruz filet of sole, and broiled halibut steak amandine comprise the seafood offerings. For beef lovers, the tournedos Taos—cooked the Zuni way, with broiled tomato, ba-nana fritters, and horseradish sauce—is a dish large enough to satisfy any appetite and then some. So are the "Texas Cut" T-bone steak; the broiled New York–cut sirloin with mushrooms and fried onions; and the steak Tampico—a skirt steak marinated, broiled, and served with Spanish rice, frijoles de la olla, salsa, and flour tortil-la. Entrees, served with salad or soup, potato or pasta, vegetable, and bread, range from $6.95 to $15.75.

The Santa Fe's late-night menu combines a number of the spe-cialties from breakfast and lunch with its South of the Border pot of chili. Prices range from $4 to $8. Sweet Santa Fe desserts expand from deep-dish apple pie for $2.50 to rich chocolate cake with fudge frosting (big enough for two) for $4.95. And all this is served with warmth, thoughtfulness, and attention to detail.

The Café Santa Fe is open daily from 7am to 11pm. The bar is open all night. The café offers a good selection of beers and wines with dinner, as well as the usual alcoholic beverages.

Ricardo's, 2380 Tropicana Ave., at the corner of Tropicana and Eastern (tel. 798-4515).

Ricardo's is a handsome haciendalike building that you might easily mistake for a new mission. The interior is every bit as attractive as the outside. As you enter, ahead is what appears to be a small Mexican plaza—pillars, tall cacti, a lovely fountain with a small balcony above, decorative tiles above and around the fountain, *Corrida de Toros* posters, and a beamed ceiling so high that it's not readily noticed. A skylight adds to the feeling of being outside. This is the main dining room. The booths and tables are well spaced. The fabric covering the cushions on the bentwood chairs and booth seats is a pleasing rust, beige, brown, and blue Mexican design.

On your right is the Cantina, a large bar room with wooden booths and tables—mobbed and friendly. Two other dining rooms and a garden dining area carry through the Mexican décor with wrought-metal chandeliers, upright leather-covered chairs, and dark-brown wood tables—more austerely Spanish than Mexican in feeling.

Ricardo's serves what I've found to be the best Mexican food in Las Vegas. It's delicious, and the portions are huge—bring a big appetite. The corn chips alone are a quarter of the size of a corn tortilla, served with deliciously hot salsa.

Ricardo's serves both meat and seafood dishes, from $9.75 to $12 at dinner. The carne Ortega is a generous portion of broiled top sirloin, thinly sliced and smothered with steaming mild Ortega chiles and melted cheese. For those who enjoy seafood, a Ricardo's specialty the likes of which you won't find anywhere else this side of the border, there's the enchilada à la Puerto Vallarta—a seafood enchilada consisting of a flour tortilla filled with shrimp, crab, and whitefish sautéed with onions, mild chiles, wine, and spices. The enchilada is covered with Ricardo's ranchera sauce and garnished with guacamole and sour cream. Or there's the arroz con pollo, prepared from boned chicken breast over Mexican rice, topped with Ricardo's special sauce and melted cheese, and garnished with mild chiles and pimentos. Specialties of the house are served with cheese salad or soup, Mexican rice, and refried beans. The tostada entrees are a truly unforgettable experience—they're massive, delicious, and inexpensive at only $5.75 to $7.50. You can have all beef, chicken, seafood, or diced pork. Whatever your choice, it's heaped on a crisp corn tortilla spread with refried beans and covered with shredded lettuce, tangy sauce, guacamole, two kinds of grated cheese, sour cream, and olives.

After several meals at Ricardo's (and I never reached the flan or deep-fried ice cream) I decided that it's all delicious, and you'll never leave feeling as though you could eat more. To wash all this down, Ricardo's has a good selection of beers, wines, margaritas (small, medium, large, and by the pitcher), fruit margaritas, sangría, and piña coladas.

Service is attentive and prompt. Two strolling guitarists look, sing, and play as though Mexico were their home—not Tante Elvira's flamenco, but gentle music to dine by.

Reservations are essential for dinner because the restaurant is usually full by 6:30pm, especially on weekends. Ricardo's is open Monday through Thursday from 11am to 11pm, on Friday and Saturday to midnight, and on Sunday from noon to 10pm.

---

4. Italian

Olive Garden Italian Restaurant, 1545 Flamingo Rd., just east of Maryland Pkwy. (tel. 735-0082).

This restaurant is quite possibly the best modestly priced restaurant in Las Vegas. Its interior is comfortable, casual, and attractive. The quality of the food is first-rate and the choices are varied and delicious. Much is offered, including attentive service and no-charge refills of their garden salad (from a huge serving bowl left at your table), the soup, and the breadsticks. The very comfortable chairs have casters that help when you're backing away from the table or tucking in. If you think that all this places the restaurant on the top of the popularity scale, you're right. I discovered the Olive Garden by following the crowd in an area replete with near-empty restaurant parking lots.

The Olive Garden is a casual country eatery that successfully combines exposed brick; trelliswork; trusses supporting a factory-high exposed-beam ceiling; Martini and Rossi umbrellas; plant dividers; white paneling; and attractive prints, photos, and posters of Italy (where else?). As you enter, it's hard to avoid seeing to your left the pizza oven, looking much more like a decorative kiln than the one in your local parlor. Straight on is a separate bar area arranged like a comfortable outdoor patio with much white and red. To the left is one of the several dining areas. There's even an atrium. Tables are decorated with fresh flowers, and each has an unopened bottle of wine. The green carpeting is about as close to the color of grass as you can get, and it matches that of the booths. If you don't happen to like green booths, there are those with a deep wine color. Ductwork and tubing overhead is painted dark green—by no means unattractive. And it somehow all works to create a pleasant setting for a meal that's relaxed and fun.

Taking it from the top, the choices of soup and salads for lunch (from $2.50 to $5.95) include a nicely seasoned minestrone soup, a seafood pasta salad, and a soup and salad combination. Garden specialties (from $3.75 to $5.75) present some toothsome pasta combinations, including a ½ cheese ravioli and ½ manicotti merger and a light pasta primavera. If you happen to be a spaghetti afficionado, there's spaghetti with truly tasty meatballs. And the toasted ravioli ($3.45) are a delectable specialty of the house. If you opt for a sandwich (from $4 to $4.65), there's a great meatball sub (for a very big appetite) and a choice of somewhat more reasonably sized sandwiches—including grilled chicken and the house's Burger Italiano. The Olive Garden has a fine selection of single-size pizzas, including the pizza Americana with cheese and tomato at $3.45. Extra ingredients are 35¢ each. A classic four-cheese pizza and the seafood pizza come in at $4.25 and $4.75, respectively.

The Olive Garden has chicken, veal, steak, and seafood entrees (from $7.75 to $12.50) to satisfy most any appetite, plus specials that change daily, all served with your choice of the daily vegetable or a pasta side dish along with unlimited refills of garden salad and fresh-baked, hot garlic breadsticks (rather like slim baby loaves of garlic bread). The garden salad is a beauty, definitely not your usual dull bits of lettuce, and it is presented in a lovely large bowl with all sorts of goodies—slim rings of red onion, julienned carrots, tomatoes, peppers (the mildly hot variety), olives, lettuce, great croutons, and a lovely dressing. Best of all, it is served with a chilled plate.

Pasta entrees (from $5.75 to $9.50) include spaghetti with various accompaniments, ravioli, fettuccine, tortelloni, and linguine with clam sauce.

If you decide that you wish to waddle out of the restaurant instead of strolling out, there are the Olive Garden's combination platters. "Substantial" is an understated description of the portions. The Northern Italian combination ($11.50) includes veal piccata, Venetian grilled chicken, and fettuccine Alfredo. The Southern Italian ($10.75) includes veal Parmesan, lasagna, and manicotti. And the Tour of Italy ($11) embraces chicken Parmesan, lasagne, and fettuccine Alfredo.

After all of the above, let me mention that the Olive Garden also has children's plates of spaghetti, lasagne, and ravioli (from $2.75 to $3.25).

If you still have room for dessert (from $1.75 to $3.25), there's a luscious chocolate mousse pie in addition to cannoli and zabaglione almonde.

The Olive Garden has a full bar, plus a good selection of wines by the glass, the bottle, and the liter (house wines).

The Olive Garden is open daily: Sunday through Thursday from 11am to 10:30pm and Friday and Saturday to 11pm. The restaurant does not take reservations. If you eat early, you will have the advantage. I've noted that it's frequently crowded for lunch by 12:15pm and for dinner by 5:30pm, but it's worth the wait. One last note: If you're off on a picnic or just touring about, stop by—most menu items are available for take out. Call ahead and your order will be waiting.

The Vineyard, 3630 S. Maryland Pkwy., off Twain Ave., in the Boulevard Mall (tel. 731-1606).

This is quite a production—a bustling indoor Italian street café with exposed brick and patinated walls; terra-cotta tile floors; street lamps; and shelves cluttered with wine barrels, crates of plastic grapes, and the like. One wall is hung with shellacked-over Italian movie posters and ads for Cinzano, Alitalia, and so on. Completing the festive ambience are high-backed rattan chairs at tables with checkered cloths and a huge salad bar, called the "Groceria," under a green-and-white-striped awning. There's more seating, as well as similar décor, upstairs. The whole thing is quite charming, and the fare is delicious. Fresh fruit and vegetables, homemade pasta, and fresh baked breads are served.

For openers, you can toddle up to the antipasto buffet and help yourself to all you want of its abundant offerings. They're included in the price of your dinner entree. You can also opt for the buffet as your entire meal: about $8 at dinner, $5 at lunch. When this fabulous smörgåsbord was last seen it included meatballs, baked spaghetti, greens, a wide choice of fresh fruits, many salads, Brussels sprouts, marinated mushrooms, big chunks of provolone cheese, pepperoni, artichoke hearts, real roquefort, hard-boiled eggs, sausages, chick peas, bean sprouts, fresh-baked breads, and more—all of it delicious.

Should you want an entree as well, dinner fare ranges from $10 to $16 for pasta dishes such as manicotti, cannelloni, and lasagne, or for steak or shrimp scampi; sandwiches and pizza also are available. Lunch fare is mostly under $6. Prices on some items are reduced for children under 10. On Sunday there's a Family Feast—all you can eat for $7.

The Vineyard is open Sunday through Thursday from 11am to 11pm, on Friday and Saturday until midnight.

---

5. German

The Alpine Village Inn, 3003 Paradise Rd., across from the Hilton (tel. 734-6888).

Wiener Schnitzel and sausages, sauerkraut and strudel—German delicacies galore are made on the premises in this outstanding restaurant, which opened in Las Vegas in 1950. It's privately owned, not a franchise in a restaurant chain with a similar name, and the attentiveness is impressive and personal.

Gemütlichkeit may be overworked to describe atmospheric qualities in German restaurants. In this case, it's appropriate. Fresh white table napery over red cloths makes an immediate cheerful impact. Roofing around the dining room's edges enhances the alpine ski-chalet/beer-garden texture. It's pretty, with little Christmas-card touches typical of the Tyrolean Alps. The service plates, bowls, and ice-water mugs are of pewter. The waiters and waitresses are in Tyrolean garb.

As a starter, a small pumpernickel loaf, cinnamon rolls, spicy gingerbreads, and salty Triscuits arrive at your table, warmed and folded in a napkin on a chopping block with a sharp knife. You'll also get a relish bowl with crackers and cottage cheese dip. Then the meal, a banquet really, begins. First comes a pewter tureen of chicken suprême soup, followed by a tossed salad. Also included in the $14 to $22 price of your entree are alpine-seasoned green beans and sauerkraut, sweet-and-sour red cabbage, potato pancakes or a jumbo baked potato, dessert (ice cream or homemade apple strudel), and tea or coffee.

If you'd like to try a few dishes, order one of the combination entrees—such as a platter of sauerbraten with fleischrouladen (beef roll) and kohlrouladen (cabbage roll). Also available are a beef roll stuffed with chestnut dressing, a tasty dish called hammelkeule—lean lamb baked with special seasonings—and Wiener Schnitzel topped with a poached egg, capers, and anchovies. Roast duckling stuffed with chopped meat, apples, prunes, celery, and onions, with lingonberry sauce, is a specialty. Ditto the fondue bourguignonne (filet beef cubes to cook at the table in a copper fondue pot). The beef cubes weigh 14 ounces, and they're lean. Steaks range from a 10-ounce filet mignon to an extra-large porterhouse. A bonus for families: Children's portions are available for most entrees at less than half price.

Downstairs, the **Rathskeller** serves lighter fare—pizzas, burgers, sandwiches, a salad bar—as well as meals of broiled chicken or catfish, complete with soup, salad bar, bread, and ice cream, all for $6 to $17.50. The Rathskeller adds songs, organ music, and, sometimes, a guitarist/folksinger; everybody sings along. If you're looking for informal fun, the Rathskeller is easy on the budget. Some people eat upstairs, then go down to the Rathskeller to round out the evening.

Both the restaurant and the Rathskeller are open from 11:30am to 2:30pm for lunch and from 5pm to midnight for dinner; both offer reduced prices for children. Reservations are required upstairs at the restaurant.

The Alpine Village Inn attracts considerable business from local people, which speaks well for its quality.

At the restaurant's entrance, there's a gift shop. You'll find pewterware, crystal, dolls, German Black Forest clocks, cuckoo clocks, musical clocks, and music boxes. The shop will mail your purchases.

---

6. Japanese and Chinese

Oh No Tokyo, 4455 W. Flamingo Rd., near Arville St. (tel. 876-4455).

As you pass through a simple granite courtyard, the small Japanese-style bridge on your left spans a pond that requires only a few koi (goldfish) to complete the tranquil introduction to Oh No

Tokyo. The entry prepares you for the lovely California/Japanese interior, vertical black blinds, shoji screens, and hanging half-curtains that divide the serving areas from the main rooms. You can choose to dine at a table or in one of several tatami rooms (assuming that everyone in your party has socks of whole cloth—remember that shoes are removed before you enter).

The last time I had Japanese food of comparable quality and diversity to that served at Oh No Tokyo was in New York City. The à la carte sushi menu is quite broad; it includes seaweed rolls and specialty rolls, among which is a superb Emperor's roll with shrimp tempura, scallops, green onion, and masago (smelt eggs). Prices are $4 to $5 for a two-piece order; quail eggs are 75¢ each. Plates of assorted sushi range from $8 to $25 and are served with soup. Other Japanese dinners, priced from $8 to $14, include such standards as shrimp and vegetable tempura; beef and chicken teriyaki; sukiyaki; and grilled mackeral, salmon, or the catch-of-the-day. Special combination plates (teisuoku) offer a choice of one appetizer and two entrees, with soup, rice, tea, and ice cream, for the reasonable sum of $16. The lunch menu also offers a choice of delectable and light udon dishes (steaming noodle soup), with egg, chicken, or beef, at $4.25 to $7.

For more occidental tastes, Oh No Tokyo adds charcoal-grilled dinners to the menu "in the tradition of Japanese boatmen." Entrees range from breast of chicken to steak and lobster, all served with soup, salad, vegetable kebab, and steamed rice. Prices begin at $9.50 and top at $26 for the steak and lobster.

Soft drinks are available, as are domestic and Japanese beers, Japanese draft beer, house wine by the glass or bottle, and plum wine by the glass.

Lunch is served weekdays from 11am to 2:30pm, and dinner is served Monday through Saturday from 5pm to 10:45pm, when the last order is taken.

Ginza, 1000 E. Sahara Ave., between Maryland Pkwy. and Paradise Rd. (tel. 732-3080).

Some of the best Japanese fare in town isn't at any of the Disney-esque extravaganzas in the major Strip hotels; it's at this simple and charmingly unpretentious little restaurant, and it costs about half the price of its dazzling counterparts. There are no waterfalls, thunderstorms, or jungles of plastic trees here—just shoji-screened windows; tables sheltered by shingled eaves; and a few Japanese prints, paintings, and fans adorning the pristine white walls. Nevertheless, knowledgeable locals, Japanese food aficionados, and Japanese tourists pack the place nightly. Kimono-clad women offer deft service.

Dishes priced from $13 to $15 are served with soup (miso or egg flower), sunomono (vinegared salad), steamed rice, and green tea. A choice of entrees includes sukiyaki, beef teriyaki, chicken teriyaki, salmon teriyaki, sashimi, yosenabe—a sort of Japanese bouillabaisse—and tempura shrimp and vegetables. A side order of nat-to oshitashi will make you wonder why anyone ever maligns spinach. As you might conclude, Ginza also has one of the best sushi bars in town. You can order sushi by the piece or as a combination of tastes. Sake can be ordered to complement your meal.

Ginza is open for dinner Tuesday through Sunday from 5pm to 1:30am.

Golden Wok, 504 S. Decatur Blvd., at Alta Dr. (tel. 878-1596).

This is your local Chinese restaurant, and the one most frequented by Las Vegas's Chinese population. It's not superb compared to the offerings in New York or San Francisco, but it is among the best in town. (It's a fair distance away, about three miles —something to consider if you must take a taxi.) The décor is unpretentious, light and airy, with bamboo-patterned wallpaper, a beamed stucco ceiling, pale-coral venetian blinds on the windows, and a number of plants here and there.

The menu encompasses Mandarin, Cantonese, and Szechuan cookery. I always begin a meal here by ordering pot stickers (Chinese dumplings) and/or, depending on the number of hearty eaters among the group, sizzling rice soup or hot-and-sour soup. If you like hot food, you might select a Szechuan entree such as princess prawns (fresh jumbo shrimp sautéed with imported mushrooms, bamboo shoots, water chestnuts, hot pepper, soy jam, and a dash of Chinese liqueur) or tso tsung-tang chicken (diced chicken served with mushrooms and green beans in a hot sauce). Less spicy, but also very tasty, are the lemon chicken and moo shu pork served with Chinese pancakes. Should you feel like a filling dessert, there are banana fritters. Entrees, multicourse dinners, and combination plates fall in the $9 to $16.50 price range (duck dishes cost more). At lunch a terrific bargain is the $6.25 buffet, where you can eat to your heart's content of eight different items, including eggrolls, fried rice, soup, and entrees. Beer and wine are available.

The chef here will usually prepare dishes not listed on the menu if you ask. Golden Wok is open weekdays from noon to 10pm, on Saturday and Sunday from 3 to 10pm.

V

A BIT ABOUT GAMBLING

Almost everyone thinks he or she might make a fortune gambling if only luck stays. This elusive dream keeps people coming back, trying out elaborate systems, reading books on how to beat the odds, betting excitedly with the house when a craps table gets hot, or casually dropping spare change into slot machines in the supermarkets during daily shopping.

From relatively small beginnings, gambling in Nevada has grown to be an enormous operation with gross revenue in 1988 totaling almost $3 billion, an increase of almost 5% over the previous year.

BUNK

According to casino managers and pit bosses, all systems are bunk. This is not to say that somebody who, say, consistently backs the same number at roulette or who always stands pat with two cards at blackjack won't occasionally strike it lucky. But, for the most part, *systems as such just don't work,* and the only one that gives the casino cause for alarm is some gamblers' habit of doubling their stake each time they lose. This, however, is countered very simply by imposing a limit on the amount of the stake, usually $1,000 or less.

Cheats, Thieves, and Slugs

Of course, some people's idea of a system is to cheat, and by now Las Vegas dealers feel that they've seen almost everything. In fact, any casino that hired amateur dealers would probably be out of business within months. The most common dodge is for a player to try to slip a little extra onto his stake when the dealer's attention is diverted (sometimes a gambler's confederate will deliberately create a diversion). Specially marked cards with identifying lettering that can be read through tinted spectacles have occasionally been slipped into the blackjack games, and shaved or weighted dice can be substituted for the original ones by a smooth crook. Dice at Caesars Palace have a little "C" printed inside to avoid such plays. It's supposed to be a secret, but you can see them almost from the far side of the room, if you keep your eyes peeled.

Play at the tables is conducted almost entirely with casino chips, and almost all the currency taken in is ostentatiously pushed through a slot in the table to fall into a locked box below. This, of course, has occasionally been a target for thieves. The boxes are removed to the counting room at the end of every shift, while play continues, and at one time the replacement box used to sit under the table waiting for its time to come. This system was changed when somebody was caught substituting a box with a false back to it, from which the dealer could extract the proceeds.

Dealers, naturally, are always under supervision, not only by the pit boss in their immediate area and various plainclothes security men wandering randomly through the casino but also by strategically placed television cameras or overhead mirrors. For anyone who appreciates style, watching an old-hand blackjack dealer, seemingly bored but actually always alert, is a study in professionalism. Flipping each player a card, noting his or her own, scooping up lost stakes, paying the winners, and filing the used cards without a wasted motion or change of expression are a graceful exhibition of manual dexterity that bears absolutely no relationship to the outcome of the game itself.

Changes have come, though, and younger-generation dealers are more prevalent. On occasion, some tend to be flippant, which is appalling to serious gamblers. But pit bosses watch dealers closely, dressing them down during rest periods (like Marine DIs chewing out new recruits) if they get out of line. Stern rules are enforced, and those who don't follow them are replaced. And that's *that*.

Obviously there have been dishonest dealers, too. Some have been caught palming money; others have slipped chips into a slit in their neckties. (In some casinos only bow ties are allowed now.) But they're allowed to take tips, as long as they signal the pit boss when they tuck one away, and sometimes, especially from a big winner, the tips are exorbitant. Cocktail waitresses have also known the joy of being tipped more for a drink than a case of scotch might cost.

Slot machines have been a frequent target for cheats. The counterpart of the gambler who paints casino chips to represent bigger value is the slot-machine player who uses slugs or Mexican coins. It's a very serious offense in Nevada (as is bad-check writing) and leads almost certainly to jail.

In attempts to beat the house, slot-machine adventurers have taken films of the spinning reels (now cameras are barred in the casinos), drilled holes into the front and sides, slipped a plastic "spoon" into the coin slot to keep it operating without depositing coins, tried to manipulate the reels with magnets, and tried to jam the jackpot mechanism.

Slot machines fixed with anticheat devices are certain moneymakers for a casino if only because they can be fixed to pay off as much or as little as possible. Most casinos adjust them to pay back up to 90% of what they ingest, because the constant tinkling of jackpots is presumed to be what keeps the players playing. The downtown casinos supposedly pay off the most often, and any place whose machines get only casual and unrepeated visits pays off the least often. Reputed to be even better than the downtown slots are those in the restaurants and bars where locals hang out. The owners of these establishments claim that locals won't play unless the slots are "loose."

SLOT HISTORY

The jackpot slot machine has an interesting history, having been devised by a young German inventor named Charles Frey while he was operating a saloon along San Francisco's Barbary Coast. His first model, the Liberty Bell (now preserved in a Reno saloon of the same name), ostensibly paid off in drinks, candy, or bubblegum but actually delivered to the winner one coin for two horseshoes all the way up to ten coins for three bells. Even in Nevada, gambling was still illegal in those days (it became legal in 1867, three years after statehood; it was banned from 1900 until 1931, when it became legal again).

Some idea of how the slot-machine business has grown since then can be gleaned from the fact that each machine now earns its operator over $6,000 per year—with about $500 per machine going to pay local and federal taxes. Various models have been tried, including one that worked on a push-button basis rather than with a handle; this model was never very successful because, even though slot players know that they have no control over the machine whatsoever, they still like to pull a handle—which gives them the illusion that they're influencing where the reels will stop. The latest models print out electronic messages every time you pull the handle: "Good Luck," "Easy Come, Easy Go," "Happy Days Are Here Again," "Columbus Took A Chance," and so forth.

If you're interested in antique slot machines, the Maxim Hotel, 160 E. Flamingo Rd., has a museum of them, most dating from about the turn of the century.

. . . AND WALK AWAY

Although all casinos impose limits for bettors, it's possible to get much more money down as a stake than at first appears possible, if all the different variations are used. This illustrates the first lesson to be learned about gambling: Learn as much as possible about the game that you're going to play. For additional lessons, see Chapter VI.

If you're lucky, you'll never need any of the Alka-Seltzer that pit bosses always keep handy on a nearby table.

The most popular games in Nevada, judging by the licenses that have been issued, are blackjack, craps, and roulette, in that order. Before you head off to play them and before I tell you where to take in a show between rolls of the dice, I will give you some pointers on how to play these games. *Then* you can walk away. And, finally, in looking for the most action for your money—downtown gambling has lower minimums than the Strip.

HOW TO BET

If you're going to try your luck at gambling, do your homework before you put your money down. Gambling with the slots—about a third of Las Vegas visitors do it—requires no headwork other than to be aware that "one-arm bandits" usually pay back 75% to 95% of what you pump in. It's hardly what you'd call a winning return. Slot machines have been called "mechanical licenses to steal and cause bursitis at the same time," although it's no longer necessary to do more than push a button. About half of the gambling group gravitates to the blackjack tables, and most of the remainder goes to craps, roulette, or poker.

IMPROVING THE ODDS

You need timing and luck to beat the odds, but you can improve your chances of winning at blackjack, craps, or even baccarat by learning the right way to play these games. You'll enjoy it more and so will the other players at your table. Here are the basics:

1. Learn the rules *before* you go to the table.
2. Set a daily betting limit and stick with it.
3. Leave the game when you're ahead—many good players hold out for a 50% profit.
4. Don't play when you're tired.
5. Raise your bet when you're winning, not losing. Some blackjack aficionados say that if you lose three times in a row, try another table.

There are thousands of systems sold for beating the house odds. It *may* be that some of them work; the question is, Which ones do?

In Las Vegas, the **Gambler's Book Club,** now over 25 years in business, can sell you a book on almost every system devised to beat the odds. The club is at 630 S. 11th St. (just off Charleston Blvd.), Las Vegas, NV 89101 (tel. 382-7555, or toll free 800/634-6243). It's the most specialized bookstore of its type and has, on hand, over 1,000 different titles on virtually every game. For the collector or researcher, the store is a treasure trove of out-of-print works—it has about 4,000 titles.

The Gambler's Book Club is not truly a club. It looks more like a Left Bank bookshop. The name was chosen because Edna and John Luckman, the owners, wanted a spot where gamblers, writers, researchers, mathematicians, and computer specialists could meet and exchange information. It's the type of store that Damon Runyon (and Harry the Horse) would have loved. There are two clerks who can give you on-the-spot expert advice on handicapping the ponies and other aspects of sports betting.

In 1990 the Gambler's Book Club (GBC) mailed out well past its one millionth catalog. (Did you ever doubt a national interest in gambling?) As to international interest, the GBC has customers in more than 60 countries. The catalog lists several hundred publications, with a description of the contents of each, and is free for the asking. Just write to the club at the address above or call. Hours are 9am to 5pm Monday through Saturday. The Gambler's Book Club motto is "Knowledge Is Protection," and it's truer than ever when it comes to gambling.

Never be too timid at the tables to ask questions of dealers at the casinos; they're advised to be pleasant, helpful, and instructive to all players. If you should encounter an unhelpful dealer, move to a more congenial table . . . or take your business to another casino. Gambling should be fun. All the experts will tell you to indulge in gambling only as a pleasant pastime.

To gamble or to imbibe in Las Vegas, you have to be at least 21. Such sports aren't for kids, and in-town activities are primarily for adults.

Schools

Special systems aside, a basic way to improve the odds is to know both the game and the rules. Many of the large hotels have free "gaming schools" where you can learn the intricacies of craps, blackjack, roulette, and baccarat. Some also have poker schools. If you're interested, ask the hotel when you call for information or when you register. Or you can simply review the list below. The list is up-to-date as of this writing, but it continues to expand as more casinos recognize the advantage of helping gamblers to increase their comfort and confidence.

Now why do you suppose a casino would spend its time and money to teach you the intricacies of gambling and betting? You're right! The house always has the edge, even if it's only in the commission.

Below is a list of casinos that do offer instruction and the times the classes are held. It's a good idea to check time and place first before going, even though advance registration is not necessary.

BALLY'S Craps lessons are every day 10:30am and 3:30pm, blackjack lessons are at 12:30pm, baccarat lessons are at 11:45am, and roulette lessons are at 2pm on the main floor.

CAESARS PALACE Craps lessons are twice daily at 10:30am and 3pm in the Olympic Casino. Blackjack lessons are at 1pm in the Forum Casino. Roulette lessons are at 9am in the Olympic Casino.

CIRCUS CIRCUS Craps, blackjack, and roulette lessons are from 10am to noon in the West Casino.

DESERT INN Poker lessons are from 11am to 7pm in the Poker Room.

FITZGERALDS Craps, blackjack, roulette, and Red Dog lessons are Sunday through Thursday from 10am to 3pm in the Main Casino.

FLAMINGO HILTON Blackjack lessons are at 10am, pai-gow lessons are at 10:40am, craps lessons are at noon, poker lessons are at 2pm, baccarat lessons are at 2:45pm, and roulette lessons are at 4pm. All lessons are weekdays only.

FOUR QUEENS One-hour sessions on craps are held in the casino at 4pm Tuesday through Friday. Poker lessons are at 1pm daily.

FREMONT Free poker lessons are given Sunday, Wednesday, and Friday between 6 and 9am in the Poker Room.

FRONTIER Instruction on the basics of poker is given at 10:30am daily, except Sunday, in the Poker Room. Door prizes are given at each session.

HACIENDA Instruction is given in craps, blackjack, roulette, and keno, Monday through Friday, in the casino from 11am until noon.

HOLIDAY CASINO/HOLIDAY INN Gaming lessons are held Monday through Friday at 9:15am and 3pm.

IMPERIAL PALACE Now here's the way to do it—the Imperial Palace has a minicasino on the fourth floor where lessons are given daily at 9am and 1pm for blackjack and roulette, 11am and 3pm for craps. Classes usually last over an hour, and mock chips are used.

LAS VEGAS HILTON Lessons are given in craps, blackjack, pai-gow, roulette, and baccarat in a special area of the casino. Classes are conducted Tuesday through Saturday; for times, call the hotel.

RIVIERA Classes are conducted Monday through Friday from 9am to noon in the Le Bistro Bar. You're given instruction and gambling hints on craps, blackjack, roulette, poker, sports betting, and keno.

TROPICANA Tuesday through Saturday, separate sessions are held on the most popular casino games. Roulette instruction is at 11:30am., baccarat lessons are at noon, craps lessons are at 1 and 5pm, and blackjack lessons are at 3:30pm. Signs in the main casino will direct you to the instruction area.

1. Craps

Because this game is played with dice, this is as good a time as any to look into the manufacture of the cubes with the dots. It's a fascinating process.

Although attempts have repeatedly been made to manufacture dice from more recently developed plastics, those used in casinos are still made of celluloid. Cotton is the primary base.

The ingredients are combined to create a viscous red mass that is strained to reject impurities and then pressed, baked, and delivered in inch-thick slabs to the Nevada Dice Company. After this, the 60-pound cellulose nitrate slabs start a one-year processing that begins with four months in the curing chambers. All this special attention is necessary to eliminate any possible instabilities that might show up later in the finished dice.

Cut into cubes slightly bigger than the finished size, the dice are hardened, buffed, and finally drilled with the requisite holes. Then a white resinous compound is applied to the sunken dots with a special brush.

In the final process, the dice are shaved down to the exact measurements (with a variability of only one ten-thousandth of an inch), then embossed and packed into boxes for delivery to the casinos. Most dice are kept in play for one day only, sometimes less, and used sets may be sold as souvenirs in hotel gift shops.

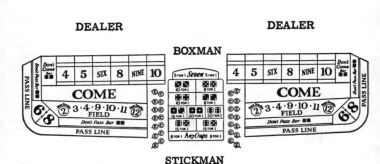

THE TABLE
The craps table is divided into marked areas (Pass, Come, Field, Big 6, Big 8, and so on), where you place your chips to bet. The following are a few simple directions.

Pass Line
A "Pass Line" bet pays even money. If the first roll of the dice adds up to 7 or 11, you win your bet; if the first roll adds up to 2, 3, or 12, you lose your bet. If any other number comes up, it's your "point." If you roll your point again, you win, but if a 7 comes up again before your point is rolled, you lose.

Don't Pass Line
Betting on the "Don't Pass" is just the opposite of betting on the Pass Line. This time, you lose if a 7 or an 11 is thrown on the first roll, and you win if a 2 or a 3 is thrown on the first roll. If the first roll is 12, however, it's a stand-off, and nobody wins. If none of these numbers is thrown and you have a point instead, in order to win, a 7 will have to be thrown before the point comes up again. A "Don't Pass" bet also pays even money.

Come
Betting on "Come" is just the same as betting on the Pass Line, but you must bet *after* the first roll or on any following roll. Again, you'll win on 7 or 11 and lose on 2, 3, or 12. Any other number is your point, and you win if your point comes up again before a 7.

Don't Come
This is the opposite of a "Come" bet. Again, you wait until after the first roll to bet. A 7 or an 11 means you lose; a 2 or a 3 means you win; 12 is a stand-off, and nobody wins. You win if 7 comes up before the point. (The point, you'll recall, was the first number rolled if it was none of the above.)

Field
This is a bet for one roll only. The "Field" consists of seven numbers: 2, 3, 4, 9, 10, 11, and 12. If any of these numbers is thrown on the next roll, you win even money, except on 2 and 12, which pay two to one.

Big 6 and 8
A "Big 6 and 8" bet pays even money. You win if either a 6 or an 8 is rolled before a 7.

Any 7
An "Any 7" bet pays the winner five to one. If a 7 is thrown on the first roll after you bet, you win.

"Hard Way" Bets
In the middle of a craps table are pictures of several possible dice combinations together with the odds the bank will pay you if

you bet on any of those combinations being thrown. For example, if 8 is thrown by having a 4 appear on each die, and you bet on it, the bank will pay eight for one; if 4 is thrown by having a 2 appear on each die, and you bet on it, the bank will pay eight for one; if 3 is thrown, the bank pays fifteen for one. . . . You win at the odds quoted if the *exact* combination of numbers you bet on comes up. But you lose either if a 7 is rolled or if the number you bet on was rolled any other way than the "Hard Way" shown on the table. In-the-know gamblers tend to avoid "Hard Way" bets as an easy way to lose their money. And note that the odds quoted are *not* 3 to 1, 4 to 1, or 8 to 1; here the key word is *for*—that is, 3 for 1 or 8 for 1.

Any Craps

Here you're lucky if the dice "crap-out"—if they show 2, 3, or 12 on the first roll after you bet. If this happens, the bank pays eight to one. Any other number is a loser.

Place Bets

You can make a "Place Bet" on any of the following numbers: 4, 5, 6, 8, 9, and 10. You're betting that the number you choose will be thrown before a 7 is thrown. If you win, the payoff is as follows: 4 or 10 pays at the rate of nine to five; 5 or 9 pays at the rate of seven to five; 6 or 8 pays at the rate of seven to six. "Place Bets" can be removed at any time before a roll.

SOME PROBABILITIES

Because each die has six sides numbered from 1 to 6—and craps is played with a pair of dice—the probability of throwing certain numbers has been studied carefully. Professionals have employed complex mathematical formulas in searching for the answers. And computers have data-processed curves of probability.

Simplified, however, suffice it to say that 7 (a crucial number in craps) will be thrown more frequently than any other number over the long run, for there are six possible combinations that make 7, when you break down the 1 to 6 possibilities on each separate die. As to the total possible number of combinations on the dice, there are 36.

Comparing the 36 possible combinations, numbers—or point combinations—run as follows:

2 and 12 may be thrown in *1 way only*.
3 and 11 may be thrown in *2 ways*.
4 and 10 may be thrown in *3 ways*.
5 and 9 may be thrown in *4 ways*.
6 and 8 may be thrown in *5 ways*.
7 may be thrown in *6 ways*.

So 7 has an advantage over all other combinations, which, over the long run, is in favor of the casino. You can't beat the law of averages. Players, however, often have winning streaks—a proven fact in ESP studies—and that's when the experts advise that it's wise to increase the size of bets. But when a losing streak sets in, stop playing!

2. Keno

This popular game is one of the oldest known games of chance. Its origin is Chinese, and it dates back to the time before Christ, when it was operated as a national lottery in China. Legend has it that funds acquired from the game were used to finance construction of the Great Wall of China.

Keno first was introduced into the United States in the 1800s by railroad construction workers from China. Looking at a keno ticket, you'll notice that it's divided horizontally into two rectangles—the upper one contains the numbers 1 through 40, the lower half contains the numbers 41 through 80.

Chinese tradition designates the upper area as Yin and the lower as Yang; and this, in Chinese lore, compares to other great opposites—night and day, for example, or heaven and earth, sun and moon, and man and woman. Significantly the Chinese believe that anything of importance occurring during the night should influence them to play in the first 40 squares, that any bad happening suggests that the lower rectangle be played.

Although the house percentage in Keno is greater than in any other game played in the casinos in Las Vegas, it's a sit-down game, offering a place to socialize with fellow players over a cool drink. Keno and bingo are the only two casino games where people have a chance to strike up a conversation between plays.

You can also play keno while enjoying free casino lounge shows, most of which provide first-rate entertainment. If you're playing keno during the show, drinks are on the house, so you might as well spend your money on keno tickets; if you don't, you'll spend the same money on booze.

Keno is easy to play, and you can win a maximum of $50,000. Each ticket consists of a series of numbered boxes, and you can mark up to 15 of the numbers and bet anything from $1 up. Then the game begins, and you compare the numbers, as they light up on the keno board, with the spots that you have marked on your ticket. After 20 numbers have appeared on the board, if you're lucky, you may have won (depending on the number of spots that you marked compared to those on the board—usually three or more will win). Winners must claim their winnings before the next game begins; if you're one of the winners, head for the cashier. A new game starts every few minutes, and helpful keno personnel will answer any questions that you might have. They are also able to show you the best ways of marking a ticket and possibly improving your bet. (Every keno writer has his or her own "system.")

3. Blackjack, or "21"

The dealer starts the game by dealing each player two cards. In some casinos they're dealt to the player face up, or one down and one up, or both down, but the dealer always gets one card up and one card down. Everybody plays against the dealer. The object is to get a total of 21 or as close to it as possible. All face cards count as 10; all other number cards except aces count as their number value. An ace may be counted as 1 or 11, whichever you choose it to be.

Starting at his or her left, the dealer gives additional cards to the players who wish to draw (be "hit") or none to a player who wishes to "stand" or "hold." If your count is nearer to 21 than the dealer's, you win. If it's under the dealer's, you lose. Ties are a stand-off and nobody wins. After all the players are satisfied with their counts, the dealer exposes his or her face-down card. If his two cards total 16 or less, the dealer must "hit" (draw an additional card) until reaching 17 or over. If the dealer's total goes over 21, he or she must pay all the players whose hands have not gone "bust." It is important to note here that the blackjack dealer has no choice as to whether he or she should stay or draw. A dealer's decisions are predetermined and known to all the players at the table.

HOW TO PLAY

Here are eight "rules" for blackjack.

1. Place the amount of money that you want to bet on the table.
2. Look at the first two cards the dealer starts you with. If your hand adds up to the total you prefer, place your cards *under your bet money,* indicating that you don't wish any additional cards. If you elect to draw an additional card, you tell the dealer to "hit" you by making a sweeping motion with your cards, or point to your open hand (watch your fellow players).
3. If your count goes over 21, you go "bust" and lose—even if the dealer also goes "bust" afterward. Unless hands are dealt face up, *you then turn your hand face up on the table.*
4. If you make 21 in your first two cards (any picture card or 10 with an ace), you've got blackjack. *You expose your winning hand immediately,* and you collect 1½ times your bet —unless the dealer has blackjack, too, in which case it's a stand-off and nobody wins.
5. If you find a "pair" in your first two cards (say, two 4s or two 10s) you may "split" the pair into two hands and treat each card as the first card dealt in two separate hands. *Turn the pair face up on the table,* place the original bet on one of these cards, then place an equal amount on the other card. *Split aces are limited to a one-card draw on each.*
6. If your first two cards total 11 or under, you may, if you choose, double your original bet and make a one-card draw. *Turn your hand face up* and you'll receive one more card face down.
7. Anytime the dealer deals himself or herself an ace for the "up" card, you may insure your hand against the possibility that the hole card is a face card, which would give him or her an automatic blackjack. To insure, you place an amount equal to one-half of your bet on the "Insurance" line. If the

dealer does have a blackjack, you do not lose, even though he or she has your hand beat, and you keep your bet and your insurance money. If the dealer does not have a black-jack, he or she takes your insurance money and play continues in the normal fashion.

8. *Remember!* The dealer *must* stand on 17 or more and *must* hit a hand of 16 or less.

PROFESSIONAL TIPS
Advice of the experts in playing blackjack is as follows.

1. *Do not* ask for an extra card if you have a count of 17, 18, 19, 20, or 21 in your cards, no matter what the dealer has show-ing in his or her "up" card.
2. *Do not* ask for an extra card when you have 13, 14, 15, 16, or more . . . *if* the dealer has a 2, 3, 4, 5, or 6 showing in his or her "up" card.
3. *Do* ask for an extra card or more when you have a count of 13 through 16 in your hand . . . if the dealer's "up" card is a 7, 8, 9, 10, or ace.

There's a lot more to blackjack-playing strategy than the above, of course. So consider this merely as the bare bones of the game.

A Final Tip
Avoid insurance bets; they're sucker bait!

---

4. Poker

Poker is *the* game of the Old West. There's at least one sequence in every western, with the hero facing off against the villain inevita-bly over a poker hand. In Las Vegas poker is a tradition, although it isn't played at every casino.

There are lots of variations on the basic game, but one of the most popular is Hold 'Em. Five cards are dealt face-up in the center of the table and two are dealt to each player. The player takes the best five of seven, and the best hand wins. The house dealer takes care of the shuffling and the dealing and moves a marker around the table to alternate the start of the deal. The house usually has a 5% "take" from each pot.

Most casinos include the usual seven-card stud and a few have five-card draw and hi-lo split. On or near the Strip there are poker rooms at the Aladdin, Bally's–Las Vegas, Caesars Palace, Circus Cir-cus, Desert Inn, Dunes, Flamingo Hilton, Frontier, Hacienda, Holiday Casino, Imperial Palace, Las Vegas Hilton, Landmark, The Mirage, Paddlewheel, Riviera, Sahara, San Remo, Stardust, and Tropicana. Downtown you can play at Binion's Horseshoe, Four Queens, Fremont, and Union Plaza.

If you don't know how to play poker, don't attempt to learn at a table. I suggest that you refer to my list of gaming schools, including those that teach poker, and learn the game before sitting down at a table.

Pai-gow poker is a variation on poker that has become increasingly popular. The game is played with a traditional deck plus one joker. The joker can be used only as an ace to complete a straight, a flush, or a straight flush. Each player is dealt seven cards to arrange into two hands—a two-card hand and a five-card hand. Rankings are based on basic poker ratings; therefore the highest two-card hand would be two aces, and the highest five-card hand would be a Royal Flush. The five-card hand *must* be higher than the two-card hand (if the two-card hand is a pair of sixes, for example, the five-card hand must include a pair of sevens or better). Any player's hand that is set incorrectly is an automatic lose. The object of the game is for both of the player's hands to rank higher than both of the banker's hands. Should one hand rank exactly the same as the banker's hand, this is a tie, *and the banker wins all tie hands*. If the player wins one hand but loses the other, this is a "push," and no money changes hands. The house dealer or any player may be the banker. The bank is offered to each player, and each player may accept or pass. Winning hands are paid even money, less a 5% commission.

---

5. Roulette

Roulette is an extremely easy game to play, and it's really very colorful and exciting to watch. The wheel spins, and the little ball bounces around, finally dropping into one of the slots, numbered 1 to 36, plus 0 and 00. You can bet on a single number, a combination of numbers, or red or black, odd or even. If you're lucky, you can win as much as 35 to 1 (see the table). The method of placing single-number bets, column bets, and others is fairly obvious. The dealer will be happy to show you how to "straddle" two or more numbers and make many other interesting betting combinations. Each player is given different-colored chips so that it's easy to follow the numbers you're on.

A number of typical bets is indicated by means of letters on the adjoining roulette layout. The winning odds for each of these sample bets are listed opposite. These bets can be made on any corresponding combinations of numbers.

---

6. Baccarat

The ancient game of baccarat—or chemin de fer—is played with eight decks of cards. Firm rules apply, and there is no skill involved other than deciding whether to bet on the bank or the player. Any beginner can play, but check the betting minimum before you

Roulette Chart Key	Odds	Type of Bet
		Straight Bets
A	35 to 1	*Straight-up:* All numbers, plus 0 and 00.
B	2 to 1	*Column Bet:* Pays off on any number in that horizontal column.
C	2 to 1	*First Dozen:* Pays off on any number 1 through 12. Same for second and third dozen.
D	Even money	
		Combination Bets
E	17 to 1	*Split:* Pays off on 11 or 12.
F	11 to 1	Pays off on 28, 29, or 30.
G	8 to 1	*Corner:* Pays off on 17, 18, 20, or 21.
H	6 to 1	Pays off on 0, 00, 1, 2, or 3.
I	5 to 1	Pays off on 22, 23, 24, 25, 26 or 27.

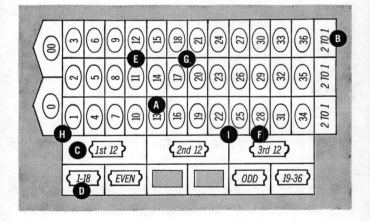

sit down. The cards are shuffled by the croupier and then placed in a box that is called the "Shoe."

Players may act as banker or play against the bank at any time. Two cards are dealt from the Shoe and given to the player who has the largest wager against the bank, and two cards are dealt to the croupier acting as banker. If the rule calls for a third card (see rules on chart below), the player or banker, or both, must take the third card. In the event of a tie, the hand is dealt over.

The object of the game is to come as close as possible to the number 9. To score the hands, the cards of each hand are totaled and the *last digit* is used. All cards have face value. For example: 10 plus 5 equal 15 (score is 5); 10 plus 4 plus 9 equal 23 (score is 3); 4 plus 3 plus 3 equal 10 (score is 0); and 4 plus 3 plus 2 equal 9 (score is 9). The closest hand to 9 wins.

Each player gets a chance to deal the cards. The Shoe passes to the player on the right each time the bank loses. If the player wishes, he or she may pass the Shoe at any time.

Note: When you bet on the bank and the bank wins, you are charged a 5% commission. This must be paid at the start of a new game or when you leave the table.

Player's Hand

Having	
0-1-2-3-4-5	Must draw a third card.
6-7	*Must stand.*
8-9	Natural. Banker cannot draw.

Banker's Hand

Having	Draws When giving Player 3rd card of	Does Not Draw When giving Player 3rd card of:
3	1-2-3-4-5-6-7-9-10	8
4	2-3-4-5-6-7	1-8-9-10
5	4-5-6-7	1-2-3-8-9-10
6	6-7	1-2-3-4-5-8-9-10
7	*Must stand.*	
8-9	Natural. Player cannot draw.	

If the player takes no third card, the banker must stand on 6. No one draws against a natural 8 or 9.

7. Big Six

Big Six is a fun game and can be easily spotted by the giant vertical Big Six wheel and the carnival-barker patter of the person spinning it. The game provides pleasant recreation and involves no study or effort. The wheel has 56 positions on it, 54 of them marked by bills from $1 to $20 denomination. The other two spots are jokers, and each pays 40 to 1 if the wheel stops in that position.

All other stops pay at face value. Those marked with $20 bills pay 20 to 1; the $5 bills pay 5 to 1; and so forth.

8. Sports Books

Most of the larger hotels in Las Vegas have sports book operations—looking much like commodities-futures trading boards. In some, almost as large as theaters, you can comfortably sit and watch ball games, fights, and, at some casinos, horse races on huge TV screens. To add to your enjoyment, there's usually a deli/ bar nearby that serves sandwiches, hot dogs, soft drinks, and beer. As a matter of fact, some of the best sandwiches in Las Vegas are served next to the sports books.

Sports books take bets on virtually every sport, with the exception of the most fascinating sport of all—presidential elections. The majority of books that I've listed below take bets on racing, but I've noted those that do not.

On the Strip there are sports books at the Aladdin, Bally's–Las Vegas, Barbary Coast, Caesars Palace, Circus Circus, Flamingo Hilton (sports only), Frontier Hotel, Holiday Casino (sports only), Imperial Palace, Las Vegas Hilton, Marina, the Mirage, Riviera Hotel, Sahara Hotel, Sands Hotel, Stardust Hotel, Tropicana, and Vegas World. Downtown, they'll take your bet at Binion's Horseshoe, El Cortez Hotel, the Fremont Hotel, Golden Nugget, and Union Plaza.

VII

ENTERTAINMENT

1. NIGHTSPOTS ON THE STRIP
2. DOWNTOWN NIGHTS
3. OTHER ACTIVITIES

The Las Vegas Strip is a postwar phenomenon, which means that the oldest structures are less than 45 years of age; renovations, additions, and improvements are proceeding so constantly that, in actuality, even the original casino/hotels are pleasant and comfortable.

Structurally most establishments on the Strip are very similar: a plush lobby opening off the street, with hotel reception desk tucked away to the left or the right past the casino; a minuscule lounge; the open casino area encircled by various restaurants (always including a 24-hour coffee shop); a theater/lounge offering almost round-the-clock entertainment; and the hotel gift shop, which is invariably stocked with such tourist-oriented merchandise as nudie playing cards, beer-stein radios, scrubbed decks of cards from the casino, slot-machine savings banks, clocks with dice as numbers, books on how to gamble, cigarettes, candy, newspapers, and magazines.

THE CASINOS

The casino activities are almost identical in every hotel: banks of slot machines . . . a few roulette tables . . . three or more craps tables . . . many tables for blackjack loosely linked together to form an enclosed area where the "pit boss" stands watching the dealers . . . a keno lounge (keno is like bingo) with rows of seats for the players . . . and, often in a roped-off corner with spectators, a baccarat game or two where thousands of dollars might change hands in a single play.

Cocktail waitresses circulate constantly; if you want service, ask the dealer to help you. It's the understandable policy of most casinos to bring gamblers free drinks, but remember to tip ("toke") the waitress.

A Warning

However tempted you might be, don't start taking photographs of the gaming action. All casinos have strict rules about cameras, both for security and for some guests' wish for anonymity, and the guards enforce them promptly. There are many aspects to security, incidentally, and as you'll soon discover, not only the men in uniform (some wearing sidearms) are keeping an eye on things. Informally dressed hotel employees wander around discreetly, and their observations are supplemented by overhead television monitors or one-way mirrors in the ceiling above the gaming tables.

THE LOUNGES AND SHOWROOMS

Surrounding the casino area are invariably at least a couple of bar/lounges, often with high-caliber entertainment. In the bigger hotels, this may be a name star who inexplicably resents being described as a "lounge performer" despite the fact that he or she might be pulling in tens of thousands of dollars per week for playing three or four shows a day, and despite the fact that these so-called lounges may accommodate as many as 600 or 700 people. The lounge policy in some hotels is to allow free admission but to insist on a two-drink minimum, with drinks costing from $3.50 to $5 apiece, depending on the show.

Most lounges keep their draperies open during the show so that nearby gamblers can play the slots and watch the show at the same time. The lounges that shut off the view are, of course, the ones with the top shows.

Almost all of the big showrooms have the same policy, which is to stage a dinner show at approximately 8pm, with dinner costing about $20 to $50 per person, minimum, depending on the performer. No tickets are issued, but reservations must be made. For the dinner show, arrive about an hour and a half early so that you'll have time to finish eating before the entertainment begins. At the late show, generally starting between 11pm and midnight, you get two to four drinks instead of dinner; in most cases, at either show, a tip to the maître d' is necessary if you want really good seats.

Occasionally on weekends or holidays or when a superstar is booked, there might also be a third show at 1am. In any case, there's always a late show playing in one of the lounges for people who like to stay up late. And in Las Vegas, visitors always do.

THE EXTRAVAGANZAS

Many major hotels have taken to staging or importing complete "extravaganzas"—either reruns of proven Broadway successes or lavish musicals such as the Tropicana's *Folies Bergère,* the Stardust's *Lido de Paris,* the Flamingo's *City Lites,* and Bally's *Jubilee.* Such shows cost a fortune to mount, but the costs are amortized over the two—and sometimes ten—years that such shows can run. Considering that a hotel offering regular talent changes might pay as much as $500,000 per week for performers' salaries, it's clear that even an initial investment of $5 million for a two-year show ends up as an economy.

The semipermanent productions, incidentally, are very imaginative with their theatrical effects: curtains of rain between audience and performers . . . film credits on giant screens onstage . . . artificial fog drifting into the proscenium . . . galloping horses . . . live camels and elephants parading through a desert oasis and nude nymphs swimming in a "mirage" pool . . . fountains and waterfalls . . . fires and hurricanes . . . and bare-breasted chorines with safety belts who descend smoothly from the ceiling on circular pedestals.

Veteran producer Frank Sennes is an outstanding name in local show-business circles. After two decades of planning Strip productions, in 1958 he started the trend to foreign imports by booking the *Lido de Paris* show and combining it with sound-and-light effects that the French edition had never dreamed of. Frederic Apcar has gone even further, imaginatively, in this direction.

THE HOURS

The gambling, unlike the entertainment—which takes a breather for a few hours a day—continues all the time. It's just as easy to find action at four or five in the morning as it is at five in the afternoon. The hotels and casinos are open 24 hours a day.

AN EXPLANATION

What follows is a rundown on the establishments along the Strip; it's basically a nightlife guide, of course, but because most of the lounge acts start early in the afternoon, the concept of nightlife per se almost doesn't exist in this town without clocks.

Bear in mind that although most people first think of the Strip for entertainment, the Golden Nugget (downtown) features some of the greatest headliners in show business—for example, Dolly Parton, Dionne Warwick, Kenny Rogers, Harry Belafonte, and Melissa Manchester.

Please keep in mind that I've already described most of these famous hotels in Chapter III. There, however, my interest was in finding a place to stay. Here I'll deal with the "hotel-as-sight-seeing-attraction-in-itself," with its casinos, theater nightclubs, and other entertainment facilities.

---

1. Nightspots on the Strip

THE MIRAGE

The Mirage, on the Strip at 3400 Las Vegas Blvd. (tel. 792-7777 for show reservations), has a magnificent showroom—**Theatre Mirage**—that presents a unique theatrical experience in the all-new Siegfried and Roy show. I guarantee that you'll see a performance unlike any that you've ever seen before. The state-of-the-art lighting and staging effects; the use of exotic animals, including the white tigers; and the entire elaborate production make it one of the most expensive shows ever brought to a stage. Siegfried and Roy perform only the first three weeks of each month, Thursday through Tuesday at 7:30 and 11pm. Tickets are $56, including two drinks and tips, for a truly unforgettable evening. The fourth week of each month features headliners, such as Cher.

BALLY'S–LAS VEGAS

Bally's–Las Vegas, on the Strip at 3645 Las Vegas Blvd. (tel. 739-4111), as befitting its super-colossal image, has not one but two major showrooms: the plush 1,400-seat **Celebrity Room** for superstar entertainment and the **Ziegfeld Room,** an 1,100-seat entertainment palace used for the super-spectacular *Jubilee.*

The Celebrity Room's opening-night mega-star was Dean Martin, who played to a full house of VIPs. He's still among Bally's stable of stars, along with Tom Jones, Frank Sinatra, and Jerry Lewis, among others.

In the Ziegfeld Room, Donn Arden's *Jubilee* replaced the famed *Hallelujah Hollywood.* The latter ran from 1974 to 1981 with a full house every night, and so far *Jubilee* is equally popular. In fact, it's a good idea to reserve your tickets when you reserve your room. *Jubilee* has a cast of more than 100 gorgeous showgirls, many of them ostrich-plumed, bespangled, and often bare-breasted. It glorifies Hollywood movies and entertainers of the last 50 years, pays a tribute to Elvis, re-creates the scene from *Samson and Delilah* in which the temple falls, shows the sinking of the *Titanic,* and includes a World War I dogfight in the air. The theater is equipped with every known theatrical device and moving stages. The costumes were designed by Bob Mackie.

Most shows in the Celebrity Room cost about $25, but the prices can escalate to $50 depending on the performer.

Jubilee has cocktail shows only at 7:30 and 11pm; there are three shows on Saturday, none on Wednesday. They're priced at $32.50 and include two drinks.

Bally's also offers comedy with *Catch a Rising Star* at Bally's Theatre. It's where you'll find eager talent seeking to make names for themselves.

CAESARS PALACE

From its opening over 20 years ago, Caesars Palace, on the Strip at 3570 Las Vegas Blvd. (tel. 731-7110), has been a tremendous hit. And the most illustrious of stars have appeared regularly in its 1,200-seat showroom, the **Circus Maximus.** In the past the room has been used for long-running Broadway hits such as *Fiddler on the Roof* and *The Odd Couple.* These days it's one of the few places still offering big-name entertainment only.

The galaxy of stars at Caesars includes Wayne Newton, Diana Ross, Joan Rivers, Julio Iglesias, Willie Nelson, George Burns, Paul Anka, Tom Jones, Rodney Dangerfield, the Judds, and the Pointer

Sisters. The room is decorated in Roman motif (natch), its plush royal-purple booths fashioned after ancient chariots. Every seat in the tiered room, which has no pillars or posts, affords a clear view.

There are no dinner shows at the Circus Maximus, only cock-tail shows at 8:30 and 11:30pm; it is closed Tuesday. Admission is usually $25 to $50, depending on the performer; drinks are often included in the price.

Another entertainment facility at Caesars is **Cleopatra's Barge,** which floats on the "Nile," five feet deep, drawing 3½ feet of water when loaded. It's off one of the hotel's wide corridors. The barge has oars (although no galley slaves man them), ostrich-feather fans, statues of the ancient pharaohs, sails (furled), and a canopied royal box where the queen supposedly entertained her Roman friends. There's a seating on the main barge, aboard two adjacent lesser craft, and on the dock. Hydraulic mechanisms rock the barge and attendant craft gently; you board via gangplanks. A small legion of Nubian-inspired waitresses—in diaphanous minitoga costumes —are on duty. A dockside fence had to be constructed, though, to keep awestruck sightseers from falling into the "Nile."

There's a live band for dancing playing nightly from 10pm to 4am, and it's really good. No reservations are required; there's no cover, just a two-drink minimum.

A superb entertainment facility at Caesars is the innovative **Omnimax Theatre,** housed in a geodesic dome with 380 seats that recline 27° and a wrap-around screen for thrilling special effects. Omnimax films allow the viewer to travel in space, under the sea, inside an atom, or through time itself. The screen explodes with glo-rious color and movement; you'll find yourself gripping your seat and actually feeling dizzy, although you haven't moved at all. The awesome visual effects are enhanced aurally by a six-track stereo-phonic "sensaround" sound system emanating from 16 behind-the-screen speakers and 56 additional speakers under the theater seats. At night, the exterior of the Omnimax dome is used to project a light show visible from the Strip. Recent offerings have included *To The Limit* and *Niagara—Miracles, Myths, and Magic,* featuring everything from a wild ride down the rapids to a high-wire crossing above the Niagara Gorge. The film also takes a historical look at the legends and tourism long associated with the Niagara River and the falls. The story of Niagara has alternated with *Speed,* an Omnimax production about man's attack on velocity, from primitive times through to supersonic jets and space travel. Caesars Omnimax Thea-tre has also been home to the magnificent story of the *Grand Canyon —The Hidden Secrets* and to *To Fly,* a paean to the exhilaration of flight.

There are continuous hourly showings from 11am to mid-night. Admission is $5 for adults, $4 for kids under 12. Don't miss this unique entertainment.

LAS VEGAS HILTON

With the construction of the International Hotel, which later became the Las Vegas Hilton, 3000 Paradise Road, at the Conven-

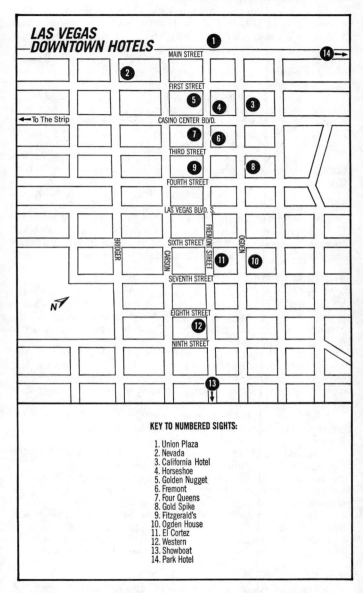

LAS VEGAS DOWNTOWN HOTELS

MAIN STREET

FIRST STREET

← To The Strip

CASINO CENTER BLVD.

THIRD STREET

FOURTH STREET

LAS VEGAS BLVD. S.

SIXTH STREET

SEVENTH STREET

EIGHTH STREET

NINTH STREET

BRIDGER
CARSON
FREMONT STREET
OGDEN

N

KEY TO NUMBERED SIGHTS:

1. Union Plaza
2. Nevada
3. California Hotel
4. Horseshoe
5. Golden Nugget
6. Fremont
7. Four Queens
8. Gold Spike
9. Fitzgerald's
10. Ogden House
11. El Cortez
12. Western
13. Showboat
14. Park Hotel

tion Center (tel. 732-5111), millionaire Kirk Kerkorian opened up what still is, even with name change and new management, a "Strip" unto itself. So huge is the 3,174-room hotel, in fact, that it almost seems a separate town all on its own.

Barbra Streisand was hired to kick off the first couple of weeks of the Hilton's 2,000-seat **Hilton Showroom** for something around $100,000 a week. An eye-popping variety of superstar headliners adds to the hotel's reputation for top-drawer entertainment. Current stars in the Hilton galaxy include Bill Cosby, Phyllicia Rashad, Wayne Newton, Engelbert Humperdinck, Dionne Warwick, and Gladys Knight.

An unusual aspect of the showroom is a 400-seat mezzanine cocktail lounge, which for the first time in Vegas allows patrons to watch dinnertime shows even if they've eaten earlier or intend to dine later. The 8pm show will set you back about $25 to $40 per person; the 11:30pm show, including two drinks, costs $20 to $25.

There's more nightly entertainment in the Hilton's **Casino Lounge,** featuring live entertainment and dancing from 8pm to 3am.

And then there's the spectacular **Hilton Center Amphitheatre,** which hosts world-championship fights and very special concert appearances. The multitalented Eddie Murphy made his first Las Vegas appearance at the Hilton Amphitheatre and packed them in. As you might expect, prices at the Amphitheatre vary considerably, depending on the event and the performer.

THE DESERT INN

The Desert Inn Hotel & Casino, on the Strip at 3145 Las Vegas Blvd. (tel. 733-4444), was expanded in the late 1970s and has just completed a multimillion-dollar refurbishment. Today it's the classiest hotel on the Strip, with a glamorous casino and first-rate facilities of every kind.

Its showplace is the **Crystal Room,** where Frank Sinatra once played in the early days; Danny Kaye, Phil Harris, and Noël Coward were also associated with Desert Inn shows. Later, the hotel followed the trend to spectaculars, featuring advanced lighting effects and dazzling feathered and sequined costumes.

Beginning in 1985 the Desert Inn went back to big-name entertainment. Today's star lineup includes the likes of Rich Little, Louise Mandrell, Bernadette Peters, and Tony Bennett.

There are cocktail shows (with two drinks) at 8 and 11pm and perhaps 9pm, depending on the day. Tickets usually cost $25 to $35 per person. Prices depend on the performer. The Crystal Room's moderate size (it seats over 600) affords the entire audience a reasonable view of the show. There is no show on Monday.

There's high-quality entertainment, too (a pianist from 4 to 8pm and top-flight lounge performers into the wee hours) in the **Winner's Choice Lounge,** a deluxe sport-themed lounge with very comfortable rattan furnishings. There is no cover or minimum.

THE STARDUST

The Stardust, on the Strip at 3000 Las Vegas Blvd. South (tel. 732-6111), was responsible for the first big show to be brought intact from abroad—the *Lido de Paris* revue, imported by veteran Las Vegas producer Frank Sennes in 1958. The show is full of beautiful dancers and artifices such as dozens of doves released over the audience's heads, a fire, ice-skating rinks, and waterfalls worked into the plot. Now joining the *Lido* is the award-winning comedy of Bobby Berosini and His Orangutans. These apes have appeared on stage, screen, and TV.

More than 13 million people so far have seen the *Lido* show at the Stardust's 1,300-seat **Café Continental,** and, with annual changes, it looks as if it might run forever. Two shows nightly are at 7 and 11pm. All are cocktail shows, with two drinks, priced at $26. There are no shows on Tuesday.

In addition, the **Starlite Lounge** provides live entertainment from 4pm to 3am.

THE FLAMINGO HILTON

The Flamingo Hilton, on the Strip at 3555 Las Vegas Blvd. South (tel. 733-3111), has presented some of the all-time greats over the years—among them Judy Garland, Louis Armstrong, Jack Benny, and Lena Horne—and provided an early showcase for such up-and-coming performers as Richard Pryor, the Smothers Brothers, Charo, Flip Wilson, Wayne Newton, and Tom Jones. In the 1950s the opening act for Mickey Rooney was the Will Mastin Trio, which featured a young multitalented dynamo named Sammy Davis, Jr. Since Jimmy Durante's name christened its marquee in 1946, the Flamingo's vocal offerings have ranged from Don Ho to Ray Charles, its comedy acts from Harpo Marx to Lenny Bruce. The late Totie Fields made her Las Vegas debut at the Flamingo as an opening act for Trini Lopez. It's a hotel with an impressive entertainment history, of which the above is only the tiniest glimmer.

In recent years the Flamingo, like many Vegas hotels, has gone the spectacular route with *City Lites,* a show packed with gorgeous showgirls, singers, dancers, and ice skaters. It offers a parade of music from *Over the Rainbow,* ice ballet to rousing country songs, an Oriental fantasy segment, and a grand finale featuring show tunes from *New York, New York* and *42nd Street.* Tickets for the dinner show (at 7:45pm nightly) start at $26.95. The 11pm cocktail show is $19.95, including two drinks. There's no show on Sunday.

There's also continuous entertainment nightly from 8pm to 4:30am in **Casino Lounge,** where disco alternates with lounge acts. There's no cover; there's a two-drink minimum on weekends only.

THE TROPICANA

When the Tropicana, on the Strip at 3801 Las Vegas Blvd. South (tel. 739-2222), first opened in 1957, it competed with everyone else for the superstars, but in 1959 it imported the famous *Folies Bergère;* this lavish show, with annual changes, has filled the hotel's **Tiffany Theatre** ever since. (Its Paris counterpart has been going for over a century!) The show never fails to dazzle audiences with its magnificent costumes and splendor, ambitious technical gimmicks, and the seminude chorus line that extends around three sides of the vast theater. The 32nd anniversary edition of the *Folies* celebrates American music, with numbers featuring such all-American products as blues and boogie.

The dinner show, with entrees priced from $21 to $40, starts at

8pm, and the late show ($15) starts at 11pm. There is no performance on Thursday.

Another Tropicana entertainment facility is the **Atrium Lounge** overlooking the shopping plaza. There are shows at 9:30pm, 11:30pm, and 1:30am in a glittering marble-and-brass gazebo fashioned after a Parisian bandstand. There's no performance on Monday.

THE RIVIERA

The Riviera, on the Strip at 2901 Las Vegas Blvd. South (tel. 734-5110), has long offered top-flight entertainment in its vast and elegant **Versailles Theatre.** Liberace, candelabra and all, was on hand for the gala opening of the Riviera on April 18, 1955. (In 1960 his opening act was a new singer named Barbra Streisand.) Appearances have also been made by top stars such as Dolly Parton, Barry Manilow, Kenny Rogers, Liza Minelli, Joan Rivers, Shirley MacLaine, and Diana Ross.

Currently running at the Versailles Theatre is *Splash,* an aquacade spectacular. It's truly an extravaganza with diving and swimming stars, mermaids, dancers, and showgirls.

Shows are at 8pm nightly, for $23.50. There's also an 11pm show, which costs $20.50. The theater is closed Wednesday. There is no nudity at the 8pm shows.

At the **Mardi Gras Plaza** is a brilliant and long-running revue, *An Evening at La Cage,* starring a bevy of female impersonators. It's clever, hilarious, and thoroughly enjoyable. The production is spectacular with its beautiful costuming and dance numbers. Shows are at 7, 9, and 11pm; admission is $11. It is closed Tuesday.

THE DUNES

Until recently the Dunes, on the Strip at 3650 Las Vegas Blvd. South (tel. 737-4110), like many other hotels, had forsaken star entertainment for one show.

Currently the **Casino Theatre** is scheduling future shows.

There are usually two cocktail shows nightly, at 9 and 11pm, on Saturday at 8pm, 10pm, and midnight. They cost $16 per person, including two drinks.

There's also nightly entertainment in **Mr. Big's Casino Lounge** from 8pm to 3:30am with no cover or minimum. And at the **Oasis,** musical groups perform from noon to 4:15am.

THE SANDS HOTEL CASINO

The Sands, on the Strip at 3355 Las Vegas Blvd. South (tel. 733-5000), represents glamour to thousands of people who've never even been to Las Vegas.

From its opening day in 1952, the Sands has been a trendsetter in entertainment. The famous **Copa Room** (made famous by Frank Sinatra) has been home to brilliant stars and unique productions. Currently appearing is *Comedy Kings* by the creators of the great TV show *D.C. Follies*—and it's just as zany and wild. Shows ($18.95) are at 8 and 10:30pm, except Mondays.

Nightly entertainment also is featured in the hotel's popular

Winner's Circle Cabaret from 5pm to the wee hours. Talented groups satisfy everyone's musical tastes with selections ranging from top-40 hits, to country/western, to Broadway hits, to rock-'n'-roll favorites from the 1950s and 1960s.

THE SAHARA

When the Sahara, on the Strip at the corner of Las Vegas Blvd. and Sahara Ave. (tel. 737-2111), was first built in 1952, it was regarded as being out of town. Today it's at the top of the Strip, at a major intersection between the Convention Center, downtown Las Vegas, and the remainder of the Strip hotels.

The **Congo Theatre** has entertainment nightly at 8 and 11pm Sunday through Friday and at 8pm, 10pm, and midnight on Saturday. The theater is closed Wednesday. Currently *Boylesque* ($10.95), the original Las Vegas female impersonation show, is on. The **Casbar Lounge** features entertainment nightly from 7pm to 5am.

THE HACIENDA HOTEL

The Hacienda, on the Strip at 3950 Las Vegas Blvd. South (tel. 739-8911), is either the first hotel on the Strip or the last, depending on which direction you're coming from. When the Hacienda first opened in 1956, its gambling license was still pending—manager Dick Taylor estimated that the wait was costing the stockholders $70 per minute—and original owner Bayley, something of a promotional genius, began to formulate plans to bring the customers in. Car drivers were handed discount folders as they paused at streetlights in neighboring cities and a DC-4 was fitted with a piano bar and was used to fly customers in free from West Coast cities. The hotel was also the first to add helicopter service from its own heliport. The casino license was eventually granted, but the Hacienda has continued many of its package plans, adding a daily free champagne party.

Currently comedy is the theme with Redd Foxx at the **Fiesta Room.** There's a show at 9pm Tuesday through Saturday and another at midnight Friday and Saturday ($16).

There's also entertainment nightly in the **Bolero Lounge** from 8pm to 1am. It is closed Wednesday.

THE FRONTIER HOTEL

Million-dollar hotels have been commonplace for a long time, but the Frontier Hotel, on the Strip at 3120 Las Vegas Blvd. South (tel. 734-0110), may be one of the first hotels to erect a million-dollar neon sign. It is 200 feet high and billboards the various entertainment attractions currently playing.

The 800-seat **Music Hall** was best known in the past for featuring singer Wayne Newton (a tremendously talented local boy whose enormous popularity here turned him into a national celebrity). Other stars who've played here include Nipsey Russell, Sergio Franchi, Joan Rivers, Steve Lawrence and Eydie Gorme, Lola Falana, Bobby Vinton, Glen Campbell, Roy Clark, and Juliet Prowse.

Entertainment runs from dusk until dawn (3:30pm to 3:15

am) in the intimate **Wild Horse Lounge,** located in the center of the Frontier's casino. There's no cover charge here, but there is a two-drink minimum.

IMPERIAL PALACE

The pagoda-roofed Imperial Palace, on the Strip at 3535 Las Vegas Blvd. South (tel. 731-3311), houses a 869-seat showroom called the **Imperial Theatre.** Presentations here vary from dance extravaganzas to *Legends in Concert,* a musical re-creation of legendary superstars in a multimedia laser extravaganza. It's a great family show. There are two cocktail shows nightly, except Sunday, at 7:30 and 10:30pm. Admission is $15.95.

HOLIDAY CASINO

The Holiday Casino and Inn, at 3473 Las Vegas Blvd. South (tel. 369-5000), presents a great new revue called *Keep Smilin' America* twice nightly at the **Holiday Theatre.** Shows are at 8 and 10:30pm except Sunday ($13).

MAXIM

When it opened in January 1977, Maxim, 160 E. Flamingo Rd. (tel. 731-4300), got off to a hot start with *Minsky's Burlesque,* a name that has been lighting up theater marquees since the turn of the century. In their heyday, the Minskys (Abe and his son, Harold) developed such comedy stars as Abbott and Costello, Phil Silvers, Red Buttons, and Pinky Lee. The famed naughty revue came to Vegas in 1950 and played at various hotels for over two decades. It featured gorgeous showgirls, exotic dancers, comedy routines, and sketches.

The Minskys are no longer at Maxim; these days the hotel has the hilarious *Wacky World of Comedy.* There is a dinner show at 7pm for $16. It is closed Sunday. There's also live musical entertainment and dancing nightly from 11pm to 4am.

CIRCUS CIRCUS

The pink-and-white-striped concrete "tent" of the $12-million Circus Circus, on the Strip at 2880 Las Vegas Blvd. South (tel. 734-0410), has been a hit since the day it opened. Almost 4 million visitors filed through in the first year to gamble and/or watch the continuous circus acts taking place overhead. Ed Sullivan once did a CBS show from here, and several movies have used it as a setting.

Bulgarian-born Alexander Dobritch, innovator of the circusy show—who also booked talent for "The Ed Sullivan Show" and even operated his own touring circus—has died, but his policies have continued. Daring and talented circus artists, performing continuously overhead from 11am to midnight, include aerialists performing on painted carousel horses, stunt cyclists, jugglers, high-wire acts, trapeze artists, tumblers, clowns, and acrobats. Kids love it, and so do their parents.

Any or all of these acts can be seen free while you're playing electronic games and pinball machines or sipping cocktails in the revolving Horse Around Carousel Bar.

LANDMARK

The Landmark is featuring *Spellbound,* with two teams of magicians, in its Showroom at 8 and 10:30pm ($17 and $20), Monday through Saturday. The Top of the Place on the 31st floor has dancing nightly from 9pm to 2am. For those who prefer just sitting, there is a spectacular view like no other in town.

---

2. Downtown Nights

Most people head straight for the glamorous Strip when they hit Las Vegas. Until the new Golden Nugget (downtown) was created by Steve Wynn, the Strip got the most publicity and the biggest spenders. Now you cannot overlook the downtown area—glamour has arrived, accompanied by the superstars of show business.

THE GOLDEN NUGGET

For your entertainment at the Golden Nugget, 129 E. Fremont St. (tel. 386-8100), there is a veritable roster of headliners who appear at the magnificent new **Theatre Ballroom** and at the intimate, informal **Cabaret.** This is where you go to see the superstars light up the sky—David Brenner, Dolly Parton (her debut engagement was in the Cabaret), Kenny Rogers, Don Rickles, the Gatlin Brothers, Diahann Carroll and Vic Damone, Jeffrey Osborne, and Yakov Smirnoff. Whoopi Goldberg made her Las Vegas debut in the Theatre Ballroom. There are two shows nightly, except Tuesday and Wednesday, at 8 and 11pm. The cost is $20 and up, depending on the performer, so it's best to call first.

THE UNION PLAZA

The major entertainment facility at the Union Plaza, 1 Main St., at Fremont Street (tel. 386-2110), is the 650-seat **Showroom,** in which Broadway-style musicals and comedies are featured. Currently it's *Nudes on Ice.* In the past there was *Oklahoma!* and Cole Porter's *Anything Goes* (based on a book by P. G. Wodehouse), *Fiddler on the Roof, The Odd Couple,* and World Class Ice Skating. There are two shows nightly, except Monday, at 8 and 11:30pm. The former costs $13 to $20 and includes dinner; the latter is $10 with two cocktails.

The Union Plaza also offers entertainment from 3pm to 3am in the **Omaha Lounge** off the casino.

---

3. Other Activities

Generally nightlife in Las Vegas means attending one or more lavish shows at various Strip hotels, with possibly a bit of gambling squeezed in at whatever casino happens to be handy. Many tourists start out at an 8pm dinner show; hop over to somebody else's midnight offering; and sometimes, if it's a weekend, take in a third show at 2:15am.

But there are a few other things to do.

MOVIES

Las Vegas isn't a big town for movies because of the wealth of live entertainment available, and a fair number of the theaters that exist show "adult" movies only. There are some conventional movie houses, however (consult their ads in local papers), including a few drive-ins. Among them is the Vegas 4, 4158 Smoke Ranch Rd., North Las Vegas (tel. 646-3565).

The biggest theater complex in town is the grouping of 11 **Red Rock Theatres**, 5201 W. Charleston Blvd., one block west of Decatur Boulevard (tel. 870-1423).

CULTURE IN LAS VEGAS

The city's hub of cultural activities (you thought everything focused on basketball?) is the campus of the **University of Nevada, Las Vegas,** on Maryland Parkway, between Flamingo Road and Tropicana Avenue. Among the regular daytime and evening activities are concerts by various music and dance groups, including the award-winning Jazz Ensemble, the Las Vegas Symphony, and the Nevada Dance Theatre.

The Department of Theater Arts, also an award-winner, stages productions of both contemporary and classic plays in two theaters —the 550-seat **Judy Bayley Theatre** (tel. 739-3801) and the 180-seat **Black Box Theatre.** Recent offerings have included both classic and contemporary plays.

The **Donna Beam Fine Arts Gallery** (tel. 739-3893) displays works by artists of national and international reputation in a spacious area with natural lighting and a loft. Among the notable exhibits that have received considerable acclaim are the *Contemporary American Collage, 1960–1986* and the *Nevada Biennial '88.*

The **UNLV Barrick Museum of Natural History** (tel. 739-3381) features traveling exhibits as well as permanent displays on the Mojave Desert, the Navajo Indians, and pre-Columbian pottery.

Lectures by prominent national speakers and leading academic experts are offered in the prestigious Barrick Lecture Series and the University Forum Lecture Series.

The university also boasts a 2,000-seat concert hall, an impressive facility that showcases many of the world's greatest classical musicians in the Master Series concerts. Among the great performers who have been featured are Aaron Copeland, Isaac Stern, Itzhak Perlman, and Andrés Segovia.

For details on university cultural events, call the Performing Arts Box Office (tel. 739-3801). For a recording of campus events, call 739-3131.

After what seemed to be a permanent transient state, the **Museum of Natural History** (*not* the UNLV Barrick Museum) finally settled into its new home late in 1990, dinosaurs and all, at 900 N. Las Vegas Blvd. (tel. 384-3466). Don't miss it. The museum is fun, fascinating, and informative for adults and kids.

VIII

SPORTS AND RECREATION

Take your sports gear to Las Vegas or you may regret it. Las Vegas has devoted more space to more sports than almost any city I know, except San Diego. Although Las Vegas has no in-town beaches, there's swimming at nearby Lake Mead and in uncounted swimming pools at almost all the Strip hotels and motels. Golf courses are among the country's finest, and there are supposed to be more tennis courts (almost all of them lit for night play) open to the public here than in any other American resort.

Bowling, rodeos, basketball, table tennis, boating, boxing, shuffleboard, horseback riding, fishing, hunting, skiing, and football are among other sports for spectators or participants, either in the city or within a short drive.

Camping, horse- and mule-packing trips, hiking and backpacking in wilderness areas in nearby Zion and Bryce Canyon National Parks (Utah) and in Grand Canyon National Park (Arizona) have increasingly been attracting entire families. Accommodations at the parks are comfortable and reasonably priced. Also appealing to families are river-float trips. Departures for adventurous white-water float trips on the Colorado and other wild western rivers can easily be arranged from Las Vegas.

The almost endless outdoor opportunities in the Lake Mead National Recreation Area, which covers 5½ million acres, and on 12,000-foot Mount Charleston, only an hour's drive from Las Vegas, are worth consideration, too.

TENNIS

A few hotel tennis courts are open to public use in Las Vegas. And there's also the dozen night-lit tennis courts at the University of Nevada, Las Vegas (tel. 739-3150). The University's courts are open from 6am to 9:45pm Monday through Friday, 8am to 8pm Saturday, and 10am to 6pm Sunday. The charge is $2 per hour for nonuniversity people (students and faculty have priority). Call before you go to find out if a court is available. Guest passes are obtained at the Physical Education Building, Room 306 or 312.

Rates are generally quite reasonable at the various courts around town. Some places charge a small fee for each player using the locker rooms. It's best to telephone in advance for rates and reservations.

The **Tropicana Hotel,** 3801 Las Vegas Blvd. South (tel. 739-2381), has four outdoor courts lit for night play. With so many possible play hours, you can usually line up a partner. Courts are for hotel guests only.

Another likable feature at the Tropicana is the cocktail lounge overlooking the courts. Those who'd rather watch than play can enjoy themselves and observe the goings-on to their heart's content. The mezzanine lounge is attractive, with wood paneling, thick wall-to-wall carpeting, comfortable chairs, and good service.

The **Riviera Hotel,** 2901 Las Vegas Blvd. South (tel. 734-5110), has two night-lit tennis courts open from 6am to 6pm. Riviera guests have preference over other hotels' guests.

Caesars Palace, 3570 Las Vegas Blvd. South (tel. 731-7110), has four outdoor courts. Patrick Du Pre is the tennis pro. The courts are open from dawn to dark for hotel guests and the public.

Bally's—Las Vegas, 3645 Las Vegas Blvd. South (tel. 739-4111), along with every other imaginable facility, has ten courts, five lit for night play. Bally's guests have preference over other hotels' guests. The pro shop is open from 9am to 5pm.

The **Las Vegas Hilton,** 3000 Paradise Rd., adjacent to the Las Vegas Convention Center (tel. 732-5111), has six courts for hotel guests only. The courts are located on an immense rooftop, stories high. All are illuminated for night action. There are several teaching pros.

The **Desert Inn,** 3145 Las Vegas Blvd. South (tel. 733-4444), has ten courts, five lit—including five new courts adjacent to the Desert Inn Spa. Marty Hennessey is the teaching pro. The Desert Inn courts are often used by celebrities and political figures. They're open from 8am to 8:30pm for all, but hotel guests have priority.

The **Sands,** 3355 Las Vegas Blvd. South (tel. 733-5000), has six courts, all lit. The courts are open from 9am to 10pm for all, but hotel guests have priority.

At the **Hacienda Hotel,** 3950 Las Vegas Blvd. South (tel. 739-8911), there are six courts, with two lit for night use; they're open from 8am to 11pm for hotel guests only.

The **Frontier Hotel,** 3120 Las Vegas Blvd. South (tel. 734-0110), has two outdoor courts, both lit for night play. They are reserved for hotel guests only and open from 8am to 10pm.

The **Aladdin Hotel,** 3667 Las Vegas Blvd. South (tel. 736-0111), has two outdoor courts on the upper-story pool deck, both lit for night play. They are open to the public, but priority is given to the Aladdin's guests. The courts are open from dawn to 10pm.

The **Union Plaza,** 1 Main St. (tel. 386-2110), has four courts, all lit for night play, located on the hotel's sports deck. Open to the public, these courts are especially handy for those staying downtown; the hotel's location is convenient to all. The courts are open from 9am to 6pm.

Apart from tennis facilities at the hotels, courts are also available at the clubs listed below. Reservations are necessary.

The **Center Court Racquet Club,** 3890 Swenson St. (tel. 735-8153), has four outdoor courts, three lighted, and ten indoor courts. Hours are 7am to 10pm on weekdays, to 6pm on weekends.

The **Las Vegas Racquet Club,** 3333 W. Raven Ave. (tel. 361-2202), has six outdoor courts lit for night play. Hours are 10am to 10pm.

The **Sports Club–Las Vegas,** 3025 Industrial Rd. (tel. 733-8999), has two indoor tennis courts. Hours are 9am to 10:30pm.

RACQUETBALL

Courts can be found in several locations around town.

Caesars Palace, 3570 Las Vegas Blvd. South (tel. 731-7110), has courts open daily from 10am to 5pm.

The **Las Vegas Athletic Club East,** 1070 E. Sahara Ave. (tel. 733-1919), has ten courts, open 24 hours a day, seven days a week.

The **Las Vegas Athletic Club West,** 3315 Spring Mountain Rd. (tel. 362-3720), has 12 racquetball courts, as well as Nautilus equipment, basketball, volleyball, an outdoor pool, and aerobics classes. The club has free child supervision. Hours are 6am to 10pm on weekdays, 8am to 6pm on weekends.

The **Sports Club–Las Vegas,** 3025 Industrial Rd., behind the Stardust Hotel (tel. 733-8999), has ten racquetball courts and two squash courts open 24 hours a day, seven days a week. (See the description of all the Sports Club's facilities, below.)

Eight courts at the **University of Nevada, Las Vegas,** 4505 S. Maryland Pkwy. (tel. 739-3150), are open Monday to Friday from 6am to 9:45pm, on Saturday from 8am to 8pm, and on Sunday from 10am to 6pm. There's a $2-per-hour charge for nonuniversity people (students and faculty have priority). Call before you go to find out if a court is available. Guest passes are obtained at the Physical Education Building, Room 306 or 312.

GOLF

Golf has reigned as the most popular outdoor sport in Las Vegas for years. Tennis enthusiasm has grown so fast, however, that golf soon may be in second place. At any rate, many major courses cater to visiting golfers.

The **Black Mountain Country Club,** at 501 Country Club Dr. in nearby Henderson (tel. 565-7933), is semiprivate, requiring reservations four days in advance. It's 18 holes, par 72. Yardage: 6,307 regular, 5,666 ladies. There are also a driving range, coffee shop, cocktail lounge, and dining room. The greens fee, including golf cart, is $25 on weekdays, $30 on weekends and holidays. The course opens at 6am.

The **Craig Ranch Golf Club,** located at 628 W. Craig Rd. (tel. 642-9700), is public. It's 18 holes, par 70. Yardage: 6,001 regular, 5,221 ladies. A driving range, pro shop, and snack bar complete the picture. The greens fee is $9, plus $6 for a cart, for 18 holes. The course opens at 6am, and you can book tee times up to seven days in advance.

The **Desert Inn Hotel and Casino,** 3145 Las Vegas Blvd. South (tel. 733-4444), also gets the nod from champions. It's an 18-hole, par-72 course. Yardage: 7,108 championship, 6,633 regular, 5,809 ladies. The Desert Inn is a PGA, Senior PGA, and LPGA tour stop. It has a driving range, putting green, pro shop, and restaurant. The golf director is Dave Johnson, and Kevin Paulsen is the head pro. This is an excellent driving course, with undulating greens. Play is restricted to guests (and those playing with guests). The greens fee is $75 weekdays, $100 weekends for registered guests, including carts; $100 and $135, respectively, for outside guests. You should call to reserve a starting time.

The **Desert Rose Golf Club,** 5483 Club House Dr. (tel. 438-4653), is 18 holes, 6,511 yards, par 71. There are a driving range, newly remodeled pro shop with rental clubs, restaurant, and cocktail lounge. The greens fee for 18 holes is $22 for nonresidents on weekdays and weekends. A cart will cost an additional $8 per person. If you need to rent clubs, they're available for $12. This is a well-managed county course, with good greens and one of the best yardage cards I've ever seen for a public course. The restaurant serves breakfast from 7 to 10:30am, including omelets and pancakes. The luncheon menu has a variety of burgers, sandwiches, melts, chicken fingers, and salads. The restaurant also has a full bar, plus draft beer by the mug, too-tall glass, or pitcher.

The **Dunes Country Club,** 3650 Las Vegas Blvd. South (tel. 737-4749), is an 18-hole championship course, 6,571 yards, par 72. There are a clubhouse, locker room, pro shop with rental clubs, coffee shop, and cocktail lounge. The greens fee is $60 for hotel guests on weekdays, including a mandatory cart, $70 on weekends; it is $70 and $80, respectively, for nonguests. The Dunes course is interesting, with its long par 5s and par 3s that have quite a few well-placed traps.

The **Las Vegas Indian Wells Country Club** (formerly the Showboat Country Club) is at 1 Showboat Country Club Dr., off Sunset and Green Valley Parkway (tel. 451-2106). This is an 18-hole, par-72, championship golf course. Yardage: 6,967 championship, 6,473 regular, 6,134 ladies. Other club facilities include a pro shop, putting green, driving range, and a clubhouse with a coffee shop and cocktail lounge. The greens fee is $55 throughout the week, including a mandatory cart. This is a challenging course and has been the site of the Seniors Open. The course opens at 6am.

The **Las Vegas Municipal Golf Course,** 4349 Vegas Dr. (tel. 646-3003), is 18 holes, par 72. Yardage: 6,335 regular, 5,734 ladies. There are a lighted driving range, pro shop, coffee shop, and cocktail lounge. The course is a good test of your short game, especially on the back side. Greens have been remodeled. The greens fee is $9 for residents and $11 for nonresidents. The course opens at 6am.

The **Sahara Country Club,** located at 1911 Desert Inn Rd. (tel. 796-0016), is a public course. It has 18 holes, par 71. Yardage: 6,815 championship, 6,418 regular, 5,761 ladies. It's a tough driving course with some water. Greens have been remodeled. There are a pro shop and a full-service restaurant and bar on the premises. The greens fee is $60, including the mandatory cart-rental fee. The course opens at daylight.

The **Tropicana Country Club,** 66 E. Tropicana Ave. (tel. 739-2457), is located across Tropicana Avenue from the hotel. It has 18 holes, par 70. Yardage: 6,647 championship, 6,107 regular, 5,787 ladies. The Tropicana has more character than most desert courses.

[handwritten annotations: "$50" near Las Vegas Indian Wells; Tropicana Country Club circled with arrow → "NO LONGER EXISTS"]

It's hilly, with many traps and trees. The country club building, lined with imposing columns, faces Tropicana Avenue. The coffee shop and cocktail lounge are located there. There are also a pro shop and driving range. The greens fee, including the mandatory cart rental, is $35 for hotel guests and $45 for visitors. The course opens at 6am.

BOWLING

After you've seen the bowling alleys at the **Showboat Hotel,** 2800 E. Fremont St. (tel. 385-9153), you'll never want to bowl anywhere else. The hotel expanded the number of lanes to 106, and they're the most modern and best-equipped in the world. There's also an excellent pro shop. They're kept busy day and night, and there's a snack bar at the alleys as well as a free kiddie playroom with a full-time attendant.

RODEO

Top rodeo stars compete for the prize money at rodeos in Las Vegas. Check local papers for events and dates, but the National Finals are usually held in December. It's a shame that most big rodeos don't schedule their Las Vegas meets far enough in advance to list them here. They're exciting western shows that appeal to everyone, a combination of carnival antics and cowboy grit.

The **Helldorado,** rated the 13th most important rodeo in the world by the Pro-Rodeo Cowboy's Association, is an annual event; it takes place in late May or early June.

A HEALTH CLUB

Although many of the Strip hotels have health clubs, none offers the amazing range of facilities that you'll find at the **Sports Club –Las Vegas,** 3025 Industrial Rd., right behind the Stardust Hotel (tel. 733-8999). Opened in 1978, this posh club for men and women is the best-equipped, best-run, and most luxurious I've ever seen. It has 12 racquetball/handball courts; two squash courts; two tennis courts; a full gymnasium for basketball and volleyball; free exercise equipment; an outdoor pool; a 60-foot-long indoor swimming pool; indoor and outdoor jogging tracks; saunas, steam rooms, Jacuzzis, and siesta rooms; sunbathing areas; a pro shop; men's and women's skin care and hair salons; a tanning salon; an excellent baby-sitting service; and a restaurant, bar, and social lounge. Aerobics classes are held at frequent intervals throughout the day. There's even a masseur on the premises. And it's open 24 hours a day.

Many celebs work out here—I've seen Susan Anton, Engelbert Humperdinck, Mike Tyson, Jerry Lewis, and J.J. Walker pumping iron at the Sports Club. The cost for a single visit is $20, or $15 if you're staying at a local hotel; reduced weekly and monthly rates are available.

HORSEBACK RIDING

About 30 minutes by car from midtown Las Vegas is **Bonnie Springs Ranch** in Old Nevada, Nevada, 1 Gun Fighter Lane (tel.

875-4191), which actually is only 18 miles from the city line, straight out of town on West Charleston Boulevard (next to the "wild west" attraction, Old Nevada). Lots of animals—pigs, goats, sheep, cows, turkeys, a buffalo, coyote, racoon, and skunks—are kept in a petting zoo at this rustic desert oasis, and horses are available for riding. Horse rental costs $12 per hour for a one-hour guided ride. There's a good restaurant and bar. The restaurant overlooks a small duck pond, the cedar tables are hand-hewn and rugged, and the menu is written on whisky bottles. The menu is surprisingly gourmet, offering mostly steak and seafood entrees as well as sandwiches, and homemade pies for dessert.

OTHER ADVENTURES

If you'd like to know some out-of-Vegas options for adventure tripping, the experts are **Adventure guides, Inc.,** 36 E. 57th Street, New York, NY 10022 (tel. 212/355-6334). You can send for their 256-page book, *Adventure Travel North America* by Pat Dickerman ($12 postpaid). It tells not only about rafting trips but also about mountaineering, cycling, four-wheel drive trips, and cattle drives. There are special trips geared to young people, as well as ranches that you can stay at, in Dickerman's other book, *Farm, Ranch, and Country Vacations* ($12 postpaid). The folks at Adventure Guides can also help you plan adventure trips using Las Vegas as a departure point.

IX

LAS VEGAS SHOPPING

There are always useful bits of information that aren't "big" enough for a special chapter—or they don't fit a particular category. Hence, this Department of Miscellany.

SHOPPING
There are shops in most of the big hotels, but for resort fashions, at boutique prices, the most complete shopping places in Las Vegas are the Boulevard Mall, the Meadows, and the Fashion Show.

The Malls
The fully air-conditioned and enclosed **Boulevard Mall**, 3528 S. Maryland Pkwy., between Twain Avenue and Desert Inn Road, has stores arranged in arcade fashion along a central walk of tile and carpeting. Plentiful benches are placed throughout the mall, and there's a big central fountain beneath a domed skylight set in high, vaulted ceilings. Potted plants and trees add a bit of charm.

Over 70 stores, snack bars, and restaurants are located at the Boulevard, and they occupy a total of a million square feet. A movie theater installed by the American Broadcasting Company shows first-run movies. Parking is provided for 5,800 automobiles.

Broadway, Sears, and Penney's are the largest stores in the mall. Each carries the wide range of products usually sold in department stores. You can also purchase a turtle, parrot, or guinea pig at the Docktor Pet Center; smoked cheese, fish, and the like at Hickory Farms of Ohio; and wonderful, sexy, skimpy bits of almost nothing at Frederick's of Hollywood. Those are just a few of the Boulevard stores; whatever you want—fabrics, clothing, hardware, shoes, automotive supplies, or trophy engraving—you'll find it here. There's also a B. Dalton bookstore; bookstores—except those selling X-rated adult literature—are scarcer than ice water in hell in this town.

From the Strip, the Boulevard Mall is a short bus ride away. It's open weekdays from 10am to 9pm, Saturday to 6pm, and Sunday from 11am to 5pm. The Boulevard Mall also has valet parking.

One of the largest of the Vegas malls, the multimillion-dollar **Meadows** opened its million square feet of shopping area at 4300 Meadows Lane several years ago. It has over 100 shops, restaurants, and snack bars, including four major department stores—the Broadway, Dillards, Sears, and Penney's—and parking space for 4,500 vehicles. Fountains and trees ameliorate the starkness of the ultramodern, high-ceilinged architecture.

You can get just about anything you can afford to pay for at the Meadows—from jogging shoes to maternity clothes; from children's toys to adult games; from health food to chow mein, burgers, and pizza. There are over 20 restaurants and snack and food stores on the premises. It's also a good place to look for shoes; you have a choice of 16 shoestores plus the department stores.

The Meadows is open weekdays from 10am to 9pm, Saturday to 6pm, and Sunday from noon to 5pm.

The **Fashion Show,** 3200 Las Vegas Blvd. South, at the corner of Spring Mountain Road near the Frontier Hotel, is a newer addition to the world of Las Vegas shopping. The doors opened February 13, 1981, giving the city an early Valentine gift. It was quite a celebration—a black-tie gala, highlighted by a fashion show of one-of-a-kind couture creations. Many of the world's leading designers—including Adolfo, Geoffrey Beene, Bill Blass, Bob Mackie, and Pauline Trigère—were on hand to show their interpretations of the "Las Vegas look." (Bill Blass described his ruffed creations for Vegas as "haute glamour and pulsating heat.") And since no event in Vegas would be complete without celebs, the Fashion Show borrowed a page from Hollywood and had the entertainers put their handprints and signatures in wet cement. The result is the mall's Promenade of Stars, which includes the prints of Danny Thomas, Doc Severinsen, Johnny Carson, Juliet Prowse, Tony Bennett, Anthony Newley, Wayne Newton, Steve Lawrence, and Eydie Gormé.

This totally enclosed and air-conditioned mall, the largest in the city, also has valet parking. It is a most luxurious environment in which to shop. There are multitiered planters filled with mature trees, flowering plants, bushes, and ground cover. A unique ramp-staircase system was designed to showcase fashion shows in the central court, and clerestory skylight windows provide natural light while conserving energy.

The 34-acre site is home to 140 shops and services. Some of the finest retailing names are represented here. Major department stores include Neiman-Marcus, Saks Fifth Avenue, Bullock's, Goldwaters, and Dillards. There are designer boutiques such as Uomo, Cache, and Lillie Rubin. And there's even a branch of Abercrombie & Fitch. Other services include four airline ticket counters: TWA, Eastern, Western, and United Airlines.

Of course, there are numerous eating places. Fast food is represented by Orange Julius, Hot Dog on a Stick, and Herbie Burgers. Fajitas, Renzios, Magelby's Muffins, Le Croissant Shoppe, Ice Cream Shoppe, Yang's Wok, Schlotzskys, and the Sbarro Italian Eatery add an international note. And for dessert, there's Häagen-Dazs, Heidi's Frozen Yogurt, Cinnabon, and Mrs. Fields Cookies.

The Fashion Show is open weekdays from 10am to 6pm (Thursday and Friday to 9pm), Saturday to 6pm, and Sunday from noon to 5pm. There's free parking for 3,500 cars.

For Gifts

For jewelry, first try **M. J. Christensen's,** 856 E. Sahara Ave., between Paradise Road and Maryland Parkway (tel. 732-0136). It's open Monday through Saturday from 10am to 5:30pm. Christensen's has two branches, one in the Meadows Mall at 4300 Meadows Lane (tel. 878-7832) and a second in the Renaissance West Shopping Center, 4001 S. Decatur, at Flamingo and Decatur (tel. 365-1211).

For silver and furniture, **Bertha's,** a few doors away at 896 E. Sahara Ave. (tel. 735-3711), is open Monday through Saturday from 10am to 5:30pm.

Very good for gifts and featuring some of the finest names in leather (perhaps a briefcase or handbag for yourself) is **El Portal Luggage and Gifts,** in the Fashion Show Mall at 3200 Las Vegas Blvd. South (tel. 369-0606). It's open Monday through Friday from 10am to 9pm, Saturday to 6pm, and Sunday from noon to 5pm. El Portal also has a shop in the Boulevard Mall at 3574 S. Maryland Pkwy. (tel. 735-6433), one at McCarran Airport (tel. 736-0076), and one at the Meadows Mall, 4300 Meadows Lane (tel. 870-3121).

For handsome turquoise and silver Indian jewelry in Navajo and Zuni motifs (among others), try **Trader Bill's,** 324 Fremont St., at Fourth Street (tel. 384-4408), open daily from 9am to 6pm. You can also buy Las Vegas souvenirs here. A special feature is a complete line of authentic moccasins for men, women, and children.

Also be sure to stop at the **Desert Indian Shop,** 108 N. Third St., between Fremont Street and Ogden Avenue (tel. 384-4977), especially notable for its authentic and imaginative collection of both Navajo and Hopi work. Artifacts of the "Old West" are a specialty here. It is open Monday through Saturday from 10am to 5pm.

Another gift shop at the **Alpine Village Inn** has select pewterware, cuckoo clocks, and such (details are in Chapter IV).

ETHEL M. CHOCOLATES

At the turn of the century, Ethel Mars and her husband began making fine chocolates in a little candy kitchen. This small enterprise developed into some very familiar names in the world of candy: Milky Way, 3 Musketeers, Snickers, Mars Almond Bars, and M & M's. With all this success, it was still Ethel Mars's dream to make the finest boxed chocolates in the world.

Ethel M. Chocolates are made only in Las Vegas in an ultramodern factory. It's open daily from 9:30am to 4:30pm for self-guided tours. Over 1,000 people a day visit the factory to watch candy being made. The best time to go is on weekday mornings when most of the activity goes on. Guests view the process through large glass windows and video monitors. All the equipment is marked to aid in the understanding of the process. If you can't time your visit for the morning, the video shows do follow the process, and people are always at work doing something. Your tour ends in the beautiful chocolate shoppe done in pinks and mauve with etched-glass and brass touches. This is where you can decide for yourself if these are the world's best chocolates. The candies, alcoholic (including the great liqueurs) and nonalcoholic, are on sale here for $11.95 a pound.

The chocolate factory is located at 2 Cactus Garden Dr., just off

Mount Vista and Sunset Road in the Green Valley Business Park, six miles from the Strip (tel. 458-8864). It's just a 15-minute drive from the Strip; take Tropicana Boulevard east and follow the signs.

An additional benefit of visiting the chocolate factory is the adjoining two-and-a-half-acre cactus garden. Designed and landscaped under the direction of Gary Lyons, curator of the Desert Garden of the Huntington Library and Botanical Gardens in California, it features cacti and succulents from all over the world. It's a photographer's paradise. Both attractions are free.

FUN BOOKS

Many of the casinos—especially those downtown—give out fun books full of coupons for free nickels, meals, double-your-money bets on blackjack, bingo cards, and so forth. One place to find coupons to get the fun books is newsletters such as *Today in Las Vegas, Tour Guide of Las Vegas, Vegas Visitor, Marquee,* and *What's On in Las Vegas;* you'll usually find them free at your hotel. They're often chock-full of additional discount coupons—sometimes so many that you could eat and gamble free for a week off one issue. Fun books are also given out at car-rental places.

X

KIDS' LAS VEGAS

It wasn't uncommon in the old days to see children kicking their heels on the sidewalk, their noses virtually pressed to the outside windows of the glittering casinos while their parents gambled away indoors.

This wasn't so bad when their parents were having a short fling, but it bordered on child neglect when a winning (or losing) streak forced the gamblers to make a day of it.

One of the most far-reaching projects for handling children is the **Hilton Youth Hotel**—a $2-million facility built specially for children, with supervision, popular activities, and even dormitories. Guests at the Las Vegas Hilton can leave children with experienced counselors for about $5 per hour or $30 for an overnight stay (calculated from midnight to 8am). The child must be three years or older and must be toilet trained. The Youth Hotel is open from 8am to 10pm all year round. It's open for overnight stays seven days a week from mid-June until Labor Day and during weekends and holidays during the rest of the year. There's a playground for the younger kids and instruction in fencing, baseball, arts and crafts, and photography for subteens and teenagers. The children are encouraged to become involved in what interests them most, even if it's only listening to the jukebox or reading. Closed-circuit television supervises the dormitories at night.

Another excellent choice for families traveling with kids is the **Circus Circus,** where so many activities are geared toward youngsters that I dare any child to ask the proverbial "What can I do?" First, of course, there are the continuous circus acts under the Big Top from 11am to midnight—clowns, acrobats, aerialists, tightrope walkers, and other thrilling attractions. All the circus acts can be seen from the mezzanine, a huge area filled with arcade and midway games, a veritable junior casino where the winnings are stuffed animals and the like. There are electronic games, balloons to shoot at, skeeball, and pinball machines galore.

One very good thing about the mezzanine is that it overlooks the casino—a very secure feeling for kids who can look down and wave to mom and dad.

Bally's—Las Vegas has a game room for kids—an arcade of about 54 machines with skeeball, pinball, electronic games, and air hockey. It also offers a baby-sitting service (tel. 737-4111) from 8am to 8pm. Sitters read stories and play games with the kids. Rates are $4 an hour ($5 an hour for those not toilet trained).

The **Omnimax Theatre** at **Caesars Palace** is a great place to take—or send—the kids. There are continuous showings from 11am to midnight, and children under 12 pay $4 (adults pay $5) for admission. Details are in Chapter VII.

Kids love **Ripley's Believe It or Not Museum** at the **Four Queens Hotel** downtown. There are over 1,000 exhibits and 54 wax figures on display. Various rooms cover nature's oddities, as well as those in art and music. The squeamish might prefer the interesting Oriental gardens to the torture cave. The exhibit is open from 9am to midnight weekdays, to 1am Friday and Saturday. Admission is $5 for adults, $3 for children under 12; it's free for those under 5.

Most kids, over and under 21, are fascinated by the **Imperial Palace Auto Collection,** at the hotel of the same name. You can ogle or drool over 200 vintage and special-interest cars, including those I've described in detail under the hotel listing in Chapter III.

You can also take the kids bowling at the 106 lanes at the **Showboat Hotel,** open round the clock. And if you'd like to bowl yourself but your children are too young for the sport, you can leave them at the Showboat's free playroom (with attendant) for up to three hours.

If these aren't enough places to amuse the kiddies, consider the above-described **Ethel M.**—the chocolate factory paradise, with its free tour. Then there's the **Las Vegas Museum of Natural History,** 900 N. Las Vegas Blvd. (tel. 384-3466), with its life-size moving (yes, I did say "moving"), roaring dinosaurs and skeletons of prehistoric creatures in a lifelike setting. It's scheduled to reopen at its new home by the beginning of 1991. And finally, **Bonnie Springs Ranch/Old Nevada,** with its petting zoo, Old West villains, shootouts, opera show, and even an old mine, is detailed below.

The **Sports Club–Las Vegas,** a 24-hour health club with 12 racquetball courts, also has baby-sitters on hand to take care of your children while you work out. (See Chapter VIII for details on the Sports Club.)

If you're not staying at or visiting any of the above establishments, you might inquire about baby-sitting at your hotel. Otherwise, you can avail yourself of the services of one of the numerous baby-sitting agencies around town.

The **Las Vegas Babysitting Agency,** 1900 Ginger Tree Lane (tel. 457-3777), charges $38 for 4 hours (minimum) for one to three children from one family; it is $9 per hour thereafter.

Reliable Babysitting, 4301 Avondale Ave. (tel. 451-7507), charges $4.50 an hour for up to two children in one family, with a minimum of $22 for one or two kids, $24 for three or four, and $26 for five or six.

Both of these agencies provide adult sitters only, all of whom have been cleared with the Health and Sheriffs departments. They also arrange their own transportation.

XI

DAY TRIPS FROM LAS VEGAS

1. PARK IN THE DESERT
2. MUSEUMS
3. BONNIE SPRINGS RANCH/OLD NEVADA

Several companies offer tours of the Las Vegas area. The **Gray Line,** 1550 S. Industrial Rd. (tel. 384-1234, or toll free 800/634-6579), offers a 6½-hour City Tour for $26 per person; it covers downtown Casino Center, the Liberace Museum, the Boulevard Mall, the University of Nevada campus, plush residential areas (past some of the stars' homes), the Ethel M. chocolate factory, and Strip attractions. Lunch is included.

The Gray Line also offers several trips to Hoover Dam, ranging in price from $17 to $30 per person. Some of these tours include lunch, a narrated boat cruise on Lake Mead, and a tour of historical museums and Sam's Town Western Emporium. There are daily tours to Red Rock Canyon; a desert tour including Valley of Fire; and Laughlin, Nevada.

Overnight trips to the Grand Canyon ($95 per person, double occupancy; $123 per person, single occupancy) and Zion/Bryce ($100 per person, double occupancy; $125 per person, single occupancy) are also available through the Gray Line. Other tours offered are Mount Charleston, Lee Canyon, a Grand Canyon Land/Air Tour, and a Colorado River Raft Tour—not a dull one among them. The Colorado River Raft Tour is an exciting float trip (without rapids) on a Coast Guard–approved river raft. It takes you through the majestic Black Canyon, where you'll see, among other things, warm water springs bubbling out of the cliffs and perhaps a bighorn sheep. Lunch is served at Willow Beach, and your trip takes you down past the Willow Beach trout hatchery. A Gray Line bus takes you back to your hotel and the glitter of Las Vegas. The tour price is $70 per person.

There are several nighttime tours offered by the Gray Line. One such is the nightclub tour, which begins with dinner and show— *Folies Bergère* at the Tropicana. This dazzling extravaganza includes French can-can acts, a Rolls-Royce onstage, live monkeys, a horse, acrobats, magicians, and elaborately costumed beauties in all their sequined-and-feathered or birthday-suit splendor. In between shows, you tour the glittering Strip. Then it's on to the Imperial Palace for *Legends in Concert*. You get two drinks at the latter show; all tips and gratuities are taken care of at both shows, and round-trip transportation to and from your hotel also is included. Price per person is $62. This tour does not operate on Thursday or Sunday.

All the tour services operate pickup systems and will collect you in time for the particular tour. Arrangements can be made either through the bell captain at your hotel or by making a direct call to the service by phone.

1. Park In the Desert

With infinite wisdom, Las Vegas has created a park in a cool oasis about ten miles out of town in the desert. This is the **Floyd R. Lamb State Park** (tel. 486-5413) at 9200 Tule Springs Rd., a shady grove of lawns and trees off U.S. 95 to the northwest.

Floyd R. Lamb State Park represents a part of the Las Vegas area's history, first as Tule Springs, an oasis and a watering stop for Native Americans, and later as a working and dude ranch. The Native Americans who first came to the oasis called themselves the "tudini" (desert people); these were the ancestors of the Southern Paiutes. During the early 1900s, Tule Springs became a major watering hole for travelers going to and from the gold fields. The town subsequently went through several incarnations—from a bootlegging center to a ranch housing gals and dudes waiting out residency requirements for divorce.

The park was the site of the Tule Springs Archeological Expedition, which found evidence of the presence of humans dating back over 11,000 years; it was thus one of the oldest confirmed sites of human habitation in western North America. Most important were findings of the remarkable fossil remains of mammoths, bison, camels, and other Pleistocene fauna.

Today the park offers a variety of daytime activities in tree-shaded groves nestled next to four small lakes. There are barbecue grills; picnic tables; and a casual collection of chickens, ducks, geese, and peacocks (none for the eating) who wander the lawns and park grounds.

Fishing is permitted in the lakes, provided that you have a valid Nevada fishing license (children under 12 do not need one). The lakes are stocked with catfish and bluegill. A trapshooting range concession open to the public is also located inside the park.

Apart from eating, fishing, and taking a break from the rigors of the gaming tables, there are lots of other things to do at the park. In the morning, you can take a bird walk around the ponds to look for yellow-headed blackbirds, great blue herons, and an elusive pair of wood ducks. Or you might want to go on the Tule Springs Ranch tour or even the arboretum walk. But above all, be sure to call and ask about the Special Events. In the past these have included demonstrations of dressage and free-style riding, games on horseback, horse-and-cart demonstrations with Morgans, and square-dancing demonstrations, among other enjoyments.

The park is open year around (closed Christmas and New Year's) from 8am to sunset. Entrance fees are $3 per vehicle.

---

2. Museums

Right on the campus of the University of Nevada, Las Vegas, 4505 Maryland Pkwy., at University Road, is the **UNLV Museum of Natural History** (tel. 739-3381), which has an interesting collection of live animals from the surrounding desert area. You can view specimens representative of the geology, biology, archeology, and ethnography of the southern Great Basin/Upper Mohave Desert natural regions. Exhibits include pre-Columbian pottery, Navajo rugs, Indian silver and turquoise jewelry, and photographs of early Las Vegas. The museum also features a large desert garden. The museum and gift shop are open Monday through Friday from 9am to 5pm and Saturday from 10am to 5pm. Admission is free.

Much more typical of Las Vegas is the **Liberace Museum,** 1775 E. Tropicana Ave., just east of Paradise Road (tel. 798-5595). The museum is a remarkable collection of memorabilia spanning the whole of Liberace's extraordinary career. Recently the museum was expanded into three exhibit areas—the main section houses the cars, pianos, and celebrity galleries; the annex displays the costume and jewelry collections as well as a re-creation of Liberace's office and bedroom; and the library contains Liberace's miniature piano collection and music arrangements and a photo history of his life and family. Guests to the Spanish-style structure are greeted at a piano-shaped desk; the marble floors reflect the sparkle of the ever-present candelabra, crystal, and jewels. A recent addition to the exhibits is Liberace's awesome stage jewelry, including a candelabra ring with platinum candlesticks and diamond flames and a piano-shaped ring containing 260 diamonds and keys of real ivory and black jade.

Included among his many costumes are a Czar Nicholas uniform with 22-karat-gold braiding and a blue velvet cape styled after the coronation robes of King George V (it's covered with $60,000 worth of rare chinchilla). As you would expect, there are many pianos in the collection, including a French Boulle, a Chickering concert grand once owned by George Gershwin, and a piano played by Chopin. Among the new exhibits is a collection of rare Moser crystal from Czechoslovakia—a magnificent service for 12 with 14 glasses for each setting. It is one of only two such handmade collections; the other is owned by Queen Elizabeth. A fleet of classic, customized cars features a red, white, and blue Rolls-Royce used in a 1976 Bicentennial salute. It all provides a peek into the world of "Mr. Showmanship," who performed to SRO audiences whenever he appeared in Las Vegas.

The Liberace Museum is open daily from 10am to 5pm and

Sunday from 1 to 5pm. The tax-deductible entry fees of $6.50 for adults, $4.50 for seniors, and $2 for children 6 to 12 (who must be accompanied by an adult) furnish 25 American colleges and universities with scholarship money.

---

3. Bonnie Springs Ranch/Old Nevada

Some 20 miles west of Las Vegas is a group of attractions that afford a variety of enjoyable experiences. Bonnie Springs/Old Nevada is a combination ranch and Old West town that can be reached by driving due west on West Charleston Boulevard. As you leave Las Vegas proper, it's fascinating to see how the terrain changes. About 16 miles out of town, you enter the **Red Rock Canyon Recreation Lands,** an area of unusual red-and-yellow sandstone hills (you can see them on the horizon from Las Vegas) surrounding flatter lands full of desert flora such as yucca, cactus, and Joshua trees. Just off the main road there's a **Visitor Center** run by the Bureau of Land Management (tel. 362-1921), which is open Friday through Monday from 9am to 4pm. Here you can get information on the numerous attractions in the canyon. You might enjoy taking in the scenery on the 13-mile loop drive that starts here. (It's open daily from 7am to 6pm.)

About five miles beyond is **Old Nevada.** It's open daily from 10:30am to 5pm from November through April (until 6pm the rest of the year); admission is $5 for adults, $4 for seniors, and $3 for children. There's plenty of parking; on weekends and during the summer, a little train acts as a shuttle between the car lot and the entrance.

Old Nevada is a microcosm of an old western town. The main "street" is lined with weathered-wood buildings fronted by covered verandas. There are country stores, an old photography shop, an ice cream parlor, and a restaurant. You can view tableaux of the Old West in the Spirit of Old Nevada Wax Museum and peek into a replica of an old barbershop. Every hour or so there's an amusing old-time melodrama acted out in the saloon, complete with moustache-twirling villain and heroic-but-helpless "maiden"; and the square in front of the Sheriff's Office (where some very unsavory characters languish in jail) is the scene for frequent "shootouts" and "hangings." The Golden Queen Mine is a bit of a fun house; also available are a horseshoe pitching and a shooting gallery. All in all, there's a lot of fun to be had by kids and adults.

Next door is the **Bonnie Springs Ranch.** Here you can go horseback riding (see Chapter VIII for details), visit the petting zoo, and enjoy a drink or dinner at the bar and restaurant.

For those without transportation, Bonnie Springs Ranch/Old Nevada runs a shuttle bus to and from the city. Call 875-4191 for information on this and any other aspects of the attraction.

FARTHER AFIELD

Nevada is a most beautiful state, well worth a day's, five days', or even three weeks' exploration. As a matter of fact, the more time that you have, the more adventure awaits you. You can venture just out of Las Vegas or all the way to the Grand Canyon; either way, you'll have a marvelous western experience.

How? If you don't have your own car, you can rent one. If you don't want to do it on your own, take a guided tour by bus . . . or by plane!

SOME SIGHT-SEEING HISTORY

Back in the 1840s, when the gold-hunters headed west hoping to make a strike, most of them were too preoccupied to notice more than the barren deserts, although even these enthrall some people. But as disillusionment set in and as the California mines began to peter out, some of the erstwhile prospectors remembered Nevada's wide-open spaces, the majestic grandeur of its rocks and canyons, and the lush greenness of its oasislike valleys.

The people who settled here first were pioneers: Mormon farmers, miners, horsemen, gamblers . . . gradually supplemented by the bankers, merchants, lawyers, and businesspeople that give every community its necessary stability. Gambling, which was outlawed officially for a while, was always taken for granted in the state, and most people were relieved when it was finally legalized in 1931.

A ROUND-UP OF WHAT TO SEE AND DO

You can find slot machines, roulette tables, and craps games all over Nevada, but 90% of them are in the Reno, Lake Tahoe, and Las Vegas areas.

An Emphatic Warning

The U.S. Department of the Interior has printed advice to those who plan to drive throughout the area, and it should be heeded.

"A word of caution to desert travelers is advisable. Many parts of Southern Nevada are accessible only by rocky dirt roads, seldom traveled by anyone. When venturing into these areas, always advise the local sheriff or someone else of your destination and when you expect to return. Always carry extra water, food, gasoline, and clothing or blankets. A breakdown or accident in these areas could mean several days of hardship before you are rescued."

As a rule, too, "desert buggies" are the only sort of vehicle that will hold up in more rugged terrain; regular passenger cars are not suited for unpaved roads. Flares and other signal devices are suggested for those venturing into remote regions, which can be hazardous. Such expeditions are not for individuals who have had no special training or preparation for desert exploration.

About 100 miles south of Las Vegas and a stone's throw from the metropolis of Bullhead City, Arizona, is the fastest-growing gambling town in the United States—**Laughlin,** Nevada. Its main attraction is gambling on the Colorado River. I will discuss Laughlin in detail in Chapter XI.

For all but the compulsive gambler, though, it's worth taking a look at some of the other things around the state. Nevada's capital, **Carson City,** with its old homes and absorbing state museum, is about 200 miles to the northwest, in the same direction as the **Lake Tahoe** resort area and **Reno** (448 miles distant). The very lively "ghost town" of **Virginia City** is also in this area, in the northwest corner of the state.

Almost as accessible from Las Vegas is Arizona's **Grand Canyon**—225 air miles away, but reachable by one-day excursion trips —or the mysteriously bizarre **Death Valley** on the California/ Nevada border.

Less than one hour's drive southeast of Las Vegas is the magnificent **Hoover Dam,** whose construction back in the 1930s finally brought prosperity to all the regions within reach of the once-rampaging Colorado River. **Lake Mead,** which is becoming saltier with silt and evaporation processes, rises behind the dam. **Boulder City,** created as a home community for the thousands who labored on the building of the dam, is one of the state's few towns that bans gambling.

Yet another "wonder," 70 miles northwest of Vegas, is what's come to be known as the **Nevada Test Site**—more than 1,300 square miles of proving ground dominated by the Atomic Energy

Commission (AEC), which employs 10,000 people in the state's second-biggest "industry," after gambling. The AEC a while back was working on a deep-space nuclear rocket for manned travel to Mars and beyond. The area is desolate and forbidding, and not only because of the physical terrain. Top security prevails, and visitors are discouraged. (The AEC maintains a public information office in Las Vegas; tel. 295-1000.)

Nevada abounds in outdoor recreation opportunities. For a complete listing of camping sites, write to the **Nevada Commission on Tourism,** Capitol Complex, Carson City, NV 89710. Some of the more popular spots in the Las Vegas area are Lake Mead National Recreation Area, Valley of Fire State Park, and the Mount Charleston Area. At Lake Mead there is Boulder Beach and Las Vegas Bay (off Rte. 41); Callville Bay, Echo Bay, and Overton Beach (off Rte. 12); and Eldorado Canyon, Cottonwood Cove, and Davis Dam (off U.S. 95). Valley of Fire is located off U.S. 15 on Rte. 40, about 45 miles from Las Vegas. North of Las Vegas (off U.S. 95) is the Mount Charleston Area. There you'll find the Charleston Recreation Area (on Rte. 39) and the Lee Canyon Recreation Area (on Rte. 52).

1. The Mountains

In summertime, the mountains that encircle **Toiyabe Park,** about 40 miles northwest of Las Vegas, are as much as 30° to 40° cooler than the sweltering desert city, and a visit to this national park is a popular daytime trip. Two ravines provide access to the Spring Mountains, in which the park is situated—Kyle Canyon and Lee Canyon—and both of them lead westward off U.S. 95, about 15 miles apart.

Nevada Rte. 39 winds up for about 20 miles through **Kyle Canyon,** beginning its climb through sparse scrubland, the cactus and Joshua trees gradually giving way to pine and fir trees and pleasantly wooded slopes. The gorge is narrow to begin with, but it gradually widens, and near the mountains several summer homes are located among the trees.

The road eventually dead-ends where the woods become thicker, a small road leading to the lovely **Mount Charleston Restaurant and Lodge** (tel. 872-5408), which is open every day of the year, 24 hours a day (food is served from 8am to 10pm weekdays, to 11pm weekends). The restaurant has one of the biggest fireplaces in the West, heaped high with enormous logs, and the atmosphere, notwithstanding the cluster of slot machines, is pleasantly homey and comfortable.

It's a twilight-zone feeling to come from hot and air-conditioned Las Vegas to this sometimes snowy region. When you're sitting before a blazing fire with a hot buttered rum, it's a mite disorienting. And speaking of hot drinks before the fire, although the lodge does serve hot buttered rum, it also has a not-to-be-missed house specialty drink. Called Mount Charleston coffee, it's a concoction of coffee (a special Jamaican blend); brandy; Drambuie; and rich, homemade vanilla ice cream, topped with real whipped cream, a touch of nutmeg, and a cherry.

Of course, you'll probably want to dine before sitting around the fire with drinks. (Reservations are suggested for dinner on weekends.) The food is excellent, lovingly prepared and served. You might begin with a shrimp cocktail. The house specialty is prime rib, and with your entree you get a salad, a stuffed or baked potato, homemade rolls, and butter. For lighter fare, there's a half-pound cheeseburger with french fries. Entrees range in price from $9 to $20. For dessert there's also homemade pie for $2.50.

Mount Charleston has entertainment in the lounge—a combo on Sunday and a pianist Thursday to Saturday nights. There are special menus for breakfast and lunch.

Campgrounds with tables, fireplaces, and toilets are located farther up the woods along an undeveloped track, and a short walk will bring you to some falls.

About 15 miles farther up U.S. 95 is the turnoff to **Lee Canyon,** where a simple ski area (see below) has been developed. However, it isn't necessary to go back to the highway, because a splendid road winds through the mountains between the two canyons, connecting Rte. 39 with Nevada Rte. 52. The drive is a positively beautiful one.

One stop along the road: **Robber's Roost** is a mountain cave about half a mile from the road up a narrow gorge—it must be traversed on foot—which may or may not have been used by fugitives. At any rate, the isolated cave today is a popular spot with young Las Vegans, who like to go there and play guitars in the peace of the mountains.

Lee Canyon Ski Area (tel. 872-5462) has a cafeteria offering breakfast, lunch, and dinner during the ski season. A ski-rental shop and a 3,000-foot chair lift and T-bar are the sum total of the development so far. The ski area and its facilities are open from Thanksgiving (if there's snow) to Easter.

The road back down from Lee Canyon to the main highway, U.S. 95, is 20 miles of sheer delight. Starting amid the coniferous trees of the mountain slopes, it soon traverses a barren but beautiful semimoorland of cactus and Joshua trees. The contrast between the greenery and coolness of the mountains and the desolate brown sand and scrub of the valley floor is quite startling. To the right of the road, gently undulating foothills look as though they have been carved and smoothed by a giant sculptor, while in the distance the sun brings out the shades and colors of the different strata of rock in the surrounding hills.

Las Vegas is 28 miles away when you rejoin U.S. 95; the round trip to both canyons, therefore, is about 94 miles. For a skier, the best plan would be to spend the day at Lee Canyon and then finish at Mount Charleston for dinner.

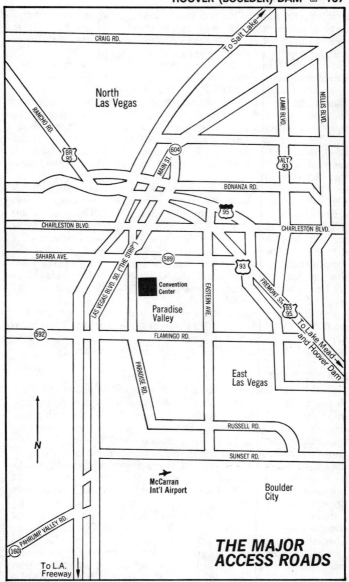

THE MAJOR
ACCESS ROADS

2. Hoover (Boulder) Dam

Until the 1930s, much of the southwestern United States
shared two natural problems—parched, sandy terrain that lacked

irrigation for most of the year and extensive flooding in spring and early summer, when the mighty Colorado River, fed by melting snow from its source in the Rocky Mountains, overflowed its banks and destroyed crops, lives, and property.

Finally, prodded by the seven states through which the river runs during the course of its 1,400-mile journey to the Pacific, Congress authorized construction of what came to be known as Hoover Dam. Completed in 1935, it not only stopped the annual floods but also became one of the world's major electrical generating plants, providing power to a score or more of surrounding communities.

Together with **Lake Mead** (the world's 16th-largest artificial lake), the dam has become a major recreation area whose boating, swimming, and fishing facilities attract more than three million visitors each year.

It's possible to take a bus from downtown Las Vegas to Boulder, about 25 miles southeast, and then on to Hoover Dam. Or you can take one of the sight-seeing tours offered by the Gray Line, 1550 S. Industrial Rd. (tel. 384-1234). The $20, 8-hour tour takes you not only to Hoover Dam—where you'll tour the plant and see a movie about the dam's construction—but also to Old Vegas and the Southern Nevada Museum. Lunch is included. Another tour, this one eight hours and priced at $30 (lunch included), visits Hoover Dam and Lake Mead. An excursion on the lake aboard the tour cruiser *Echo* is part of the trip.

What many people do, however, is drive. The best route is southeast, along Hwy. 93/95 through the industrial city of Henderson, past the new Las Vegas Downs racetrack, and on into Boulder City. If you do drive, try to avoid Saturday and Sunday.

BOULDER CITY

Although the city limits embrace an area of 33 square miles and shelter a population of about 13,000, Boulder appears to be little more than a main street to transient visitors driving through. Actually it's a pleasant, well-planned town—built only half a century ago as a model city to house the managerial and construction workers for the building of the vast dam. Located here are laboratories of the University of Nevada's Desert Research Institute, as well as similar facilities for the U.S. Bureau of Mines, the headquarters of the National Park Service for Lake Mead, and the regional headquarters of the Department of Energy. The city rose up in just a year, turning a desert waste into a community of 6,000—with homes, four churches, stores, restaurants, hotels, and even a 700-seat theater. The workers came from all over the country.

Today it harbors a dozen or so motels, tennis courts, swimming pools, and a park with picnic facilities. One of the most interesting spots is the Gold Strike Inn, where there's a lobby display of old-time slot machines, all in mint condition. Drop by the **Hoover Dam Visitors Bureau,** 1228 Arizona St. (tel. 293-1081), to see a free showing of the 28-minute movie, *The Story of Hoover Dam* (screened from 9:30am to 4:15pm), which was made during construction. The Bureau is open daily from 9am to 4:30pm.

ONWARD TO THE DAM

Some 200 or 300 yards past Boulder City, at the top of a slight incline, Lake Mead comes into view. It's quite eerie-looking, surrounded by sandy-colored rocky hills on which nothing seems to grow, sloping down to the water's edge.

You'll pass the Alan Bible Visitor Center, outlet for information about the Lake Mead National Recreation Area (about which I will say more later). And so on to the dam (which, curiously enough, crosses a state line and a time zone; it's an hour later on the east than it is on the west!). Hoover Dam is a magnificent project whose $175-million cost is gradually being repaid by the sale of inexpensive power to cities (Burbank, Glendale, Pasadena, and Los Angeles), states (Arizona and Nevada), and the water and electrical utilities of southern California.

A massive, horseshoe-shaped wall, more than 600 feet thick at the bottom and tapering to 45 feet thick where the road crosses it at the top, it acts as a plug between the canyon walls to hold back the millions of gallons of water in Lake Mead. Four concrete intake towers on the lake side drop the water down about 600 feet to drive turbines and create power, after which the water spills out into the river and continues south.

Because it was a product of the WPA period, all the architecture is on a grand scale: Even the rest rooms and the exhibition hall reflect an ornateness more typical of Radio City Music Hall than an engineering project.

The best way to understand the dam is to take one of the 35-minute tours ($2 for adults, children under 16 are free) that are conducted at regular intervals daily between 7:30am and 7:30pm Memorial Day to Labor Day (9am to 4:15pm the rest of the year). This is preceded by a free ten-minute orientation in the exhibition hall—a taped explanation of the course of the Colorado River and why it was necessary to dam it in the first place.

In addition, the exhibit building, open to the public, houses a model of a generating unit and a scale model of the Colorado River, with further information about the river and the workings of the dam. Over 22 million people have toured the dam and its immense power complex since guided tours were instituted in 1937. Last year over half a million visitors took the conducted tour through what has been called one of the Wonders of the World.

The tour begins with a one-minute elevator ride that drops you 44 stories (528 feet), almost to the level of the river on the Nevada side. Here the rocky cliffs are honeycombed with over seven miles of tunnels, but the tour takes you along only half a mile of them (all that space and not a slot machine to be seen!), a guide pointing out the seven-story-high turbine generators, each of which contains 800 tons of rotating units. The turbines are so complex and so enormous that each takes almost three years to manufacture and assemble.

The heroic scale of the dam is reflected in the art around it. On one side (Nevada) there is a magnificent pair of 30-foot-tall seated figures, the *Winged Figures of the Republic,* cast in bronze by sculptor Oskar Hansen. The sculptures are on black diorite bases.

When the dam was first being built, almost all the incredibly heavy pieces of equipment had to be lowered 600 feet to the river level from a cable railway at the road level overhead, and looking up now you can still see the control room for this cable operation overhanging the steep cliffs. The heads of people standing on the road and peering over look from here like the tiniest specks.

Across the river and through another long tunnel the tour pauses in a hollowed-out chamber above a section of one of the 30-foot-wide pipes that carry the water down to the turbines.

LAKE MEAD

Most of the lake's major attractions lie along its western shore, adjoining Nevada Hwy. 166; easiest access is from **Alan Bible Visitor Center,** maintained by the National Park Service. At the center, Hwy. 93 and Lakeshore Road (tel. 293-8906), overlooking the lake, you can pause to watch an educational movie and pick up a folder that lists nearby facilities and also carries safety tips both for wilderness areas (hiking and camping are popular in this region) and for those using boats on the lake. Two miles from here is Boulder Beach, with good swimming, a boat dock, a restaurant three miles from the Visitor Center, motels, trailer court, store, and camping facilities.

Waterskiing is an almost year-round sport on the lake, with complete equipment available for rent. And boats are also much in demand by fishermen, who came to fish by day or night in its clear, blue waters. Bass (largemouth and striped) is the most popular fish, with channel catfish and rainbow trout also numerous.

Farther up the lake, a mile or two north of Boulder Beach, is **Lake Mead Resort and Marina,** 322 Lakeshore Rd., Boulder City, NV 89005 (tel. 293-3484), departure point for boat tours and locale of a floating restaurant. It's open Monday through Friday to 9pm, Saturday and Sunday to 10pm. There's live music occasionally in the summer, and the bar stays open nightly until the action winds down.

You can also rent boats here. There are boats of all sizes available, from a 16-foot 15-horsepower fishing boat that rents for $15 per hour with a two-hour minimum ($50 per day) to a 19-foot 140-horsepower ski boat that costs $45 per hour with a two-hour minimum ($125 for four hours, $200 per day). Ski equipment and more sedate patio boats can also be rented. For example, you can rent a pontoon boat (with a gas barbecue and cooler) for $30 per hour (two-hour minimum), $90 for four hours, or $150 for the day. This marina is run by Seven Crown Resorts, Inc., which also operates the Echo Bay and Temple Bar marinas on Lake Mead. At **Echo Bay** (tel. 394-4000) you can even rent houseboats that sleep six to ten people, from $580 to $860 for a three-day weekend or $970 to $1,300 for a week. For information and advance reservations, you can call Seven Crown Resort's toll-free number, 800/752-9669.

Down the road apiece, the **Lake Mead Lodge,** 322 Lake Shore

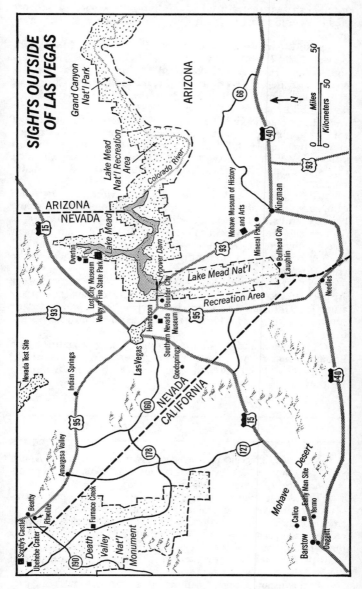

Rd., Boulder City, NV 89005 (tel. 702/293-2074), offers 43 re-modeled units with lake views. Facilities include a swimming pool, a steak-and-seafood restaurant, a coffee shop, a retail store, and a lounge. Rates are $47, single or double occupancy, and $62 for a room with two queen-size beds. Additional persons pay $6 per night. All units have bath but no phone or TV. Boat rentals are available.

Lake Mead Yacht Tours operated by the Lake Mead Ferry Service, 2200 E. Patrick Lane, Suite 21 (tel. 293-6180), has daily sight-seeing cruises from Lake Mead Marina, 23 miles from Las Vegas. They depart four times daily, year round, except Christmas, at 10:30am, noon, 1:30pm, and 3pm. Cost of the cruise is $8 for adults; children under 12 pay $4.

The average depth of Lake Mead is 250 feet. Different levels of the surrounding mountains expose layers of civilization. Precambrian rock on one island, for example, is estimated to be 750 million years old. Wild burros, cougars, big-horn mountain sheep, golden eagles, deer, and wild horses all roam the surrounding Sierra Madre ranges.

The entire 550-mile perimeter of Lake Mead is dotted with campsites, eight of them equipped with running water, picnic benches, and stoves. These are administered by the National Park Service, and rangers are on call (tel. 293-4041) 24 hours a day in case of emergency or for information. Camping is restricted to 30 days. A small charge of $5 per night (per campsite) is exacted at the entrance to each campsite.

Wildlife is very prevalent in the area, and hiking and exploring are popular, except in the middle of summer, when daytime temperatures top 100°. Sunglasses and a hat are strongly recommended for summer visitors; warm clothing is recommended for those visiting in winter.

Park rangers and naturalists present evening programs at the **Boulder Beach Amphitheater** in spring, summer, and fall; in fall, winter, and spring all-day conducted hikes leave from the Alan Bible Visitor Center.

---

3. Valley of Fire

Most people's conception of desert is of the Lawrence of Arabia variety—countless wastes of undulating sand broken only by an occasional ridge of dunes or oasis of palm trees.

The desert of America's Southwest bears hardly any resemblance to that romantic image. It stretches for hundreds of miles around Las Vegas in every direction—a seemingly lifeless tundra of reddish earth, shaped by time, climate, and subterranean upheavals into a million canyons and ridges. But it is far from lifeless: Deserts are natural homes for many fascinating species of plant and animal life.

In the distance, always seeming but a short walk away, the rugged cliffs and crags punctuate the irregular terrain as though in a giant's rock garden, changing through the color spectrum as the day gets shorter and the viewer gets nearer.

The **Valley of Fire State Park,** about 60 miles northeast of Las

Vegas, is the major example of bizarrely colorful rock formations in this part of the country. It's a popular one-day trip for visitors to the city and can be combined with a visit to Lake Mead, whose north-western shore almost skirts it, or made the subject of a separate excursion. This is the largest state park in Nevada—46,000 acres.

By car, the most interesting route is Las Vegas Boulevard north, then eastward along Lake Mead Boulevard. This will take you along North Shore Road through part of the Lake Mead National Recreation Area. Facilities for camping, fishing, picnicking, and swimming are available along this route. Visitors can stop for a meal at Callville Bay, Echo Bay, or Overton Beach. No concession facilities are available in the Valley of Fire.

The turnoff into the Valley of Fire is about four miles beyond the Overton Beach exit. A small interpretive station at the entrance has a display of maps and helpful information for park visitors.

The most scenic aspects of the Valley of Fire are the dominant Aztec sandstone formations. Wrinkled, etched, and scoured by time, these ancient rocks were formed in the Jurassic period, 135 to 150 million years ago.

Photographers, naturally, find the intricately shaped and brightly colored rocks fascinating, and in recent years Hollywood movie producers have begun to exploit this intriguing landscape. Burt Lancaster, Lee Marvin, Eva Marie Saint, Claudia Cardinale, and Gregory Peck have all shared starring roles with the natural wonders. The park is noted for its many diverse and whimsical formations—a duck, beehives, the "Rock of Gibraltar," the "Seven Sisters," and as many varied creatures as imagination can create. Most of these features are the result of chemical erosion aided by natural breakage of the brittle sandstone.

Fascinating Indian petroglyphs pecked into the rock walls and boulders can be seen throughout the park. These ancient rock writings are dramatic reminders of earlier cultures who traveled through this area on food-gathering and hunting expeditions. Fine examples of this rock art are found at **Atlatl Rock** and **Petroglyph Canyon**—both easily accessible from the main park roads.

At several park locations you can see petrified wood—the remains of ancient forests that washed into the area some 225 million years ago!

The many plants and animals seen in the park have developed elaborate strategies to survive the desert temperature extremes. Plant life includes creosote bushes, numerous types of cactus, primroses, and other vegetation. Desert animals such as kit foxes, jackrabbits, ground squirrels, lizards, and snakes avoid extreme desert conditions by venturing out only in the cooler evening hours. Often the only evidence of these mammals and reptiles is delicate tracks left in the fragile sand dunes. A lucky visitor, however, might even get to see a desert tortoise. Birds are also common within the park, and a great number of species can be observed.

A good place to begin your visit to the Valley of Fire is the air-conditioned **Visitor Center** on Hwy. 169, six miles west of North Shore Road (tel. 397-2088). It's open seven days a week from

8:30am to 4:30pm. Exhibits explain the origin and geologic history of the park's colorful sandstone, describe the ancient people who carved their cryptic rock-art panels on the canyon walls, and identify the plants and wildlife that you're likely to see. Postcards, books, slides, and film are on sale there.

Hiking trails, several picnic sites, a group-use area, and two campgrounds are available in the park. Most sites are equipped with tables, grills, water, and rest rooms. A fee ($4 per night per vehicle, $2 from June through August) is charged for use of the campground.

Although it is possible to drive right through the park and rejoin the main highway at the other side, an alternative route is to double back and visit the tiny town of **Overton,** in a surprisingly fertile valley replete with trees, vegetable crops, horses, and herds of cattle. You might find it a welcome contrast after the topography of the last 60 miles. Here you can obtain gas, food, and lodging.

Now primarily a residential area, Overton, settled in the late 1800s, once produced excellent lettuce, radishes, onions, melons, tomatoes, and alfalfa in quantities sufficient to supply large markets in southern California, Utah, and Las Vegas.

About one mile south of Overton (which is little more than a main street and a couple of bars and cafés) is the **Lost City Museum** (tel. 397-2193), commemorating the ancient Native American village that was discovered in 1924. The city's population reached one of the highest levels of Native American culture in the United States. Artifacts dating back 12,000 years are on display, and exhibits tell the story of the ancient Lost City settled and inhabited by prehistoric dwellers of the area.

The museum's main display is of the ancient Pueblo culture that inhabited this area between A.D. 300 and 1150. Old clay jars, dried corn and beans, arrowheads, necklaces of tiny seashells, and straw baskets—all are displayed, as are a few macabre skulls and bones. A large case full of local rocks—petrified wood, fern fossils, iron pyrites, green copper, and red iron oxide—together with manganese blown bottles, turned purple by the ultraviolet rays of the sun, occupies most of the rear room of the Lost City Museum.

Admission is $1 for those 18 and over. The museum is surrounded by reconstructed pueblos. It is open daily from 8:30am to 4:30pm.

---

4. Death Valley

It's barely possible to drive from Las Vegas to Death Valley and back in the same day, but it wouldn't make much sense. The nearest entrance to this famous national park is about 140 miles to the northwest (take U.S. 95 and turn off at Lathrop Wells).

In winter, spring, and fall, the only times when it's cool enough to be comfortable, the few accommodations in the valley itself are usually booked up several weeks ahead—so advance reservations are a must. These are the resort hotels at **Stovepipe Wells** and **Furnace Creek.**

The Furnace Creek Ranch, Hwy. 190, P.O. Box 1, Death Valley, CA 92328 (tel. 619/786-2345), is rustic and very "western" in feel, with accommodations in sprawling cabins, fairway-view units, and pool-view units. A green desert oasis, it offers an astounding number of facilities in addition—of course—to horseback riding. There are an 18-hole golf course, a large swimming pool, Ping-Pong, shuffleboard, bicycling, volleyball, basketball, two tennis courts, even movies and bingo. For dining there are a steak house, a coffee shop, and a cafeteria. As for the horseback riding, there are two escorted two-hour rides a day, which cost $10 per person.

The ranch is open year round, although some activities are not available in summer. During the summer accommodations are $65 per night for a redwood cabin with a shower. From October to June, it's $60 per night. Deluxe rooms, which are like modern hotel rooms with TVs, phones, and refrigerators, are $94. Rates are for one or two people.

Up the road apiece (a mile to be exact) is the luxurious and exclusive **Furnace Creek Inn,** P.O. Box 1, Death Valley, CA 92328 (tel. 619/786-2345), with its own supper club, the Oasis, offering nightly entertainment and gourmet fare. Typical entrees range in price from $25 to $35 and include filet mignon béarnaise and breast of capon Marengo; flambé desserts are a specialty. The Oasis is justly famous for its $15 champagne Sunday brunch, served from 11am to 2pm. Other facilities include four tennis courts, a restaurant/cocktail lounge, a swimming pool, and very lovely rooms. Of course, guests can also avail themselves of all the facilities back at the ranch.

The tile-roofed inn was built of adobe bricks by the Panamints over half a century ago in the opulent pre-Depression days. These days it's owned and operated by the Fred Harvey Company, about which I will say more later in this chapter. (The ranch was established even earlier—in the 1880s—originally to provide accommodations for men working in the borax mines.)

The inn is open from mid-October to mid-May only. Rates are on the Modified American Plan, which means that breakfast and dinner are included. They range from $200 to $230 per day, single occupancy, and $235 to $265 per day, double occupancy. An extra person is $50; children aged 5 to 11 can stay in their parents' room for $25 each.

Needless to say, Death Valley must be seen in daylight, and the jagged mountains with their subtly changing tones . . . the rippling sand dunes . . . snowy-looking salt flats . . . and endlessly undulating flatland—all hold their special beauty for the visitor who has time to appreciate it.

The best starting point is actually the Visitors' Center at **Furnace Creek,** a quarter mile north of the ranch on Hwy. 190 (tel. 619/786-2331). The center functions as a combination information area, auditorium, museum, and camping ground (trailers are very popular around here, and there are facilities for camping), which is open November 1 through Easter from 8am to 8pm seven days a week, to 5pm the rest of the year. There is an 18-minute orientation film shown hourly.

In 1988 Death Valley began charging a fee for entry into the National Monument. The fee per motor vehicle for a seven-day visit is $6, and for a bicycle or pedestrian the fee is $2.50. An annual area pass good for the calendar year is $16.

Big-horn sheep (stuffed), burros, hummingbirds, and kangaroo rats can all be inspected in the museum, which is probably the only place visitors do see these animals. There are many explanatory displays about the valley's geological evolution—how numerous flash floods over the ages have covered the floor with water, only to be dried out again throughout long centuries of baking sun.

In some places, salt is many feet thick on the valley floor, and a salty creek that runs north to south, disappearing underground and re-emerging from time to time, actually contains a tiny species of fish whose ancestors can be traced back to the beginning of the Ice Age. Although streams run down from the surrounding mountains at some times of the year, the valley receives less rainfall—less than two inches a year—than anywhere else in America. (By comparison, New York City receives 43 inches each year; Los Angeles, 15; and San Francisco, 22.) There have been occasions when Death Valley's entire annual supply of rainfall has been dumped from the clouds within one hour's storm—not in summertime, though, when temperatures of 110° F and 120° F are fairly common.

Roughly speaking, temperatures rise by 5½° for every 1,000-foot drop in elevation, and the heavy, cool air that drops down between the mountains is compressed (and heated), rising to make room for more cool air to take its place (so glad you asked). All you need to know about this is that if you're going to wander around the valley in summertime, be sure to have plenty of water with you; if your car breaks down, stay—sheltered—as close to it as possible.

Some things can live in the desert with little or no water—creosote bushes and mesquite trees, which put down deep, spreading roots, and the kit fox, which gets its moisture from other animals (it catches and eats sidewinder snakes, lizards, and bats).

The museum's evidence that the mastodon stalked across the land was removed as the track area was closed to the public. A cast of a Titano skull, an ancient rhinolike mammal, is displayed, however. Other milestones of history are uncovered in the different layers of rock—twisted and distorted from their geological sequence by the earthquakes that shattered the region eons ago.

The various living conditions that exist for plant life in the valley are defined poetically as "shady streamsides, mountaintops, sunbaked slopes, and salty flats."

Native Americans have always lived here and still do; they are believed to have been around when the luckless prospectors ("the 49ers") on their way to California were trapped by the valley's hostile environment and soon died of thirst and starvation. Their beads, baskets, arrowheads, and cornhusks are on display, side by side with old prospectors' tools and supplies. Many adventurers have tried their luck for gold and silver, and the northeast edge of the valley nearest Las Vegas is still dotted with ghost towns, such as Rhyolite (near Beatty), which were once thriving communities. Borax, a salty white mineral used for chemicals, paint, gasoline, glass, and detergents and as a preservative and a water softener, has been mined extensively in Death Valley for years, and another small museum, devoted to this activity, is located next to the Furnace Creek Ranch.

One of the most interesting attractions in Death Valley is an elaborate $2,000,000 structure, **Scotty's Castle.** It was built in the early 1920s by a Chicago millionaire, Albert Johnson, in association with a notorious pseudoprospector, storyteller, and publicity seeker, Walter E. Scott, better known as "Death Valley Scotty." Their story is one of a unique friendship that lasted for almost a half century.

The structure was originally called **Death Valley Ranch,** but Scotty publicized it—and the press always touted it—as Scotty's Castle. Spanish and Moorish in style and lavishly furnished in antiques and custom-made pieces, the castle stands in the northern section of Death Valley. It's about an hour's drive from either Stovepipe Wells or the Monument's headquarters at Furnace Creek.

Scotty was a frequent guest of Johnson's and is credited with suggesting the site for his desert home. After Johnson's death in 1948, Scotty lived on here until the end of his own life. No one has ever been able to discover whether Scotty, an ex-performer with Buffalo Bill's Wild West Show, actually had a gold mine in the desert or not. He did spend almost half a century prospecting in Death Valley, supported by various grubstakes, the most famous of them being from Albert Johnson. Up until his death in 1954, Scotty was frequently trailed into the desert, but no one ever located his mysterious mine. It appears now that there never was a mine, and that Scotty's real gold mine was Johnson.

The castle and grounds are open to visitors every day of the year, and there are regularly scheduled 45-minute tours of the interior. The tour is $5 for adults and $3 for children.

Near the castle is a volcanic crater, **Ubehebe Crater,** 490 feet deep, and two hours' drive from there is a fascinating mud playa called the "racetrack" because of the heavy stones that have been moved across it by strong winds, leaving clear tracks behind.

Another attraction in the extreme north section of the valley (starting just outside the old ghost town of Rhyolite with its house made of bottles and its abandoned mineshafts) is the 26-mile **Titus Canyon,** so narrow that traffic is one way throughout its entire length from Rhyolite to the northbound highway through the valley.

Near Furnace Creek is **Zabriskie Point,** a fascinating area of badlands and multicolored rock that was the scene of an Antonioni movie of the same name. A 1½-hour round trip will take you to **Dantes View,** which is the only place accessible by road from which you can view the entire panorama of the 130-mile valley.

There are, of course, numerous other sight-seeing spots for visitors with the time to spare. A comprehensive map of the valley can be obtained at the Furnace Creek Visitors' Center, from which various expeditions are regularly conducted.

5. Ghost Towns

The shadowy phenomenon of ghost towns—once-flourishing areas that were later deserted and abandoned—has always been an intriguing and romantic image to just about everyone.

Many of these towns began with a lone traveler who serendipitously stumbled on mineral-rich rocks while out on another pursuit —perhaps tracking game, strayed livestock, or criminals. He would mark off his area, stuff his pockets and knapsack with specimens, and rush off to the nearest mine with his claim. If there was anything to it, adventurers, drifters, and raggedy prospectors would soon flock to the area, set up meager lodgings, break out picks and shovels, and set to work.

Often this initial feverish effort would quickly prove fruitless, but if the yield seemed in the least bit promising, word would spread and entrepreneurs would arrive with provisions. Soon a main street would develop around a general merchandise store, followed by other shops and the inevitable mining-camp saloons, gambling houses, and red-light district. A camp newspaper would come into being, and more stores and more permanent buildings of stone, brick, and concrete would be erected. Eventually a real town would evolve, with schools, churches, and perhaps electricity and even a railroad station.

But then the mines would begin to dry up. Little by little, businesses would fold, and the population would dwindle. Vandalism, wind, and fire would ravage the remaining structures, leaving only ghost-inhabited remnants of what had been. And so the town died.

Nevada has at least 40 such towns, ranging from those that still (or again) have a small population centered around a store, a bar, and perhaps a post office, to those that are now merely relics and rubble. The latter are perhaps the more mysterious and evocative.

A third category are the Disney-esque artificially revived-for-tourism towns, often with rides and attractions, not to mention cutesy misspelled "olde" signs. One of these, Calico (in California), is actually owned by Walter Knott of the Berry Farm fame.

The following listings run the gamut. To some you need to bring a vivid and perhaps visionary imagination. Others, such as McDonald's, "do it all for you." These are the ones that you should probably seek out if you're traveling with kids.

All are within driving distance of Las Vegas since most are in Nevada; some are in accessible areas of adjoining states.

GOODSPRINGS

To reach this ramshackle town 35 miles from mid-Strip Las Vegas, follow Rte. 15 for 28 miles almost straight south toward the

California border, then turn onto Rte. 161 (at the sign that indicates Jean-Goodsprings). The road is good all the way.

There are two specific reasons for mentioning Goodsprings: First, it's close to Vegas; second, the **Pioneer Saloon** in the center of town (tel. 874-1484), open daily from 10am to 10pm, is an authentic leftover from time past. It's the only complete metal building still standing anywhere in the United States.

As you enter Goodsprings, you'll pass the cemetery first. It's down-at-the-heel, not the sort of place where perpetual care has been a big thing. The graves appear to be only shallow mounds in some cases, but I was assured that "coffins are set just as deep as anywhere, even if they have to dynamite to get down six feet." A couple of markers are wood, weathered almost to the point of no identification. The only standard headstones are in a segment of the yard that has been fenced off by a low rail. All of these stones belong to the Fayle family, who were top brass in Goodsprings for some years. In the area near the cemetery, you can search for Native American arrowheads, spearheads, and other artifacts. They're difficult to recognize, however, unless you've had some experience studying them in museums.

"Slots—Cocktails—& Booze" says the painted sign on the side of the building as you approach the Pioneer Saloon. The saloon is a metal building with pressed-tin walls and ceiling on the inside, more metal (which almost looks like cement or stone blocks until you inspect it and feel it cold to the touch) on the exterior. There are a potbelly stove; linoleum so worn that it no longer has a pattern; drapes (they never were *draperies*) that don't match; a swamp cooler; and a long, saloony bar.

The Pioneer Saloon has been in business since at least 1913. There's a 1916 copy of the *Goodsprings Gazette* that carries an advertisement for the saloon. And the Goodsprings Hotel was advertised in New York newspapers as "the finest in the West." In those days Goodsprings had a population of 2,000 (which had shrunk to 62 by 1967; today it's about 100), and people from Las Vegas went to Goodsprings "to shop, gamble, dine out, drink, go to the theater, and to live it up." The thriving metropolis had nine bars, several restaurants, a theater, churches, other businesses, and homes, and it was a regular stop for Barnum & Bailey. It was the biggest town in Nevada in its time. A narrow-gauge railroad carried ore from the surrounding mines to the Union Pacific tracks at Jean.

On January 16, 1942, Goodsprings made headlines because it was the closest town to Potosi Mountain (25 miles distant, but it seems nearer in the clear desert). A flight, lost in a storm, crashed there with Carole Lombard, the famous movie star, aboard. There's a piece of the wreckage on top of the potbelly stove, and people who drop in at the saloon remember details as if the tragic event had occurred only yesterday. Clark Gable, the actress's husband, stayed at the Goodsprings Hotel. Later the hotel burned to the ground, and the last big blow to Goodsprings occurred when the old General Store was torn down and used to construct part of the Long Branch Saloon in Las Vegas.

Surrounding Goodsprings are the rotting remains of mining

companies, such as the Argentine and Yellow Pine Zinc & Lead, and discarded wrecks of old, abandoned cars on the far outskirts of town.

NELSON

Like Goodsprings, Nelson has the advantage of proximity to Las Vegas. Head south along U.S. 95 and turn off at Rte. 60.

The Spaniards, in the 1770s, were the first to discover gold in this region; they called it Eldorado but did little about mining the area's riches. The gold remained unextracted until about 100 years later, when good old American know-how took over. Unfortunately the consequent Techatticup Mine was riddled with violence from the start. Disagreements between labor and management, not to mention heated ownership disputes, led to so many killings that the town of Nelson was among the West's most notorious.

Nevertheless, several millions in gold, lead, silver, and copper were mined successfully. Today huge cyanide vats (cyanide was used in processing gold ore), all that is left of the old settlement, remain an imposing sight.

MINERAL PARK, ARIZONA

Mineral Park, Arizona, is less than 90 miles from Las Vegas, five miles from U.S. 93 near Kingman, Arizona. It was a thriving town in 1877, when it was designated as county seat of Mohave County. And in those days, a good-sized emporium, blacksmith shops, attorneys' offices, an assayer's building, an apothecary, and several bars were kept busy by seekers and finders of gold in the surrounding hills. Silver was known in the 1860s, but marauding Native Americans got in the way of any serious attempts to mine. It wasn't too long until miners established a foothold, however, and Mineral Park had "made it" when the first post office was opened there in December 1872. But the town fathers of Mineral Park put too many hopes into "the railroad" to keep things humming. Their prediction went bust. In 1887 the Mohave County seat was switched to Kingman, and the only newspaper in the town and county closed shop and moved to Kingman, too. The railroad, alas, never came closer to Mineral Park than 12 miles.

Today Mineral Park is dominated by a mining venture of the Duval Copper Division. It's a relatively clean and neat setup, but much that had survived of the lean-to town is buried under heaps of rock and by new buildings put up by Duval. Still, a few things from the past may be seen.

An old edifice with a cupola houses a kiln that must have been used to evaluate ore samples, and it continues to hold its own, somewhat awry and out of kilter. Verbena blooms in the yard. And the remains of a wan but sturdy adobe brick house of some substance valiantly struggle against time. Outside walls had been whitewashed —you still can see that—and faded flowers bloom from the tattered wallpaper inside, peeling from the walls in sheets. Vandals have done their work, and windows and doors and floors have been damaged. The roof is still intact, though, and the fireplace (also of adobe brick) stands proudly.

The road from U.S. 93 is kept clean, and it isn't a bad drive. For those interested in the ecology of copper mining, Duval provides a look toward the problem of getting rid of tin cans. They're used in the extraction of copper from the ore. You'll probably also see rock blasting. The smelting, incidentally, is performed not in Mineral Park but in El Paso, Texas.

About 15 miles away is **Kingman,** where the **Mohave Museum of History and Arts,** 400 W. Beale St. (tel. 602/753-3195), was opened in 1963. Ancient Native American carvings and stone implements and a superb collection of carved turquoise are on display here along with pioneer wagons, mine equipment, and other implements that the early people of Kingman used. Well-known artist Roy Purcell did much of the artwork in the museum, including a fascinating mural that adorns the front lobby. However, one of the most popular exhibits is that including portraits of the Presidents and First Ladies by Laurence Williams. There's a restored 1926 pipe organ and a room devoted to actor Andy Devine, who grew up in Kingman. A gift shop on the premises features Native American craft articles. The museum is close to two nice parks, at the junction of U.S. 93/Historic Route 66 and I-40.

The museum is open weekdays from 10am to 5pm, and Saturday and Sunday from 1 to 5pm; closed on most major holidays. There is a nominal admission fee.

CALICO, CALIFORNIA

Calico, California, is 160 miles from Las Vegas off sleek Interstate 15, on above-average roads all the way. You turn from I-15 between Yermo and Barstow onto a paved side road when signs point to Ghost Town Road. As you enter Calico, you'll go between the old Boot Hill Cemetery and a trailer camp that's been planted with trees. (I've never quite understood why so many ghost towns located their cemeteries on the approach roads.)

Calico has had a silver lining. Silver made it big in 1881 and kept the town humming for 15 years while the associated businesses that go with a boom town thrived. Silver from coffers of Knott's Berry Farm was poured into restoration of the sagging town more recently, and the town was deeded by the Knott family to San Bernardino County. It's now maintained by the regional parks system of San Bernardino County, and you can enjoy it as a restoration (if a somewhat touristy one) that approximates Calico during its heyday.

Calico's vast riches were discovered by chance when a Panamint stole a horse from one Lafayette Mecham. Mecham pursued the thief across miles of desert into the Calico Mountains. He never did catch the Panamint, but he did observe what looked like indications of silver in the mountains. There had been talk of silver in Calico before this, and Mecham's sons, Frank and Charles, on hearing their father's story, decided to investigate. They assembled a group and, grubstaked by John C. King, sheriff of San Bernardino County, set out in the spring of 1881.

Charlie made the first important find in September 1882. Silver King (named in honor of the expedition's sponsor) was for a time the richest mine in California.

By 1885 the mine had yielded about $1 million worth of silver bullion. Word spread, and soon the Mechams' lone tent was joined by hundreds of lean-tos, sun-bleached adobes, shanties, and rustic frame houses.

It became a thriving mining community of some 3,500 men, women, and children, including 40 Chinese residents who set up a small Chinatown at the eastern end of the town, complete with a Chinese restaurant. Their town boasted two hotels, a church, a one-room schoolhouse, and 13 saloons! During the boom years they extracted close to $20 million in silver ore from the Calico Hills. (Some estimates say $86 million is closer to the true figure, and there are old miners who claim another $86 million in silver ore is still buried in the hills.)

The entire town was totally devastated by fire twice, in 1884 and in 1887, and completely rebuilt. But a more important disaster to the inhabitants was the continuing drop in the price of silver. When Charlie found his first lode, the price of silver was $1.13 an ounce; by 1894 it had dropped to 64¢ an ounce, and many prospectors had already begun to abandon Calico to search elsewhere for something more lucrative—gold.

By 1896 the price of silver was a mere 53¢ an ounce, and the stamp mills were shut down. The discovery of borate (Twenty Mule Team Borax originated in Calico) kept things going until 1907, after which the swift exodus began, and desert winds and sands began to claim the town.

The legendary folk of Calico included many colorful characters. Wyatt Earp was a frequent visitor, although the town was notably law-abiding and peaceful compared to its counterparts elsewhere. As on TV's "Gunsmoke," there was the town physician, Dr. Goodenough, dubbed by local wags "Dr. Drunkenough," and Diamond Lil (known as Madam de Lil), Calico's answer to Kitty. And then there was old Quartz Davis, so tough that when a black scorpion bit him, it died.

Perhaps the most intriguing legend concerns an unlikely pair, a miner, Pat Hogan, and his Chinese friend, Wong Lee, a Calico cook. They arrived in town together in the early 1880s, and every night, after work, they would go to watch the gambling and revelry at Lucky Joe's Palace. Lee never betted, but he would always study a certain roulette wheel. He also studied the stars from an old Chinese astrology text. Finally the auspicious night arrived. He stepped up to the wheel with a silver dollar of Hogan's and a $5 gold piece of his own. He won and kept winning, wiping out the owner and then politely refusing further play. An argument ensued, and Wong was killed, but Hogan escaped with the winnings. He soon turned up in Vegas, where, several days later, he was shot in a drunken brawl. His last words were "the gold—it's buried in Calico three feet from the big rock." But he never said which rock, and people are searching for Hogan's gold to this day. Or so the story goes.

Legends were all that remained of Calico until Walter Knott

decided to purchase the town and surrounding areas in 1950. Knott had a sentimental interest in the preservation of Calico. He was the nephew of Sheriff John King, who had grubstaked the original mining expedition, and as a young man he had even spent a summer working one of the mines.

He rebuilt Calico over a period of about 15 years, trying to reflect the spirit of the town as he remembered it although adding such necessary conveniences as modern plumbing, piped water, and parking lots. Several old-timers were called in as consultants in the reconstruction. Although Calico now bustles with activity during the day, without the large number of tourists it is still a ghost town of just a few residents.

If you prefer to explore Calico on a more-than-one-day trip and don't wish to use the trailer park, several motels are located within reasonable distances, and nearby towns offer nighttime recreation. There are also camping sites ($10 per night per camper, plus $1 for off-road vehicles) located in shaded canyons; call 619/254-2122 for information. A parking lot is located just below the town, and a fee of $3 per car for daytime-only parking helps pay for maintenance. From the parking lot, you can either climb flights of stairs to Main Street or ride up the steep incline on a tramway ($1 to $1.50 for adults and 50¢ for kids, round trip).

Shops that retain the atmosphere of Calico have opened on Main Street and along some of the short side streets. You may dine in several places.

Fees are charged for several of Calico's attractions, but not for all of them. The ones that do charge—such as old-time melodramas at the Calikage Playhouse—are reasonably priced, and most are worth it. Calico also features the Maggie Mine tour, the Calico-Odessa R.R. Museum, and a shooting gallery. In this regard, visitors should remember that Calico is not supported by taxes. So anything you may drop into the coffers to help keep up the town is encouraging and perhaps an incentive toward preservation and restoration of other such places. At any rate, while other ghost towns fade and sag in sad disrepair, Calico plays host to thousands of visitors every year. Annual celebrations include Calico Days in October, the March Hullabaloo, and the May Spring Festival.

Nearby Mohave Desert Sights

While you're in the area, you might want to take in some other Mohave Desert attractions. One is an archeological dig, the **Calico Early Man Site** (tel. 619/256-3591), located 15 miles northeast of Barstow via Interstate 15, then 2½ miles north on Minneola Road (the last two miles of the road are unpaved, but it's quite passable by car).

Excavations since 1964 have unearthed over 11,500 artifacts. Lab and field analyses have established human presence in North America for more than 50,000 years. It's the oldest site on the continent and unique as the only site in the Americas ever worked by famed anthropologist Louis S. B. Leakey. The site was developed by the National Geographic Society and the San Bernardino County Museum and is significant as a "stone tool" workshop. The area is open for tours Wednesday at 1:30 and 3:30pm and Thursday through Sunday every two hours from 9am to 3:30pm (major holidays excepted). Admission is free.

Visitors may enter the excavations on guided tours; observe tools and methods of excavation; visit the small museum to handle stone tools, casts, and replicas; and view photographs of work.

Detailed desert recreation information, maps, and brochures are available at the **California Desert Information Center,** 831 Barstow Rd., one block north of Interstate 15 (tel. 619/256-8617). It's open from 9am to 5pm daily. The center is managed by the Bureau of Land Management and the Barstow area Chamber of Commerce. It houses displays on the high desert's natural history, its wildflowers, and its wildlife. The staff can tell you about area lodgings, camping, hiking, and driving in the desert; they're also a great resource for information on canyons, petroglyph sites, things to see and do in the Barstow area, and local services. All in all, the California Desert Information Center is well worth a visit if you plan to explore the area.

As long as you're in Barstow, there are several points of interest that you might want to investigate for some historical and geological background on the area. First, stop at the California Desert Information Center and pick up their folder called *Begin in Barstow with 5 One-Day Adventures.* Directions and maps in the folder are more detailed and helpful than any other maps you may have.

Note, then, that Barstow is home to the **Mojave River Valley Museum,** 270 E. Virginia Way (tel. 619/256-5452), open daily from 11am to 4pm. The museum is dedicated to the preservation of the heritage of the Mojave River Valley and has artifacts and displays relating to the area, a number of them from the famous Calico Early Man Site. The museum also displays a variety of materials from Paleo-Indian sites found throughout the desert. Specimens of local gemstones on exhibit present a selection of the minerals still being mined in the Mojave Desert. You might want to check into the field trips the museum conducts to local sites of historical interest.

And while you're in Barstow, stop at the **Barstow Station,** 1611 E. Main St. (tel. 619/256-0366), open daily from 9am to 9pm. This unique early-1900s railroad station and complex has a wide variety of interesting shops.

If you'd like to peruse a portion of the nearby foothills of the Calico Mountains on horseback, the **Pan McCue Ranch** would be the place to begin. Pan McCue is not the name of the ranch's owner but of a stallion—one the founding sires of the American Quarter Horse Association. The ranch conducts western trail rides for both the novice and the more experienced rider, taking them through the high desert with its magnificent scenery and varied terrain. You might also want to join in on one of the ranch's old-fashioned cookouts or hayrides. The Pan McCue Ranch is eight miles east of Barstow via I-15 (tel. 619/254-2184) and is open daily from 7am to sunset, later by reservation.

About 20 minutes north of Barstow lies **Rainbow Basin/Owl Canyon** (tel. 619/256-3591). This area was formed a bit before our time, perhaps between 10 and 30 million years ago. It contains fossilized remains of insects and animals, said to be among the best-preserved specimens found anywhere. Erosion has revealed richly colored sedimentary layers of remarkable beauty. The four-mile loop into and out of the area is narrow but passable for small vehicles. If you have an RV, the Owl Canyon campground, one mile east, accommodates 31 units and has picnic tables, grills, fire rings, drinking water, and trash receptacles for $4.50 per night.

The Rainbow Basin area is frequently visited by university groups interested in the fossil remains found here. In 1972 the Rainbow Basin was designated a "National Natural Landmark" by the Secretary of the Interior. Its sediments are textbook examples of folds, faults, and other disruptions of the earth's crust. And because of the quantity and quality of fossils found at the Rainbow Basin, the locality is a reference standard for the age of Barstovian land mammals who lived 12 to 16 million years ago in North America. Hiking through the Owl Canyon wash, next to Owl Canyon Campground, you will pass through three different geologic formations, evidencing a time span of millions of years.

In a more contemporary vein, and if you're a careful observer, you may see a variety of wildlife, including the kit fox, desert tortoise, and bobcat. The barn owl, the red-tailed hawk, and the turkey vulture frequently are sighted in this area. Bear in mind that all species are protected by the State of California, unless designated as game animals; therefore desert tortoises and birds of prey may not be removed or harassed. Furthermore, hobby collection of fossils is restricted; all significant fossil finds must be reported to the Bureau of Land Management. As noted above, the California Desert Information Center in Barstow has a wealth of information on this area and guidelines for its use, including a map that outlines roads, trails, campsites, viewpoints, and the natural area boundary.

When you run out of archeological sites and the children are beginning to squirm, head for **Lake Dolores** (tel. 619/257-3315 or 254-2009), about 20 miles northeast of Barstow via I-15. The area is open from Palm Sunday weekend (the weekend before Easter) through Labor Day weekend from 8am to 5:30pm. The water park has the West Coast's first and biggest high-speed water slide—80 feet high and 200 feet long; you can reach speeds of up to 50 miles per hour. For the Tarzan in you, there's a 350-foot-long cable extending over one of the lakes; aspiring circus performers can trapeze into the middle of a 15-foot-deep lake. Once that excitement dies down, there are skeeter boats to whip around a half-mile course, or the gentler wet-and-wild bumper boats. Kiddies can play in a shallow lake with teeter-totters, swings, and slides. When you come out of the water, you can enjoy a leisurely game of miniature golf, have a picnic, or use the snack bar facilities. Showers also are available. Admission to Lake Dolores is $6 for those 9 years old and up, $3 for kids 3 to 8; there is no charge for those under 3.

GOLD POINT

You have to turn off a good highway and cover about seven miles of graded gravel to get to Gold Point, about 180 miles from Las Vegas. But it isn't overly rugged. The town is located between

Beatty and Goldfield. You take U.S. 95 most of the way, then turn onto Nevada Rte. 3.

The weathering of the years is the only real debilitation that Gold Point has suffered. It's been saved from the depredation and disgrace of vandals, mostly because the vigilant postmistress stayed on to serve the population of eight. (It takes only one strong-willed individual to save a town in some Nevada precincts.) The number of residents in Gold Point recently jumped somewhat, because of a new glimmer of interest in mining. Now there's some consternation about the newcomers, who have a bright chance to do more harm than good—parking their trailers among the old buildings, digging all over the place. "They're not environmentalists interested in preservation," snorted one state official.

I won't suggest that you attempt to drive a regular passenger car out into the rough desert from Gold Point. But if you have access to a desert buggy, which can stand more rigorous terrain, you might look into both Oriental and Gold Mountain, nearby mining centers that have fallen into sagging relics since their prime days in the 1870s and 1880s. Plenty of old diggings can be seen in the weathered hills.

Funny thing about Gold Point: It started out as Hornsilver, after an earlier metallic lure, and even had a newspaper, the *Hornsilver Herald,* an accomplishment that gave towns of that era a certain cachet.

During the good old days, the population zoomed to 2,000. Silver turned to gold and so did the town's name, in 1929, but that's "way back in history" in these parts of Nevada. The year 1929 is when some mine operators started digging again and stayed on through several ensuing years. And it's probably why the town hasn't given in as much as most of its less recently occupied contemporaries. Good points about Gold Point: It's about 60 miles beyond Rhyolite, one of Nevada's most famous ghost towns, and also within a reasonable distance of Death Valley, for an entirely different travel sensation.

GOLDFIELD

Returning to U.S. 95 from Gold Point, you might want to continue north a bit and explore two more ghost towns, Goldfield and Tonopah.

The first you'll reach is Goldfield (182 miles north of Las Vegas). It's now boarded up and abandoned, but in the early 1900s it was a thriving community of 30,000. When prospectors Billy March and Harry Stimler first staked their claim in 1902, the town was called "Grandpa," but the region's vast resources suggested the name change.

It was a rip-roarin' town, with all the shoot-outs, labor disputes, and other disorders so typical of turn-of-the-century mining settlements. Of course, there were numerous flourishing saloons, the best known run by Tex Rickard. Rickard had made a fortune in the Klondike and lost it. In addition to running a bar so huge that it required 80 bartenders to handle it, Rickard moonlighted as a fight promoter. A nationally publicized bout for the lightweight championship of the world in 1906 between Gans and Nelson ran 42 rounds, with Rickard offering the largest purses in fight history— $20,000 to the champ, Nelson, and $10,000 to the challenger.

In the beginning years, the abundant Goldfield mines produced between $5 million and $11 million worth of ore annually, but by the early 1920s, production had dwindled to a fraction of that amount.

Today Goldfield is one of the more interesting of Nevada's ghost towns, since so many structures are still standing intact— despite a flash flood and a huge fire. The boarded-up Goldfield Hotel, once a beautifully appointed showpiece, remains at the center of town. Its lobby is still furnished under layers of dust, its dining room set up for an evening meal that never took place. And there are old mines and dumps to see at the foot of the Columbia Mountain. You can also see Tex Rickard's home, but like the hotel, it's not open to visitors.

TONOPAH

Proceeding about 25 miles farther north, you'll reach Tonopah, where, during the boom years of 1905 and 1913, $250 million worth of gold and silver was mined.

There are quite a few stories about the discovery of mineral wealth in Tonopah. According to expert Lambert Florin, author of a series of books about western ghost towns, the most likely version concerns two prospectors, Jim Butler and William Hall, who were en route to a mining camp called Southern Klondyke in 1900. They camped overnight at Tonopah, and the ornery Hall, unable to waken Butler from a sound slumber the next morning, went on alone. Butler finally woke, tracked down the party, and was just on the point of flinging an angry stone at the burros when he noticed that the stone showed signs of valuable ore.

Butler's wife, on hearing the story later, called in expert Tasker L. Oddie, who estimated that the area could produce $350 per ton of rock. She then staked a claim in one of the richest-producing mines in the region—the Mizpah Mine.

The town was laid out, grew, prospered, and then diminished —but never completely. Some mining is still in progress today, although mostly for semiprecious stones. Hence, Tonopah is not, strictly speaking, a ghost town. It has a thriving main street of shops and restaurants centered around the five-story Mizpah Hotel. An unusual feature of the town is its high curbs designed to channel the floodwaters that occasionally rush through the town.

RHYOLITE

There are several roads going into Death Valley National Monument off Hwy. 95. One such is the Nevada approach from Beatty and onto Hwy. 374. En route, about 2½ miles west is the ghost town of Rhyolite (about 118 miles from Las Vegas). What you'll see are the remnants of what once was a town of 12,000 inhabitants in 1907. It was abandoned when its gold mine failed.

What still stands out are the railroad depot, which is now boarded up, and the **Bottle House,** which is unfortunately fenced off. Originally the Bottle House was built by a bartender (who else?). The materials were used partly in fun, I understand, but the bottles proved to be practical; they were available in quantity (miners imbibe in the desert!), and they cost the builder nothing. The house has outlasted more pretentious buildings that once graced the city of 12,000. (Of course, it helped that it was restored for a movie setting in 1925 by Paramount.)

Rhyolite began with the Bullfrog Mine. Gold was dug there at a fantastic clip, and speculation ran high. The precious metal was discovered by Frank (Shorty) Harris and Ernest L. Cross in August 1904. As Shorty later described it in the *Rhyolite Herald:* "The quartz was full of free gold. . . . Talk about rich! Why, gee whiz, it was great! . . . The very first boulder was as rich in gold as anything I had ever seen. . . ." As the news traveled, scores of rainbow-chasing prospectors poured into the camp; by September there were already 75 residents.

H. D. and L. D. Porter arrived with an 18-mule team laden with merchandise and set up the town's leading store. By mid-March the population was 200, most of them lodged in tents and other ramshackle affairs.

In the course of time, a gentleman named Pete Busch showed up. As he shivered through the winter on the uncomfortable slopes of the mining camp, he dreamed of promoting a livable town. He liked the idea of wide streets and good buildings. Apparently a lot of other miners liked the idea, for Rhyolite blossomed into a city within a matter of months. Miners who had been paying $5 for a barrel of water, men who had lived in drafty tents, now lavished their golden bounty trying to outdo each other with grand houses. The miners were rip-roaring men, free with their new wealth.

Water was piped into Rhyolite, a new post office was built, and a school building was constructed for the (then) outrageous sum of $50,000. In 1906 three railroads fell over each other to reach the city first. The Las Vegas and Tonopah Line arrived first, connecting Rhyolite with the famous Union Pacific tracks. In its hey-day Rhyolite had electric light and power, a telephone system, three newspapers, and a stock exchange. There were banks, office buildings, churches, a hospital, a jail (much needed), restaurants, hotels, an opera house, many stores, and over 20 saloons and a thriving red-light district.

Unlike other mining towns built of canvas, adobe, and thrown-together wood structures, Rhyolite was built of stone and concrete —it was built to last. Its population peaked at over 12,000. A real town, Rhyolite offered its citizens not only the usual boom-town saloon/gambling-hall entertainments but also such genteel activities as Sunday school picnics, church socials, dances at the opera house, a tennis court, and concerts—even the circus came to Rhyolite.

But by 1907 financial panic had begun to sweep the nation, and Rhyolite was hard hit. The railroads, so hungry to be in the city only a year earlier, were as anxious to leave as they were to get there. They ripped up their tracks, sold the metal and the ties, and deserted the depot.

After three frustrating years, only about 700 people remained in the city. By 1911 the Montgomery-Shoshone Mine, the last working mine, had overextended. It, too, closed shop. The remaining 700 workers lost little time in packing up their belongings and moving out.

It must have been discouraging for those remaining 700 people to see what had happened to their town. They had watched, helpless, as friends and neighbors hightailed it to other places, watched as thousands abandoned their businesses, paper still on their desks, houses full of furniture. Undoubtedly they wondered how a city that had once held so much promise could fade so quickly.

The *Herald* reported the town's demise:

April 1910: The street lights were turned off, and there were no longer funds available to pay for water.

May 1910: There were no more banking facilities; H. D. and L. D. Porter sold out their entire stock of merchandise at everything-must-go prices; the Commercial Hotel was sold to a D. Pecetto, who moved the entire structure, furnishings and all, to Las Vegas.

March 1911: The Montgomery-Shoshone closed down; two issues later *Herald* editor Earle R. Clements published his "Goodbye, Dear Old Rhyolite" editorial and fled for the coast. His newspaper died that May.

By 1920 there were only 14 residents left in Rhyolite. Some stayed until they were so poor that they couldn't afford to move their belongings when they left.

In 1922 a visiting motor tour from the *Los Angeles Times* found only one remaining inhabitant, a 92-year-old Frenchman, J. D. Lorraine.

What was once Nevada's biggest city is now its biggest ghost town, creaking—and, somehow, noble—in the wail of the desert winds.

PIOCHE

Want to visit the site of the wildest, baddest shoot-'em-up boomcamp in the West? It's Pioche, 175 miles northeast of Las Vegas via U.S. 93.

Discovered in 1863 by William Hamblin (friendly Paiutes led the lucky prospector right to the ore-laden hills), the area was developed by a Frenchman from San Francisco named F.L.A. Pioche, who bought Hamblin's claim.

By 1870 the camp was well on its notorious way, with the first 75 deaths a result of shootings! During 1871–1872 over half the killings in the state of Nevada took place in or around Pioche. A murderer's row, fenced off from the more respectable dead, was started in the town's Boot Hill; it eventually became the resting place for about 100 killers. You can still see some of the graves today, and above them the remnants of a tramline that was used to carry ore buckets from the hills.

Although the camp produced over $40 million in ore, it is best remembered for myriad tales of violence. For example, there was the bartender named Faddiman whom everyone warned not to take a job in Pioche. (No bartender had ever survived more than a year there.) But he needed a job desperately, even one in a barely civilized town. During his second week on the job, he refused to serve a drunk another round. The drunk bounded over the bar, killed Faddiman with a six-shooter, stepped over the body, and helped himself to the contents of the till. Then continuing his rampage, he stepped next door, slit the throat of the buxom proprietress of the butcher shop, and emptied her till. The sheriff arrived and shot him full of holes. And so the graveyard grew.

Today you won't get shot at in Pioche, but you will see some interesting relics, among them the old Lincoln Courthouse. A museum and library are provided to acquaint visitors with Pioche history.

6. The Grand Canyon

There's really no way to describe the Grand Canyon, and oft-used phrases such as "awesome panorama," "Eighth Wonder of the World," "timeless spectacle," and "nature's finest monument" cannot begin to evoke the reality.

More interesting is the story of the earth-building erosion that formed it, a story that spans two billion years of the earth's history.

The Grand Canyon is indeed *grand*. It spans 280 miles of the reddish-brown Colorado River, a powerful body of water that begins in the Rocky Mountains of Colorado and travels down 1,450 miles to the Gulf of California, with many canyons along its course.

Spaniards searching for gold discovered the Grand Canyon as early as 1540, but no attempts were made to comprehend its origin until the 1850s, when geologist John Strong Newberry explored the region. The subject is still a matter of debate, but all agree that it was carved by the dramatic upheavals of earth and the erosions caused by the powerful river.

The earliest rocks, dark and vertically layered, date from the early Precambrian era. During this era these rocks, sediments, and volcanic lavas were metamorphosed into mountains (as high as any in the world today) and then eroded, bit by bit, to a plain near sea level. This stage began about 2 billion years ago and came to an end about 1.2 billion years ago. Although no fossil traces have been found in rocks dating to this period, scientists have uncovered signs of organisms and single-celled plants believed to have existed here. Perhaps the titanic forces of mountain building and erosion erased fossil evidence.

In the next stage of development, the late Precambrian era, sediments began to build in the shallow water that covered the eroded mountain remnants. The first layer was of algae-formed limestone reefs, and next came a brilliant vermilion rock, above which came deposits of a hard quartz-sand rock. Other layers accumulated until the thickness of rocks created in this era was over 12,000 feet. Approximately 600 million years ago, this second stage, which also included the formation and erosion of another mountain range, was completed. Late Precambrian rocks can be seen today along the

South and North Kaibab trails, in the Shinumo amphitheater to the west of Grand Canyon Village, and on the floor at the eastern end of the canyon.

During the Paleozoic era that followed (it ended about 230 million years ago), the upper two-thirds of the canyon walls were formed, only to be covered in Mesozoic times (those were the days when dinosaurs roamed the earth) with sediments of 4,000 and 8,000 feet.

Then in the present era, the Cenozoic (it began about 65 million years ago), the Mesozoic rocks were eroded; you can still see the remnants of them at Cedar Mountain, the Painted Desert, and Zion Canyon. It was in this final period that the most widespread erosion took place and the earth was sculpted as we see it today. The last series of violent changes took place over a million years ago, when molten rock from deep within the earth spewed forth, creating volcanoes.

And, of course, geology never comes to a standstill, even at America's major tourist attraction. Ultimately, after millions of years have passed, the Grand Canyon may one day be a level plain with the tired remains of the Colorado River flowing across it.

TO THE GRAND CANYON'S SOUTH RIM BY AIR

You can fly to the South Rim of the Grand Canyon from Las Vegas, spend the day sight-seeing, souvenir hunting, and enjoying lunch with a view, and be back in your Las Vegas hotel by early evening. What's more, the flights in twin-engine, nine-passenger Cessnas dip hundreds of feet below the canyon's rim—for the ultimate in spectacular views.

The **Gray Line** offers a daily Grand Canyon Land and Air Tour, including a buffet lunch and a motorcoach tour to Hoover Dam. The flight through the Grand Canyon leaves Boulder City, flies over Hoover Dam and the entire length of Lake Mead, and dives into the rugged wilderness of Grand Canyon. Cessna Aircraft are used for the best possible viewing. The price, including lunch, is $99 per person. There is hotel pickup and return.

Scenic Airlines, 241 E. Reno Ave., Las Vegas, NV 89119 (tel. 739-1900), runs deluxe, full-day, air-ground tours for $181 per person, that price including lunch at the Grand Canyon, plus all air and ground transportation with guides. For children aged 2 to 11 the cost is $141. A three-hour air tour (basically a round-trip flight, to and from the South Rim airport) is $126.

In addition to the standard nine-passenger planes used by most Grand Canyon tour operators (every seat is by a window), Scenic Airlines features deluxe Vista Liners. The wings of these planes are above the oversize windows so the view is completely unobstructed. Six of the Vista Liners' 19 seats are on the aisle, but the windows are large enough that even views from these seats are terrific. The unique individual narration system translates to eight languages simultaneously. It costs an extra $10 each way to take the Vista Liner; it's well worth the price to try it at least one way.

Note: Both the nine-seaters and the Vista Liners are very small planes, so they are much more at the mercy of air currents than larger craft. If you are susceptible to air sickness, it would be wise to take an air-sickness preventive before your flights. (But don't let this minor inconvenience prevent you from experiencing this trip of a lifetime!)

The South Rim of the Grand Canyon is 225 miles from Las Vegas on the route flown east; the westbound return flight, more direct, is 185 air miles. Flying time to Grand Canyon Airport is an hour and 15 minutes.

The hues of the cliffs and slopes along the canyon's walls, mostly red sandstone, change with the passing day, painted by the sun and varied weather conditions. Its lowest points are a mile deep, a distance from which the mighty Colorado River appears no bigger than a thin stream. Boulders, rocks, and sediment are the grinding tools of the Colorado, employed for eons to cut deeper and deeper into the chasm.

From your first glimpse of the Colorado River, you're flying mostly over federal lands, "high desert" in local parlance, which means mountainous territory, as barren and dramatically sparse as the lower deserts you'll see around Las Vegas. The Colorado River and its contributing sources flow through the high-plateau country and on to the Gulf of California, 1,450 miles from their beginnings. The Grand Canyon was hewn from the southern slopes of the Kaibab Plateau. Its North Rim is about 8,200 feet above sea level; the South Rim is about 7,000 feet above sea level.

The plateau reaches an elevation of 9,000 feet to the north. In width, the canyon averages 9 miles, with various distances measuring from 4 to 18 miles. The total area of the Grand Canyon, administered by the National Park Service, is 1,052 square miles (673,575 acres).

The South Rim of the canyon is open all year. Most visitors are concerned only with the South Rim, where hotels, dining, and shopping multifacilities are run by the Fred Harvey Company under a sort of grandfather-clause contract that's guaranteed him almost-exclusive commercial rights since 1904.

The Fred Harvey Company

Many of us who hail from east of Chicago first encountered the Fred Harvey name in the Judy Garland movie *The Harvey Girls,* which was famous for the tune "The Atchison, Topeka, and the Santa Fe." The film romanticized history about how Harvey moved groups of chaperoned young ladies west to work in his restaurants in such places as railroad junctions. That's where the action used to be, in the century before air travel. Not surprisingly, many of the Harvey girls married and settled down to help populate the American West.

Harvey made several fortunes with his concessions, eventually settling into a good number of the great national parks, building hotels and stores, lucrative operations that have outstripped gold mining for income by far. It appears that the empire he built in the West will go forever. He moved into the South Rim of the Grand Canyon in 1904. The Fred Harvey Company now is owned by

Amfac, Inc. (canyon address: Grand Canyon National Park Lodges, P.O. Box 699, Grand Canyon, AZ 86023).

When you consider that the Harvey folks have practically no competition, they do a very good job. If you plan to stay over for a couple of days at the canyon, you'll snuggle into one of the Harvey hotels. And if you take a two-day mule trip down into the canyon, you'll ride one of the Harvey-trained mules.

Rooms at the canyon are as scarce as hen's teeth during the summer. You must—repeat, *must!*—make reservations in advance of your visit. Off-season, rooms are plentiful.

The hotel and lodges described below are part of the Grand Canyon National Park Lodges organization. For reservations at any one, call 602/638-2631.

The 70-room **El Tovar Hotel** is the classic lodge, spacious and rambling, with broad porches. Open year round, it's built of native boulders and great pine logs. All accommodations here were renovated a few years back. The better rooms offer views across the canyon. All rooms have bath with tub and shower, TV, and a switchboard phone. There's a big lobby with a fireplace. Nightly rate is $110 to $140, single or double occupancy; it is $7 for an extra person in a room. A few suites and posher digs run $160 to $250 per night.

The El Tovar's dining room serves both table d'hôte and à la carte meals. The food is hearty, all-American fare. Breakfasts are whooping affairs, dished out with the gusto of ranchhand informality. A cocktail lounge adjoins.

The **Bright Angel Lodge** offers a wide range of rustic accommodations year round. Rim cabins with bath, sleeping up to four people, are $65 to $80 for single or double occupancy; the same with fireplace are $80 a night. An extra person pays $10. A coffee shop and cocktail lounge are on the premises.

The **Kachina Lodge**, adjacent to El Tovar, is a modern two-story facility. All rooms are equipped with bath/shower, TV, and phone; some are canyonside. Single or double rooms rent for $95 to $110. The adjoining **Thunderbird Lodge** offers identical rates and facilities.

The **Yavapai Lodge East and West,** situated in pine and juniper woodlands, is a two-story facility offering rooms with bath, TV, and phone; it's open from Easter to November only. It is approximately three-quarters of a mile from the main village area but is adjacent to the Mather Shopping Center. Rates are $70 to $80, single or double; it is $8 for each additional person.

In the southwest corner of the village area, just minutes from the canyon rim, the **Maswik Lodge** offers rooms with two double beds, bath, TV, and phone for $67 to $95, single or double; it is $8 for each additional person. It's open year round.

At the very bottom of the canyon, a vertical mile down, the **Phantom Ranch** offers a central lodge, rustic cabins, and a night of rest on a dozen acres. Dormitory facilities are $20 per person per night. Since cabin facilities are limited, it is necessary to call the main number given above for rates and availability.

Outside the park boundary, six miles from Grand Canyon Village, is **Moqui Lodge,** a rustic accommodation offering rooms with two double beds and bath but no phone. It's open from March to December. Rates are $65 to $75, single or double; it is $8 for each additional person.

Mule Trains

Long-eared mules have been used for visitor descents into the canyon since 1912. Unbroken stock is purchased in Tennessee and Missouri mainly, and the mules are trained at the canyon. They're big animals, bigger than most horses, and strong.

Some mules never measure up to carrying people, and they're used for packing supplies only. When a mule starts carrying riders, he's been trained as a pack animal for at least a year. Mules are considered to be the only animals sure-footed enough and fit for the strenuous work of descending into and climbing back up out of the canyon.

The two-day trail trip by mule (tel. 602/638-2631) includes guide, mule, box lunch, two meals, and overnight accommodations at Phantom Ranch for $277 single and $478 for a couple. One-day rides to Plateau Point are also available at $70 per person, including box lunch.

This trip isn't for the faint of heart. The minimum height for descent into the canyon is 4 feet 7 inches. And you must weigh under 200 pounds and be of good physical condition and sufficient stamina to take the heat and the saddlesore seating that you get on a mule. I suggest that you make reservations six to nine months in advance for in-season (April 1 to October 31) trips.

For Your Information

In Grand Canyon Village, illustrated and informal talks are given by Park Service lecturers every summer evening. Talks are scheduled at specific times, which are posted on bulletin boards at the lodges.

Material covering geology, biology, prehistory, and other features of the canyon is exhibited at the **Park Headquarters and Visitor Center,** the **Yavapai Museum,** and the **Tusayan Ruin and Museum** (farther out on the East Rim Drive).

LAUGHLIN

If the frontier-town spirit is in your soul and if you love country music (Charlie Pride, Johnny Cash, and Merle Haggard), casual dress (jeans, sneakers, and T-shirts), camping, and RV life but can still enjoy Las Vegas comforts, Laughlin may be your style. It's in Clark County but a bit closer to Los Angeles than Las Vegas.

Laughlin is about 100 miles south of Las Vegas (take U.S. 95 to Nev. 163 east). Once you're on 163 headed east, there's a four-lane highway, and you may believe that you're not far from town life; but the four lanes disappointingly become two lanes at the end of a mile. Be very patient for the next 20-plus miles and pass cautiously. One alternative to driving is **States West Airlines** (tel. toll free 800/759-3866), which serves the small Laughlin/Bullhead City Airport that's about a mile across the Colorado in Bullhead City, Arizona. The airline has scheduled flights from Los Angeles and from several cities in southern California and Arizona. At the airport you can pick up a rental car from Avis (tel. 602/754-4686), Budget (tel. 602/754-3361), or Hertz (tel. 602/754-4111).

Laughlin is a town on a roll. In 1964 Don Laughlin bought a down-at-the-heels motel and bar in what was then called South Point. He parlayed his purchase into the Riverside Hotel and Casino; in the process, the name of the town was changed to Laughlin. In 1981 Laughlin had less than 450 hotel rooms, but by the end of 1992, it is expected to have about 13,000 rooms and will have added well over 100,000 square feet of casino space—enough to accommodate a lot of gaming elbows and craps table "yo's."

To no one's surprise, hotels along the Laughlin side of the Colorado are springing up and expanding at a frenetic pace. And why not? Low room rates and bargain restaurant prices make Laughlin especially attractive, the idea being that you will use for gambling the money that you don't have to spend on food and lodging. However, dinner with wine in a few of the fancier restaurants can still run about $80 to $90 for two. What's more, the coming of the newer and splashier hotel/casinos may well begin to raise the average room tab for the gaming crowd.

What you won't yet find in Laughlin are the big, splashy, show-room extravaganzas; the top-notch lounge acts; and most of the world's favorite performers.

For the moment, January to August occupancies in Laughlin generally run over 98%. Gaming revenues have increased at a whop-ping rate of 21%, compared with 10% in Las Vegas. (Casino gaming is not allowed in Arizona.) The thought of getting in on the act may be appealing, but you'll have to hock more than the house, the spouse, and the kiddies. The price of Laughlin land along the Colorado zoned for hotel/casino development is over $1.5 million per acre. Still, Don Laughlin estimates that there will be as many as 18 action-packed casinos in ten years.

It's getting more difficult day by day to cross Casino Drive (the main street through Laughlin). There are the bare beginnings of air pollution despite some very breezy days. January through March are windy and chilly, as they frequently are in Las Vegas. The summer months can elevate temperatures to over 110°. But then you can al-ways take refuge in the casino or by the pool or head to Lake Mohave and enjoy the mild breezes at Katherine Landing (see below).

Las Vegas is still the fastest-growing major city in the country, but Laughlin is in a bursting-at-the-seams mode. Bullhead City, Ari-zona, across the Colorado may not be the center of urban sophistication, but for the moment it's definitely the place to go for vital necessities—such as a full-size service station (except for that at Harrah's RV Convenience Center), a supermarket, and the culinary comforts of a fast-food establishment for the kiddies. Don Laughlin was good enough to build a $4-million bridge for folks to get across the river, just beyond his Riverside Hotel and Casino. The bridge also enables Don to drive to his holdings on the Arizona side of the Colorado. If you want to survey all the hotel/casinos in town, you could walk the mile or so from one end of Casino Drive to the other. But to get you back to the gaming tables faster, Laughlin has a bus that runs every 30 minutes between casinos. The fare is 50¢.

For up-to-the-minute information on all of what's going on in Laughlin, stop at the **Chamber of Commerce,** 1725 Casino Dr., P.O. Box 2280, Laughlin, NV 89029 (tel. 702/298-2214, or toll free 800/227-5245). The Chamber is located in a tired-looking mobile home on your right, next to the bank, as you head south on Casino Drive.

---

1. Hotels/Casinos

You have several choices, and no two hotel/casinos are much further apart than one mile from the Best Western Riverside at the north end of Casino Drive to Harrah's at the south end. Newer facilities include the Flamingo Hotel Laughlin, Harrah's, and the Ramada Express.

Best Western Riverside Hotel and Casino, 1650 Casino Dr., P.O. Box 500, Laughlin, NV 89029 (tel. 702/298-2535, or toll free 800/227-3849).

Almost from the day it opened, the Riverside (owned by Don Laughlin) has been under expansion; today there's a 660-room hotel, a 900-seat Celebrity Theatre, a three-screen film theater, three restaurants, and two pools.

For those who head east from Hwy. 95 into Laughlin, you can't miss the Riverside Hotel—it's the first hotel at the north end of Casino Drive. The Riverside is all decked out in an attractive white-and-gold color scheme, once an exclusive of the Golden Nugget in Las Vegas. The interior has a turn-of-the-century look with frosted-globe chandeliers, etched glass, and red-and-black carpeting. However, there's nothing old-fashioned about the women serving drinks—they are attired more like bunnies than like Great-aunt Bertha. You'll also find a marvelous collection of antique slot machines, including two that can still be played, with bells, bars, cherries, oranges, lemons, and plums. There are also a few ingenious devices for spending money that you may never have seen before (one dating back to 1898), such as dice machines, some designed to look like juke boxes and some created as baseball games.

As to the rooms, all have a pleasant southwest look and color scheme, the style of choice among most of the newer hotels. Woods are dark and set against beige walls and carpeting—a flattering contrast to the draperies and spreads, which have an orange-and-beige Native American pattern. Most rooms overlook one of the pools, the Colorado, or the mountains; or all three. All rooms have color cable TV, phones, and most of the conveniences you expect of a contemporary hotel.

Gaming facilities at the Riverside include everything from 5¢ and 25¢ slots on up to poker, blackjack, craps, roulette, keno, bingo, and a sports book—all to bend the elbow and pocketbook to your heart's content.

The Riverside has the only major showroom in Laughlin, and it has hosted such acts as Crystal Gayle, Vikki Carr, Helen Reddy, Mel Tillis, Eddie Arnold, and Charley Pride. Most shows are priced between $20 and $35. From time to time, you may also see women wrestlers and female impersonators performing at the Riverside, although these have not yet achieved star status. For those who want other than country music or women wrestlers, the Riverside has a three-screen theater complete with Dolby sound and inexpensive ticket prices of $1.50 by day and $3 by night. And then there's more activity—weekly dances at the Riverside's Western Dance Hall, swing-dance classes, and a free Sunday tea dance in the Starview Showroom.

When you've finished with all of the above, the two pools I mentioned are a great place to relax, if you can find the time.

Rooms at the Riverside Hotel, single or double, are $34 to $39

Sunday through Thursday, $48 to $58 Friday and Saturday, and $64 on holidays. The higher prices are for rooms with a view. Small pets are welcome. There is 24-hour ferryboat service back and forth across the Colorado.

Adjacent to the casino is the **Riverside RV Park.** There are 600 spaces with full hookups, laundry facilities, showers, and a dump station. Pets are welcome there, too.

Restaurants

For dining, the **Prime Rib Room** offers prime rib carved tableside from 4 to 11pm. The **Gourmet Room** serves such delectables as fresh oysters; clams casino; escargots bundled in brioche; and elegant entrees such as quail and beef and veal specialties. All of this is beautifully enhanced by a superb view of the Colorado. Reservations are suggested for the Gourmet Room. Of course, there is a 24-hour eatery, the **Riverview Room,** plus the **East and West Buffet.**

Edgewater Hotel, 2020 Casino Dr., P.O. Box 642, Laughlin, NV 89029 (tel. 702/298-2453, or toll free 800/257-0300).

The Edgewater is situated next to the Colorado Belle. There are some 600 pleasant rooms that are a bit more spacious than most, with furnishings of natural-tone woods and hues of red in the southwest prints of the spreads and drapes set against beige walls. Some of the rooms and one-bedroom suites have patios and balconies overlooking the Colorado River. And before you ask, there are color TV, phones, and air conditioning. Currently the Edgewater is in the process of expanding with a 25-story tower that will have another 1,000 rooms; it is scheduled to be completed in late 1991.

The casino area repeats the southwest look, although it may be a bit difficult to see around and above the slots (just look at the walls and carpeting). You will find the usual collection of games in the casino—blackjack, craps, roulette, and a sports book.

Rooms at the Edgewater, single or double, are $31 Sunday through Thursday and $49 Friday and Saturday. Suites are $120 throughout the week.

Restaurants

For sustenance, there are three places to dine in the Edgewater —the **Embers** for steak and seafood, the 24-hour **Fountain Room,** and the **Buffet.** For relaxation, there are a pool and spa as well as a video arcade for the little ones.

Colorado Belle, 2100 Casino Dr., P.O. Box 2304, Laughlin, NV 89029 (tel. 702/298-4000, or toll free 800/458-9500).

The Colorado Belle is a model of the paddlewheelers of the Mississippi River landlocked on 22 acres beside the Colorado. The Belle has over 1,200 rooms, two pools, and a spa.

The lower deck has 64,000 square feet of casino gaming space.

You'll find slots (over 1,200), blackjack tables, roulette, craps, poker, and keno.

As to the accommodations, single or double, each has a king-size bed or two queen-size beds. Rooms and suites are nautically themed, all decked out in reds and blues with ship's wheel head-boards. As with just about all hotels these days, there are color TVs, phones, and full baths. Rates are $31 for all standard rooms Sunday through Thursday and $49 on weekends and holidays. If you want a river view, staterooms are $59 and suites are $85 to $120.

Restaurants

For serious food or light sustenance, there's a place to fit every taste and purse. The top-of-the-line **Orleans Room** serves steak, sea-food, and pasta. **Mark Twain's** has chicken and delicious barbecued ribs. The **Mississippi Lounge and Seafood Bar** offers fresh oysters, clams, and shrimp. **Captain's Food Fare** is the Belle's buffet. **Huckleberry's Snack Bar** is the light-food establishment. And the **Paddlewheel** is the 24-hour full-service restaurant.

Ramada Express Hotel/Casino, 2121 Casino Dr., P.O. Box 658, Laughlin, NV 89029 (tel. 702/298-4200, or toll free 800/272-6232).

It's easy to spot the $60-million Ramada Express, which steamed into town in June 1988 and stopped at the first traffic light on the right. The building bears a marked resemblance to a bright-yellow sprawling church with an enormous steeple or a decidedly old-fashioned but interesting railroad station. It isn't on the river, but it is a fun place to be, and the view is great from the upper stories.

The interior is done nicely and in good fun. The registration area and desk are in white and dark green and resemble photos of an old-time ticket counter. The chandeliers are circular brass with chimney lamps. The lovely people behind the registration desk are dressed with a turn-of-the-century look: Gentlemen wear striped shirts, garters on their sleeves, vests, and black trousers; gentle-women wear dresses with leg-of-mutton sleeves. Carrying out the theme, the paintings behind the desk are scenes with famous trains—the New York Special, the San Francisco Limited, the Orient Ex-press, and so forth. A sign helpfully tells those coming aboard of the Ramada Express departure and arrival times.

The railroad theme is carried into the casino's main room, which resembles the waiting room of a station—a high-pitched roof is supported by visible trusses and cross-members. Even the green carpeting has a red locomotive design. As to the gaming, there are slots, slot contests, blackjack, roulette, craps, keno, and mini-baccarat.

Rooms are done attractively and appointed comfortably, with a pleasant un-Vegas look. Woods are dark, and a relaxing green pre-dominates in the furnishings. Spreads and draperies in floral prints of green, rose, and light blue add airiness to the rooms. Prints on the walls are sure to tell you where you are since they are of handsome old locomotives. And what would room amenities be without color

TVs (with stations from Arizona), phones, and roomy baths. Hallways are carpeted, and each floor has the name of a railroad. Even the personnel at the Ramada Express have a touch of old-world courtesy and helpfulness.

As to what to do for an encore after gaming, there is always the swimming pool and sunning area. For the kiddies, there's a video arcade. Or everyone can hop aboard old Number 7, a full-size 2-4-0 train that runs around the Ramada Express. Entertainment is at the **Caboose Lounge** Tuesday through Sunday nights.

Rates are $34 for all rooms, single or double occupancy, Sunday through Thursday, and $54 and $59 (higher price for the higher floor) on Friday and Saturday or holidays.

Restaurants

The Ramada Express has four fine places to dine or snack. The **Steakhouse** has a reasonably varied menu that features, as you might expect, excellent steaks nightly. The **Dining Car** is the 24-hour coffee shop. The **Round House Buffet** offers an extensive selection of choice breakfast repasts, luncheon and dinner entrees from 7am to 10pm. The **Whistle Stop** has all kinds of snacks. The **Seafood Bar** behind the Caboose Lounge serves crab legs and a shrimp cocktail from 11am to 7pm on Saturday and Sunday.

Flamingo Hilton Laughlin Hotel/Casino, 1900 Casino Dr., P.O. Box 2290, Laughlin, NV 89029 (tel. 702/298-3103, or toll free 800/292-3711).

This $185-million showplace was opened in July 1990 and is all decked out in flamingo-pink reflective windows. In keeping with the bigger-and-bigger philosophy of the Nevada hotel/casino business, the Flamingo Hilton Laughlin Hotel/Casino (sometimes the names get longer, too) has twin towers with 2,000 riverview rooms. But that's only the beginning: For the now-and-then outdoor types, on the roof there's a huge pool and a sunny recreation deck with tennis courts.

Then there is 50,000 square feet of casino—enough space to game to your heart's content with 1,200 slot machines, including those that will willingly accept 5¢ and 25¢ donations. There are blackjack tables, roulette, craps, poker, pai-gow poker, and a race and sports book.

Rooms are quite attractive. All accommodations have drapes and wallpaper in coordinated color schemes. They're handsomely furnished and offer great views of the Colorado. Room rates vary depending on the location and view—for the moment, at least, they are the same for weekdays and weekend: from $22 to $65, single or double; one-bedroom suites are $150, and two-bedroom suites are $200.

Restaurants

There are four restaurants from which to choose. The **Alta Villa** has classic Italian cuisine enhanced by a superb river view. The **Steak House** offers thick and tender steaks and chops. **Lindy's** deli/coffee shop is open round the clock. And the **Flamingo Fantasy Buffet** offers a view of the Colorado to buffet by. Live entertainment, apart from the games, can be found at the Flamingo Hilton Laughlin Lounge.

Harrah's Del Rio, 2900 Casino Dr., P.O. Box 5608, Laughlin, NV 89029 (tel. 702/298-4600, or toll free 800/447-8700).

Harrah's is snuggled into a natural cove along the bank of the Colorado River at the south end of town. It's a handsome south-of-the-border, hacienda-style complex with 958 rooms and suites, nonstop casino action, a pool with Jacuzzi, and a lovely guest beach —all situated on a 50-acre site.

Harrah's has a fun and festive look and sound with now-and-then strolling mariachi bands, a casino designed to resemble a Mexican courtyard, and nightly entertainment in the Club La Bamba with or without margaritas. In May look for the *Cinco de Mayo* festivities.

Harrah's casino has over 1,000 slots, blackjack, roulette, craps, poker, pai-gow poker, keno, and a sports book. Action for the kiddies is at the video arcade in the north hotel tower.

Each of Harrah's rooms has walls of exposed slump block, reflecting an old Mexico theme. All have an airy, outdoor look with contemporary furnishings done in southwestern pastels set against dark-blue carpeting. The rooms offer a pleasant place to relax before or after the pool, the beach, or the trials of the casino. You'll also find color TVs and phones; in the higher priced rooms you get a lovely view of the Colorado River.

Room rates vary according to the day of the week or holidays or location, the riverfront being the higher price. All rates are single or double occupancy. Standard rooms are $33 to $38 Sunday through Thursday; weekend and holiday rates are $49 to $59. Patio rooms are $75 daily, and minisuites are $90. There is no extra charge for children under 12 staying in the same room with their parents. An extra person is $7. Harrah's has over 2,000 parking spaces, including 500 spaces of free, covered parking for guests—a distinct blessing during the hot months.

Harrah's **Del Rio RV Plaza** has 300 parking places for RVs, with a complimentary shuttle to Harrah's casino. The convenience center at the plaza has two islands to service vehicles with gasoline and diesel fuel. The store at the center offers fresh deli and bakery goods, RV necessities, beer, wine, soft drinks, and picnic items.

Restaurants

At the point when you must eat, you have several choices. The **La Hacienda Mexican Restaurant** serves such specialties as freshly made chile rellenos and sizzling fajitas to be enjoyed to the tune of mariachi music. Or if you prefer dining on a supremely substantial steak or seafood while enjoying a great view of the river, **William Fisk's Steakhouse** (named for Harrah's founder) is the place to go. And there is a **Del Rio Buffet** and a 24-hour full-service coffee shop, the **Colorado Café**. For those who don't want to miss out on a minute of the action, the **Gringo Grill** is prepared to provide fast food.

The Golden Nugget Laughlin, 2300 Casino Dr., P.O. Box 2281, Laughlin, NV 89029 (tel. 702/298-7111, or toll free 800/237-1739).

As of this writing, the Golden Nugget is bustling to expand 35,000 square feet of casino space and create over 2,200 rooms for a total tab of some $70 million. While Steve Wynn's newest Las Vegas Mirage is a Y-shape configuration, the Golden Nugget Laughlin will have a T-shape design to offer the best in room views. Look for two 26-story towers done in the Steve Wynn color combination of white with gold accents. It should be a beauty.

---

2. Entertainment

For adults, the largest showroom in town is the 900-seat Don's Celebrity Theatre at the Riverside, where big names in the world of country music appear quite regularly. It's also where you may see female wrestling and female impersonators.

Most of the hotels have good lounge entertainment nightly at no charge and with no minimum. You usually have a choice of styles —from mariachi music, to the big-band era, to hard rock, to everything in between. At the **Riverside** there is the Western Dance Hall featuring country/western music; the Loser's Lounge, which has such interesting now-and-then events as Coors Best-Chest-in-the-West contest (for women); and the Starview Showroom, which has big-band music and a live radio broadcast. **Harrah's** has the attractive Club La Bamba, which features name groups and also has a dance floor. **Sam's Town Gold River** has Roxy's Lounge with a river view and a big dance floor—done in an 1890s saloon style. At the **Colorado Belle**, the Riverboat Lounge has an ongoing roster of individual entertainers, and every Sunday evening you can dance to the big-band music of the 1930s and 1940s. The **Ramada Express** has the Caboose Lounge with live entertainment.

For adults and children, the Best Western Riverside Hotel has a three-screen theater with Dolby sound. Admission is $1.50 by day and $3 by night.

More daytime entertainment is that found on the Colorado River. It's one of the big draws in Laughlin. You do not spend dreamy hours on its banks. The brownish Colorado bursts by, carrying water taxis ferrying passengers to hotels and casinos or taking them across the river to Bullhead City in Arizona. Swift-moving and cold (usually about 58° F), the Colorado is not the place to take an unprotected dip. But if you'd like a fun break from gambling, there are daily river cruises.

The **Little Belle**, P.O. Box 526, Laughlin, NV 89029 (tel. 702/298-1047 or 298-2453 ext. 2118, or toll free 800/228-9825), a 150-passenger sidewheeler, leaves from the Edgewater Casino on a 1½-hour sight-seeing cruise along the Colorado River. You can enjoy the passing countryside from beneath a canopy on the open-air upper deck. The entertaining and informative tour is narrated. The enclosed lower deck has a snack spot and a full-service bar. Cruises are every two hours from 11am to 7pm. Adults are $10, and children are $6. Tickets can be purchased at the Edgewater Casino dock.

A day-long 7½-to-9½-hour narrated cruise from Laughlin to Lake Havasu is offered by **Blue River Safaris.** The variation in time is because of fluctuating levels of water released by Davis Dam and coincident changes is what's to be seen. All tours (Safaris 1, 2, and 3) begin at the Best Western Riverside Hotel. The tours take you down the Colorado to Lake Havasu, where you take a bus to the English Village, the new home of the famous London Bridge. The day also may include a side trip to the old mining town of Oatman. All tours include lunch at the English Village. Safaris 1 and 2 are $50, and Safari 3 is $35. Prices for children 10 years and younger are $40 for Safaris 1 and 2 and $30 for Safari 3. There is no charge for toddlers.

Finally, if the outdoors is your bag, you're only 6 miles from Katherine Landing and Lake Mohave, just a bit beyond Davis Dam (see below).

---

3. Excursions from Laughlin

KATHERINE LANDING/LAKE MOHAVE

Katherine Landing offers a marvelous opportunity for an extraordinary addition to your Laughlin vacation. Consider the possibility of staying at the motel or on a houseboat cruising around the lake, fishing, anchoring at a beach during the day, and taking in some of the great Ranger-conducted activities and talks. Then when you feel the irresistable urge to play the slots or dine at one of the elegant hotel establishments, simply drive the six miles into Laughlin. (Katherine Landing falls within the limits of Bullhead City, Arizona; hence there are no slots or other forms of casino gaming there.)

On your way to Katherine Landing from Casino Drive (the Nevada side), continue north past the bridge that leads to Arizona and Bullhead. Signs will direct you to Davis Dam (which you will cross) and then to Katherine (or Katherine Landing). As the crow hops, it's about 6½ miles from the bridge that you ignored. On the other hand, if you're going to Katherine Landing from the Arizona side, simply head north on Hwy. 95, pass the turn to the bridge, turn left at the Davis Dam sign (*not* Davis Camp), then turn right at Katherine. Shortly thereafter you will be at Katherine Landing. If you prefer staying at the lake (Mohave) or on the lake in a houseboat with comfortably gentle breezes, it's seldom more than 15 minutes from Katherine Landing to a casino.

Whether or not you stay there, Katherine Landing is a beautiful place to swim, sail, sunbathe, fish, or just loaf. Almost any water sport is especially enjoyable because during the summer the water near Katherine Landing warms up to about 80° F.

Lake Mohave Resort and Marina at Katherine Landing has boat slips, boat rentals (including houseboats), a launch ramp, and beaches with picnic areas; there's also a campground with RV hookups.

To reserve one of the 60 motel rooms at Katherine Landing, Bullhead City, AZ 86430-4016 (tel. 602/754-3245, or toll free 800/752-9669), be sure to give yourself enough lead time. Reservations for Memorial Day or Labor Day weekend should be made five to six months in advance, or you may be disappointed. Singles with a king bed are $57, doubles with two double beds are $65, doubles with a kitchen are $69, and kitchen suites (suitable for one to three persons) are $79. Each additional person is $6. Children 5 years or under stay free when sharing an adult's room. Some of the rooms have a shower only rather than a tub and shower. All rooms have air conditioning/heat and color TVs. End rooms of the two-story segment of the motel have small patios or balconies. My choice is room 50, which overlooks the lake and has a small balcony.

Katherine Landing also has a fine restaurant—the **Tail O' the Whale** (tel. 754-3245), located right at the Marina with a great view of the lake, mountains, ducks, and carp jumping for breakfast. The restaurant is geared to accommodate motelers and boat people from breakfast through dinner. It's open daily (except Christmas) from 8am to 9pm during the winter and at other times from 7am to 9pm. The restaurant is nautically attired with halyards, stanchions, ships' lamps, booms, tabletops of varnished hatch covers, captains' chairs, and red leather booths. The food is very good, and the service is pleasant. Breakfast can be anything from one egg, to a tall stack of large pancakes with or without strawberries and whipped cream, to one of several varieties of three-egg omelets. On the other hand, you might prefer steak and eggs or a pork chop and eggs. Breakfast will average $2 to $5, with the steak and eggs at $7.50. The luncheon menu includes a good selection of hot and cold sandwiches; soups; salads; and some hot entrees, including a fish fry and shrimp fry. One of the very nice touches is that when you order a cup of coffee or a glass of ice tea, a pot or a pitcher is left on your table for complimentary refills. As to dinner, specials change nightly. Menu entrees offer a variety of choices from chicken and french fries to fish and chips, to shrimp, scallops, steak, and pasta (from $6 to $14); top of the line is the filet mignon. Wine is available by the glass or by the carafe; several varieties of beer can be had from the bar.

The **Katherine Landing RV Park** is also under the auspices of Lake Mohave Resort. Reservations can be made at the above numbers for the motel. All spaces are available with full hookups—electric, sewer, and water. Rest rooms with showers are on the premises, as are coin-operated laundry facilities. Rates are $15 per night for two persons and $2 per night for each additional person over five years; those under five years stay free. Reduced monthly rates are available.

Lake Mohave is part of the Lake Mead Recreation Area, and the Park Service manages two campsites at Katherine Landing.

Campsites are $6 per night ($3 per night if you have a Golden Age Passport) for two motorized vehicles and no more than eight persons—assuming that you're arriving with an RV and a car in tow or a car with a towed trailer. The Park Service does not take reservations; it's strictly first come, first served. Bear in mind that during the summer, when the temperature begins to rise toward 115° F, a campsite can get quite hot. You may be much more comfortable at the RV Park.

During the cooler months, from approximately November 1 to mid-April, there are excellent Ranger-conducted activities (tel. 602/754-3272)—including talks; slide presentations; films; and Ranger-guided wildlife, bird, and wildflower walks. Evening programs are held in the Katherine Campground Amphitheatre. You can learn all the fascinating details of such subjects as what a desert is; tales of the Mohave, legends and stories about the region; or the history of steamboats on the Colorado. The Rangers also schedule sunrise and sunset walks. You can get information at the Ranger station on hikes to Katherine Mine (over $12 million worth of gold was mined here); to Davis Cove; and through Grapevine Canyon—a remarkable trip through time when you see the prehistoric Native American petroglyphs. The Canyon also has wild grapes (no one seems to know how they got here), a small waterfall, and some magnificent scenery. (Sturdy hiking boots and binoculars can make these excursions even more enjoyable.) The Ranger station has all sorts of goodies, from maps of the Lake Mead National Recreation Area to descriptions of the week's activities open to the public. You can get an education on cacti just by stopping at the entry to the Ranger station and reading the small signs in front of the many species there.

Nonlandlubber types can take to the water and rent a houseboat for a few days and tour the lake. Reservations for houseboats and boats of other types (ski boats, pontoon boats, fishing boats, and bass boats) should be made at the above numbers for the motel. You can also rent fishing tackle by the hour, day, or week, but be sure to get a license at the marina. Lake Mohave offers some of the best sport fishing in the country—largemouth bass, rainbow trout, and striped bass are some of the popular catches. It's open season on all species of fish year-round, but do find out about the catch limits.

During the "value" season from September 16 to May 14, you can move about for three days on a fully equipped houseboat for $580—complete with instructions on how to handle it. The boat is suitable for sleeping six: This amounts to less than $33 per person per day. Assuming that you plan to eat and sleep during the voyage, you will need to bring your own food and linens. All houseboats are equipped with generators and air conditioning. For a seven-day trip during the "value" season, the cost will be $970. From May 15 to September 15, the peak season, the three-day rate increases to $860; for seven days, it's $1,290. It's still a bargain, though: The seven-day excursion amounts to $31 per person per day, assuming that you have a full complement of six people. Houseboats are also available with sleeping space for ten.

If you haven't been to Lake Mohave before, bear in mind that the water temperature at the upper end of the lake is about 55° F in the summer, while that near Katherine Landing is more like 80° F. Equally important, during the summer the air temperature can rise to 115°F; even though it's dry desert heat, that's still hot. A final note relative to beaches, swimming, and generally lazing around: Starting about Memorial Day and lasting throughout the summer, there is high water on the lake, which is to say that there's very little beach for you to use. This can obviously limit your activities.

For general information on Lake Mohave, the Lake Mead National Recreation Area is a most helpful source of information (tel. 702/293-8907).

BULLHEAD CITY, ARIZONA

There's a bridge that connects Laughlin, Nevada, and Bullhead City, Arizona, and it also separates the gaming and nongaming worlds. Don Laughlin spent over $4 million building this link to afford easy access to his properties in Arizona and for his employees who lived in Bullhead City. About one mile over the bridge and south on Hwy. 95 (the main street through Bullhead) is where you'll find a small airport, service stations, small motels, and a variety of fast-food establishments. Continue south for another three miles, and you will find the Motel 6 I've discussed below. Go a bit farther, and you'll see a mall with all the refinements of civilization—a supermarket, a laundry, more fast food, and so on but no slots or casino gaming. And as unlikely as it may seem, you are now quite close to an exceptionally good Chinese restaurant, which I've also discussed below.

Bullhead City has a brand new **Motel 6,** 1616 Highway 95, at Merrill Avenue, Bullhead City, AZ 86430 (tel. 602/763-1002). It's right across the river from Laughlin, about four miles south of the Laughlin/Bullhead bridge on U.S. 95, and it has a delightful and most helpful couple managing it. You'll also find some pleasant surprises uncommon to other Motel 6s. Each room has a good-size bathroom with sink, shower, and tub. The end tables have convenient shelves. What's more, each single room has a large table that's actually quite suitable for working. End chairs are as comfortable as the bed, which, by the way, has a headboard and lamps with enough light to read or work by. As with all other Motel 6 facilities, there are color TVs and new and efficient air conditioning. Local calls are still free; if you plan to make calls to Laughlin, remember that it's not a local call since you are calling another state.

If you plan to stay at Motel 6 in Bullhead, make reservations at least a month or two in advance. Currently the occupancy is running at 100%.

The name of Bullhead City would hardly inspire belief that therein lies an excellent Chinese restaurant that's worth the brief time it takes to cross the Laughlin/Bullhead bridge and head south on Hwy. 95 (the main street) for about five miles. This restaurant is **China Szechuan,** 1890 Hwy. 95, Bullhead City, AZ 86430 (tel. 763-2610).

There's nothing chi-chi about China Szechuan, but the local folk are quite familiar with the excellent quality of the food. The restaurant is done in red, gold, and black. If you want chopsticks, ask for them. There are a number of delicious luncheon specials, such as the hot and spicy Kung Pao chicken—diced chicken with green onions, peanuts, and water chestnuts—and tasty Imperial shrimp prepared with broccoli and Chinese peas. These are served with egg roll, fried wonton, and fried rice. On Saturday and Sunday, the extra goodies also include barbecue beef. Luncheon specials range from $3.55 to $4.55 and are served daily from 11:30am to 2:30pm.

The dinner menu has a long list of appetizers and soups, including an exceptional Imperial Soup with chicken, shrimp, and egg white. Entrees include seafood, beef, pork, poultry, and vegetable dishes, plus a number of chow mein and rice offerings. If you feel a little flamboyant, the shrimp with sizzling rice is a delight to see and listen to and even better to eat. For those who especially enjoy beautifully seasoned meat dishes, the beef with Chinese pea pods and black mushrooms is truly outstanding. Dinner entrees average $6.55 to $9.55; the price of lobster dishes varies seasonally. If you choose to precede dinner with an appetizer or soup, count on adding another $3 to $5. Family dinners, with appetizers included, range from $7.55 per person to $9.95—the selection of entree is from a list of seven to nine menu items.

The restaurant has a full bar and offers Chinese beer (Tsingtao), Heineken's, and a variety of domestic beers. There's also wine by the bottle or glass, sake, and plum wine if you wish it for dessert.

China Szechuan is open Sunday through Thursday from 11:30am to 9:30pm and Friday and Saturday to 10:30pm.

OATMAN, ARIZONA

As long as you're in the Laughlin/Bullhead City area, there's an interesting town that both adults and children can wander through and learn a bit about one segment of the history of gold. It's not Disneyland style; as a matter of fact, it's more like a part of the past that's been somewhat revived and restaged.

To get to Oatman from the Arizona side of the Laughlin/Bullhead bridge, head south on Hwy. 95 for about 15 miles until you see a sign to Oatman. Then head east from Hwy. 95 on what once was old U.S. 66 for about 13 miles. As a matter of fact, once you turn off Hwy. 95 you may think that you're on your way through the edges of the city dump. Then the thought may occur to you that they've misplaced Oatman. Despair not. When you arrive at the sign saying "Historic 66" and a road somewhat in need of repair, you'll know that you're almost there. And you will begin to understand the unidentified isolation that must have been a joy to Clark Gable and Carole Lombard on the first night of their honeymoon spent at the Oatman Hotel. (If you're not over 50, you may not know of this famous cinema couple and the unfortunate demise of Miss Lombard—see the entry on Goodsprings in Chapter X.) One of the most interesting sights just before you enter Oatman is a number of the houses at the outskirts of the town—they are constructed from local wood, rock, and corrugated tin.

Oatman had its beginnings in 1906 as a tent camp; then it grew into a gold-mining center that produced over $36 million dollars in gold, at 1930 prices. Before the Great Depression, Oatman had a population of more than 12,000. (At the moment, Oatman has a population of about 100.) The spectacular scenery in the area offered superb settings for such films as *Foxfire* and *How the West Was Won*. Currently Oatman's construction is of corrugated tin, batten, and board (new and old). Early in the morning, all the shop owners and their dogs visit on the street before the tourists arrive. The only disturbing morning sounds are the motorcycles of some of the residents. You may not see the burros then, but evidence of their presence is left there. I'd advise you to come later in the day if you want to see and feed the wild burros. I'm sure that the animals know exactly when most of the tourists arrive and plan their forays for food accordingly. (Burro food is sold at Fast Fanny's.)

Oatman merchants strive to keep their town as authentic as possible. You'll find the old Oatman Hotel (now listed on the National Register of Historic Buildings), an antiques shop that once was a drugstore and professional building, a ghostly old lumber company building, and a variety of other buildings once part of the mining town.

Since Oatman is, indeed, a town, you can always drive through and find breakfast, although most of the shops don't open until about 10am. There are saloons; general stores; antiques shops; variety stores; gift shops; jewelry shops; a rock and gift shop; and Fast Fanny's, where you can buy T-shirts and the aforementioned burro food. There's even a firehouse and a community hall with restroom facilities. You'll also find the remnants of an old mine near the town entry. On weekends, the Oatman Gunfighters (768-3470) stage gun fights.

The real beauty of Oatman lies less in the town itself than in nature's jagged rock towers and canyons, which surround what must have been busy mining territory at one time. American Mining still has "no trespassing" warnings at various spots behind the main road through town.

If you're planning to go from Oatman to Topock, the original roadway directly south is patchy and unpaved and not recommended by the locals. Instead, just head back to Hwy. 95 and proceed south.

INDEX

GENERAL INFORMATION

SIGHTS AND ATTRACTIONS

Las Vegas

Day-Trip Areas

Excursion Areas

Laughlin

ACCOMMODATIONS

Las Vegas

KEY TO ABBREVIATIONS: B = Budget; E = Expensive; HB = Houseboats; I = Inexpensive; M = Moderately priced; RV = Recreational Vehicle facilities

Excursion Areas

Laughlin

RESTAURANTS

Las Vegas

KEY TO ABBREVIATIONS: *B* = Budget; *E* = Expensive; *M* = Moderately priced

Laughlin

NOW, SAVE MONEY ON ALL
YOUR TRAVELS!
Join Frommer's™ Dollarwise® Travel Club

Saving money while traveling is never a simple matter, which is why the **Dollarwise Travel Club** was formed 31 years ago. Developed in response to requests from Frommer's Travel Guide readers, the Club provides cost-cutting travel strategies, up-to-date travel information, and a sense of community for value-conscious travelers from all over the world.

In keeping with the money-saving concept, the annual membership fee is low—$18 for U.S. residents or $20 for residents of Canada, Mexico, and other countries—and is immediately exceeded by the value of your benefits, which include:

1. Any TWO books listed on the following pages.
2. Plus any ONE Frommer's City Guide.
3. A subscription to our quarterly newspaper, *The Dollarwise Traveler*.
4. A membership card that entitles you to purchase through the Club all Frommer's publications for 33% to 50% off their retail price.

The eight-page **Dollarwise Traveler** tells you about the latest developments in good-value travel worldwide and includes the following columns: **Hospitality Exchange** (for those offering and seeking hospitality in cities all over the world); **Share-a-Trip** (for those looking for travel companions to share costs); and **Readers Ask . . . Readers Reply** (for those with travel questions that other members can answer).

Aside from the Frommer's Guides and the Gault Millau Guides, you can also choose from our Special Editions. These include such titles as *California with Kids* (a compendium of the best of California's accommodations, restaurants, and sightseeing attractions appropriate for those traveling with toddlers through teens); *Candy Apple: New York with Kids* (a spirited guide to the Big Apple by a savvy New York grandmother that's perfect for both visitors and residents); *Caribbean Hideaways* (the 100 most romantic places to stay in the Islands, all rated on ambience, food, sports opportunities, and price); *Honeymoon Destinations* (a guide to planning and choosing just the right destination from hundreds of possibilities in the U.S., Mexico, and the Caribbean); *Marilyn Wood's Wonderful Weekends* (a selection of the best mini-vacations within a 200-mile radius of New York City, including descriptions of country inns and other accommodations, restaurants, picnic spots, sights, and activities); and *Paris Rendez-Vous* (a delightful guide to the best places to meet in Paris whether for power breakfasts or dancing till dawn).

To join this Club, simply send the appropriate membership fee with your name and address to: Frommer's Dollarwise Travel Club, 15 Columbus Circle, New York, NY 10023. Remember to specify which single city guide and which two other guides you wish to receive in your initial package of member's benefits. Or tear out the next page, check off your choices, and send the page to us with your membership fee.

FROMMER BOOKS
PRENTICE HALL PRESS
15 COLUMBUS CIRCLE
NEW YORK, NY 10023
212/373-8125

Date_____

Friends:

Please send me the books checked below.

FROMMER'S™ GUIDES

(Guides to sightseeing and tourist accommodations and facilities from budget to deluxe, with emphasis on the medium-priced.)

☐ Alaska.....................$14.95	☐ Germany.....................$14.95
☐ Australia...................$14.95	☐ Italy........................$14.95
☐ Austria & Hungary.......$14.95	☐ Japan & Hong Kong...........$14.95
☐ Belgium, Holland & Lux-	☐ Mid-Atlantic States.........$14.95
embourg..................$14.95	☐ New England.................$14.95
☐ Bermuda & The Bahamas....$14.95	☐ New York State..............$14.95
☐ Brazil.....................$14.95	☐ Northwest...................$14.95
☐ Canada....................$14.95	☐ Portugal, Madeira & the Azores......$14.95
☐ Caribbean.................$14.95	☐ Skiing Europe...............$14.95
☐ Cruises (incl. Alaska, Carib, Mex, Ha-	☐ South Pacific...............$14.95
waii, Panama, Canada & US)..$14.95	☐ Southeast Asia..............$14.95
☐ California & Las Vegas.....$14.95	☐ Southern Atlantic States........$14.95
☐ Egypt.....................$14.95	☐ Southwest...................$14.95
☐ England & Scotland........$14.95	☐ Switzerland & Liechtenstein........$14.95
☐ Florida...................$14.95	☐ USA.........................$15.95
☐ France....................$14.95	

FROMMER'S $-A-DAY® GUIDES

(In-depth guides to sightseeing and low-cost tourist accommodations and facilities.)

☐ Europe on $40 a Day......$15.95	☐ New York on $60 a Day...........$13.95
☐ Australia on $40 a Day....$13.95	☐ New Zealand on $45 a Day.........$13.95
☐ Eastern Europe on $25 a Day.$13.95	☐ Scandinavia on $60 a Day.........$13.95
☐ England on $50 a Day.....$13.95	☐ Scotland & Wales on $40 a Day......$13.95
☐ Greece on $35 a Day......$13.95	☐ South America on $35 a Day.......$13.95
☐ Hawaii on $60 a Day......$13.95	☐ Spain & Morocco on $40 a Day......$13.95
☐ India on $25 a Day........$12.95	☐ Turkey on $30 a Day.............$13.95
☐ Ireland on $35 a Day......$13.95	☐ Washington, D.C. & Historic Va. on
☐ Israel on $40 a Day.......$13.95	$40 a Day....................$13.95
☐ Mexico on $35 a Day......$13.95	

FROMMER'S TOURING GUIDES

(Color illustrated guides that include walking tours, cultural and historic sites, and other vital travel information.)

☐ Amsterdam..............$10.95	☐ New York....................$10.95
☐ Australia.................$9.95	☐ Paris........................$8.95
☐ Brazil....................$10.95	☐ Rome.......................$10.95
☐ Egypt.....................$8.95	☐ Scotland....................$9.95
☐ Florence..................$8.95	☐ Thailand....................$9.95
☐ Hong Kong...............$10.95	☐ Turkey......................$10.95
☐ London....................$8.95	☐ Venice......................$8.95

TURN PAGE FOR ADDITONAL BOOKS AND ORDER FORM

0690

FROMMER'S CITY GUIDES

(Pocket-size guides to sightseeing and tourist accommodations and facilities in all price ranges.)

☐ Amsterdam/Holland	$8.95	☐ Montréal/Québec City	$8.95
☐ Athens	$8.95	☐ New Orleans	$8.95
☐ Atlanta	$8.95	☐ New York	$8.95
☐ Atlantic City/Cape May	$8.95	☐ Orlando	$8.95
☐ Barcelona	$7.95	☐ Paris	$8.95
☐ Belgium	$7.95	☐ Philadelphia	$8.95
☐ Boston	$8.95	☐ Rio	$8.95
☐ Cancún/Cozumel/Yucatán	$8.95	☐ Rome	$8.95
☐ Chicago	$8.95	☐ Salt Lake City	$8.95
☐ Denver/Boulder/Colorado		☐ San Diego	$8.95
Springs	$7.95	☐ San Francisco	$8.95
☐ Dublin/Ireland	$8.95	☐ Santa Fe/Taos/Albuquerque	$8.95
☐ Hawaii	$8.95	☐ Seattle/Portland	$7.95
☐ Hong Kong	$7.95	☐ Sydney	$8.95
☐ Las Vegas	$8.95	☐ Tampa/St. Petersburg	$8.95
☐ Lisbon/Madrid/Costa del Sol	$8.95	☐ Tokyo	$7.95
☐ London	$8.95	☐ Toronto	$8.95
☐ Los Angeles	$8.95	☐ Vancouver/Victoria	$7.95
☐ Mexico City/Acapulco	$8.95	☐ Washington, D.C.	$8.95
☐ Minneapolis/St. Paul	$8.95		

SPECIAL EDITIONS

☐ Beat the High Cost of Travel	$6.95	☐ Motorist's Phrase Book (Fr/Ger/Sp)	$4.95
☐ Bed & Breakfast—N. America	$11.95	☐ Paris Rendez-Vous	$10.95
☐ California with Kids	$14.95	☐ Swap and Go (Home Exchanging)	$10.95
☐ Caribbean Hideaways	$14.95	☐ The Candy Apple (NY with Kids)	$12.95
☐ Manhattan's Outdoor		☐ Travel Diary and Record Book	$5.95
Sculpture	$15.95		

☐ Honeymoon Destinations (US, Mex & Carib) $14.95

☐ Where to Stay USA (From $3 to $30 a night) $10.95

☐ Marilyn Wood's Wonderful Weekends (CT, DE, MA, NH, NJ, NY, PA, RI, VT) $11.95

☐ The New World of Travel (Annual sourcebook by Arthur Frommer for savvy travelers) .. $16.95

GAULT MILLAU

(The only guides that distinguish the truly superlative from the merely overrated.)

☐ The Best of Chicago	$15.95	☐ The Best of Los Angeles	$16.95
☐ The Best of France	$16.95	☐ The Best of New England	$15.95
☐ The Best of Hong Kong	$16.95	☐ The Best of New York	$16.95
☐ The Best of Italy	$16.95	☐ The Best of Paris	$16.95
☐ The Best of London	$16.95	☐ The Best of San Francisco	$16.95

☐ The Best of Washington, D.C. $16.95

ORDER NOW!

In U.S. include $2 shipping UPS for 1st book; $1 ea. add'l book. Outside U.S. $3 and $1, respectively.
Allow four to six weeks for delivery in U.S., longer outside U.S.

Enclosed is my check or money order for $_____

NAME_____

ADDRESS_____

CITY_____ STATE_____ ZIP____

0690